D0252499

PRAISE FOR *CHANGE MAKER*

"John has condensed years of his hard-earned experience into a thoughtful, beautiful book. This is the kind of resource that shaves years off your learning curve."

— UJ RAMDAS
Co-Creator of *The Five Minute Journal*, Co-Founder at Intelligent Change

"John has a unique way of breaking down lofty concepts like 'passion' and 'purpose' and transforming them into real, actionable steps and daily practices. He has fundamentally changed the way I think about (and pursue) goals, skills, and self-development in my own life. Both systematic and heartfelt, this book is a reliable road map to making real change, and loving the journey."

— CAMILLE DEPUTTER
Author of *Little Poems for Big Hearts*, Creator of Storytelling with Heart

"This is the book I wish I had when I first started in fitness. Even now, I find myself revisiting certain chapters and picking up new insights. True to its name, *Change Maker* will fundamentally change the way you see the world—and it may just change your life."

— NATE GREEN
Author of *Built For Show*, Writer for *Men's Health* magazine

"*Change Maker* picks up where certifications leave off. It gives health and fitness pros the secrets to building successful, sustainable businesses by helping clients transform their lives."

— GERALYN COOPERSMITH
Author, Speaker and Industry Consultant

"I literally have more faith in humanity because of the way that John Berardi and his team have achieved such success. *Change Maker* delivers integral lessons from someone who's done it—and done it right!"

— GEOFF GIRVITZ
Founder of Bang Fitness, Creator of Dad Strength

"John Berardi's guidance and wisdom have positively impacted my life and my business. If you want a long, impactful, and lucrative career, I highly recommend this book."

— CASEY SASEK
Co-Director of Girls Gone Strong, Owner of Wildcat Mattress

"*Change Maker* exceeds all expectations. It really is the complete roadmap to achieving your greatest ambitions. It might even make you a better human, too."

— ADAM CAMPBELL
Best-selling author and former Chief Content Officer of *Men's Health*, *Women's Health*, *Prevention*, and *Runner's World*

"Eleven years ago, I opened my first fitness business: a facility based on principles I learned training people in special operations. During this process, JB's advice and insight played an invaluable role in shaping my new business into what I wanted it to be. If you're starting a career in the fitness industry, this book should be on your desk."

— CRAIG WELLER
USN SWCC, founder of Barefoot Fitness, Co-founder of Ethos Colorado, Precision Nutrition Coach

"Congratulations on finding this book! You've chosen an industry that has the ability to change the world. And the right guide to help you navigate it."

— JONATHAN GOODMAN
Author of *Ignite the Fire*, Founder of The PTDC

CHANGE MAKER

CHANGE MAKER

TURN YOUR PASSION FOR HEALTH AND FITNESS INTO A Powerful PURPOSE AND A Wildly SUCCESSFUL CAREER

JOHN BERARDI, PhD

with TED SPIKER

BENBELLA

BenBella Books, Inc.
Dallas, TX

Copyright © 2019 by John Berardi Consulting, Inc.

All rights reserved. No part of this book may be used or reproduced in any manner whatsoever without written permission except in the case of brief quotations embodied in critical articles or reviews.

BenBella Books, Inc.
10440 N. Central Expressway, Suite 800
Dallas, TX 75231
www.benbellabooks.com
Send feedback to feedback@benbellabooks.com

Printed in the United States of America
10 9 8 7 6 5 4 3 2 1

Library of Congress Control Number: 2019945097
9781948836555 (print)
9781948836807 (electronic)

Editing by Claire Schulz
Copyediting by Scott Calamar
Proofreading by Michael Fedison and Cape Cod Compositors, Inc.
Indexing by WordCo Indexing Services
Text design and composition by Rodrigo Corral
Cover design by Rodrigo Corral
Printed by Versa Press, Inc.

Distributed to the trade by Two Rivers Distribution, an Ingram brand
www.tworiversdistribution.com

Special discounts for bulk sales are available.
Please contact bulkorders@benbellabooks.com.

To my wife and children:
For helping me live my purpose,
using my unique abilities,
in harmony with our shared values.

++

To change makers everywhere:
For pursuing your passion,
making your life matter, and
helping the world become a better place.

CONTENTS

FOREWORD

I was lucky.

During my time as a student at the University of Western Ontario, I emailed legendary nutrition researcher and Western faculty member Dr. Peter Lemon to ask for career advice. Graciously, he invited me to his office and spent hours guiding me, focusing me not on *what* to think, but *how* to think, when it comes to learning more about, and pursuing, a career in health, fitness, and nutrition.

While I was there, Dr. Lemon showed me a study from 2002. His co-author on it was a young (and unknown) doctoral student named John Berardi, who I've since come to know as JB. As Dr. Lemon was his PhD advisor, he talked about JB's work, his work ethic, and the high hopes he had for him.

Although we've been friends for years, and JB has become one of my most influential mentors, I never told him this story before. But he had a hand in guiding my career long before we first spoke. And, trust me, worthwhile guidance in the field of health and fitness is hard to come by.

As JB and I are both avid readers, I know he'll appreciate me using a line from Tolkien to illustrate what happens to many new health and fitness professionals: "Out of the frying pan and into the fire." Unlike many other fields, the health and fitness industry seems to throw people into the profession headfirst. It's a certification or training course and then . . . sink or swim.

Sure, there's the opportunity for continuing education along the way. But, in most cases, there's a woeful lack of guidance on which courses to take, which skills to build, and which career paths make the most sense for now and into the future.

Until now.

In *Change Maker*, JB provides authentic, insightful, wise counsel, the kind so many health and fitness pros need regardless of whether they're just starting out or in the middle of their professional careers.

He begins by busting the myth that the path to a powerful purpose and wildly successful career is simplistic and one-dimensional. Indeed, as he discusses, there are *many* opportunities for you, opportunities that don't *just* involve seeing clients and patients in person or one-on-one.

He also highlights several ways to use your passion to make a real difference, while also bringing together your own unique purpose, talents, and values. The good news is that even if you haven't yet found the right fit, it's never too late to switch your focus and bring all three into alignment.

Beyond discussing all the great opportunities available now—and the ones that will emerge in the coming years—he also shares how to get laser focused on what matters to you, to the people you serve, and to your career. This way you can put your energy into the things that make a real difference while ignoring what's unimportant or, at least, unimportant for now.

If we're going to solve the problems of obesity, lifestyle disease, and overwhelming health-care costs for future generations, we need to think prevention. And movement, nutrition, sleep, and stress management are the best preventatives we have.

However, as I've said before: your ability to write a quality program is less important than your ability to get someone to do the program. In this area, JB's a master. And in this book, he shares an exciting frontier in coaching, one centered in behavioral psychology and rooted in long-term sustainable change, not yo-yo dieting or fitness fads.

With a mix of humility and candor, JB shares some of my favorite lessons: business and professional development strategies that helped him become one of the most successful people in the history of the industry, growing the world's largest nutrition and lifestyle coaching, education, and software company.

In the end, this is a full-circle moment for me. The man whose work was introduced to me during my first real guidance session in this industry has asked me to write the foreword for a book that will guide you (and hundreds of thousands of others) to personal and professional success.

So congratulations on finding this book. You've chosen an industry that has the ability to change the world. And you've chosen the right book—and the right guide—to help you navigate it.

Jonathan Goodman
Author of *Ignite the Fire*
Founder of the PTDC

INTRODUCTION

How I Found My Calling and How to Find Yours Too

In nearly every aspect of life, we need some sort of infrastructure. A house without a foundation would blow over in a breeze. A city without pipes, roads, and power lines would crumble. A body without bones would be a fleshy blob of goo.

So why do we have almost no structure in the health and fitness industry?

Sure, there are lots of choices: a buffet of books, websites, workshops, certifications, and friendly (or not so friendly) advice to randomly gorge on. But while there's an abundance of options, almost no one's connected the dots. There's no curriculum, no path to follow, no guidelines for what to do and how to act, no steel girders to give you the structure to launch yourself into a successful career.

If you work in health and fitness, you're pretty much on your own.

Sure, you may know a lot about exercise or nutrition or the inner workings of the body. But where will you learn how to choose your specialty, attract clients, run a business, manage difficult situations, protect your reputation? Where will you be exposed to the inner workings of success?

Herein lies one of the biggest problems I see in the health and fitness industry: **Too much information, too little context.** It's easy to get overwhelmed or to focus on the wrong things. And that can lead to unclear vision, frustrating (or no) personal development, and—ultimately—lots of good professionals feeling stuck in careers they once dreamed about being a part of.

To illustrate my point, there's currently a 40 percent annual turnover rate among health and fitness professionals—meaning that by this time next year, four in ten will have left a field they were once deeply passionate about.

This book is designed to change that.

In *Change Maker*, I'll share a road map, a curriculum, a way to connect the dots that'll help you achieve success on your own terms. Of course, defining success depends on your perspective, your goals, and your stage in life. But the way I define it is:

CHOOSING A PROFESSIONAL PATH
that brings you the most meaning,

MAKING ENOUGH MONEY
to be financially secure,

HAVING THE FLEXIBILITY
to create your own schedule,

BALANCING YOUR PERSONAL AND PROFESSIONAL LIVES
so they support one another, and

SEEING PHENOMENAL RESULTS
with your clients and patients.

That last one is why you're in this business, right? It's certainly not because the industry is full of trainers, nutritionists, and functional medicine docs driving Maseratis and doing biceps curls with gold bricks. Instead, you're probably here because 1) you were called (by someone or something) to help change lives and/or 2) the health and fitness industry changed *your* life, just like it did mine.

How health and fitness changed— no, saved—my life

Maybe it's because I was small and weak, always sneezing and wheezing. Or maybe it's because skinny kids like me got picked on a lot growing up. Whatever the reason, by the time I got to high school, I had a chip on my shoulder and was mad at the world. I skipped a lot of classes; I was always drunk and high; I wasn't that fun to be around; and I had no prospects for continuing my education.

Then, one night, after drinking and driving with friends (go ahead and judge me; I deserve it), we crashed a car. As we spiraled out of control into a wooded area, I had one of those cinematic near-death experiences: Everything slowed down. I saw visions of my childhood. I watched myself being lowered into the ground while my parents loomed overhead, grieving and ashamed.

But, miraculously, we narrowly missed the trees. We didn't hurt ourselves or anyone else. All we did was scrape the car and knock off a side mirror during the crash. When the dust settled, we sat up in a whoa-what-was-that? stupor. "Let's get the car out of this embankment," said the driver. "My parents are gonna kill me."

I had a wholly different reaction. *Holy shit!* I thought. *I have to do something different with my life.*

Although we were miles from my house, I decided to walk home. My buddies drove away, getting arrested later that night.

I agonized over what to do next. I knew I needed to do *something*. But I had no skills. All I knew was the party lifestyle, and I was so small and weak that my upper arm and wrist circumferences were nearly identical. Even so, I was unmistakably drawn to the idea of living better. Part of me wanted to get more sleep, eat better food, and start working out to build some muscle. So I joined a local gym.

I didn't know anyone. I didn't know what to do. I just showed up.

You've probably heard the saying: "When the student is ready, the teacher appears." Well, that's what happened next. One day, while I was flailing around on a leg-press machine, the gym's owner, Craig, approached. He shared some tips, and I guess I took them well, because he invited me to work out with him the next day.

Craig was every young guy's hero. He was big and strong, a 230-pound bodybuilder. He had a business degree and owned a few well-respected gyms. He was well-read. He drove a nice car. He was handsome and girls loved him.

What Craig saw in *me*, I have no idea. However, during the next two years, he became a trusted coach, a good friend, and my greatest mentor. He gave me books to read. He taught me about health and fitness. He talked about the business of owning a gym. He even gave me a job at the front desk and showed me how things worked.

Craig's mentorship didn't just change my life; it *saved* my life. I didn't go back to partying. Instead, I went to a community college. To pay for school, I took personal training and lifestyle coaching courses and started working with a few clients at Craig's gym.

I'd found my calling.

I went on from community college to study medicine, biology, chemistry, psychology, and philosophy as I progressed through advanced degrees at five different universities. While working on my mind, I also built my body, entering bodybuilding and powerlifting competitions. I eventually went on to win a national bodybuilding championship, earn a PhD, and co-found Precision Nutrition, which is now the world's largest nutrition coaching, certification, and software company.

When I discovered health and fitness, I needed a makeover

When I started working out, I needed to build a new body, mind, and perspective.

Later on, I needed to rebuild my perspective again.

I paid my way through ten years of postsecondary education by coaching clients. Yet, halfway through the journey, I was feeling unsettled in my work. This was strange because the health and fitness industry saved my life. I believed in the power it had to save other lives too.

At the same time, when I looked around, I saw a big disconnect between the people working in health and fitness and the people we were supposed to be helping.

It seemed as if the entire field was set up to cater exclusively to people like me and my fellow fit friends: the people who already worked out in gyms, shopped at organic markets, and had a commitment to living a healthy lifestyle.

Think about the implications of that.

We were putting all our energy into serving a tiny percent of the population—the small segment of people who, ironically, needed our help *the least*. Not only did this present an ethical dilemma, it also presented a business problem. How was I supposed to stand out when competing with everyone else trying to serve the same market as me?

In addition, we were ignoring the people in pain, the millions who didn't have any experience with health and fitness, the ones who needed our help *the most*. This really hit home for me when I realized that no matter how "expert" I was becoming, I still didn't have the necessary skill or ability to help my loved ones, the people closest to me, avoid fads and make positive changes in their lives.

Once I had this realization, I couldn't *unrealize* it.

Again, I knew something had to change

I needed to learn a different way of seeing my clients—plus a new way of thinking about my work.

That's when I decided two things.

First, I didn't want to *only* help fit and healthy people get *more* fit and healthy. I also wanted to help *everyone* who was ready and willing to make changes in their lives—no matter who they were, what they looked like, or where they were starting from.

Second, I wanted to make sure that my help was the real deal—the kind of help that facilitates lasting, meaningful change in a person's life. No quick fixes, no Band-Aids, no solutions that only work when the conditions are perfect.

Sadly, early in my career, I wasn't doing either

I wasn't doing either of those two things—helping those who most needed it, and offering lasting change—on my own. And I wasn't even doing them during the early days of Precision Nutrition, which I started with my friend Phil Caravaggio in a basement in the early 2000s.

Precision Nutrition began as a passion project, a fun way to indulge our love of health and fitness while expressing our geeky science- and technology-loving genes.

In our early years we wrote articles, created educational DVDs, sold e-books, and otherwise ran what people call an "information product" business. During this time we collected lots of testimonials and people told us we were doing great work.

But I wasn't quite sure.

Phil and I started to suspect that articles, books, and DVDs—while offering *some* value—could only do so much. We were beginning to realize that people who want change in their lives don't benefit from big chunks of information dumped into their laps at once.

Careful, patient, compassionate *coaching* makes the real difference

Phil and I started to realize that this kind of deep-level coaching was almost entirely missing from the health and fitness industry. So we set out to find better ways to reach more of the people who needed us— especially the people who weren't yet "into" health and fitness.

THIS BEGAN WITH *REALLY LISTENING* TO PEOPLE and, in turn, speaking to their deepest needs when describing our programs.

THEN, ONCE THEY BECAME CLIENTS, COACHING THEM BY USING NEW METHODS—borrowed from more established fields like behavioral psychology—known to facilitate sustainable change.

FINALLY, IT MEANT COMMITTING TO BUILDING A BETTER BUSINESS, one that'd be around for a long time—long enough to help create industry-wide change.

Thankfully, we've made great strides.

Today, Precision Nutrition is on its way to directly help millions of people eat, move, and live better while also empowering health and fitness professionals to do the same with their own clients and patients.

As of 2019, we've worked with more than 150,000 coaching clients and mentored more than 75,000 health and fitness professionals from all over the world.

We've coached professional sports teams and Olympic athletes at the highest level of sport.

We've consulted with some of the most respected companies in the world including Apple, Equinox, Nike, and Virgin.

Our methods have been validated in several peer-reviewed scientific journals.

Our team has been recognized by Fast Company as one of the world's most innovative organizations.

Our co-founder, Phil Caravaggio, has been named one of Canada's Top 40 Under 40, recognizing outstanding, visionary young achievers in Canadian business.

And I've been repeatedly named one of the 100 most influential people in health and fitness.

Now, I'm not bringing all this up to brag. This track record of success, I hope, will help you trust me to guide you toward a more fruitful, empowering career yourself. Because that's exactly what I plan to do.

How can *you* become the ultimate change maker?

While I'm hopeful for the future of the health and fitness industry, I'm frustrated by all the noise out there today. I've watched too many change makers get stuck in the matrix—minds influenced by the bad thinking of pseudo experts, the persuasive power of unscrupulous marketing, and the short attention span of health and fitness media—unable to figure out what's true, useful, or important.

But if you think it's bad on the professional side, consider what it's like for the public. These are the people who desperately need our help. In an industry full of diet books, late-night infomercials, and a million diagnoses from Dr. Google, they don't know where to turn, or who to turn to.

Of course, I want them to turn to *you*.

But only if you're willing to think differently about who you are, why you're here, how you can make a great living, and how you can make a real difference.

Because, if you can do that, I know you'll be able to:

turn your passion into a rewarding, life-changing career that you're proud of;

make enough money to do (and have) the things you want;

learn whether the things you want (and have) are actually the right things for you;

make your own schedule, work on valuable projects, and make a difference; and

surround yourself with people who push you to be better and celebrate your successes.

Even more:

You have the opportunity to change, even save, lives

Think about all the people out there who are suffering, or in pain, or frustrated.

Maybe they're shooing their daughter away at the park, saying, "I can't play right now; Daddy's knee hurts too much."

Maybe they're giving their mom her first shot of insulin, saying it's just going to be a little pinch.

Maybe they're sitting in the middle seat of an airplane, trying to ask the flight attendant (as quietly as possible) for a seat belt extension and avoiding the judgmental eyes of everyone around them, wishing they could somehow shrink and disappear inside themselves.

Maybe they're sitting on the wax-paper-covered table at the doctor's office, hearing how they're not going to live to see their kids finish high school.

Lucky for them, you're here. Lucky for them, you're ready and willing to help.

But let's do it right

Let's turn your passion into something real. Let's put you on track to becoming the ultimate professional, one capable of making change for others and for yourself. Let's put a structure in place where you not only learn to help others live up to their potential, but where you live up to yours.

With this book, I hope to offer that structure.

To begin, *Change Maker* is organized into seven chapters that'll teach you how to turn your love of health and fitness into an invigorating purpose and a sustainable career. Whether you're already working in the field or you're thinking of switching from another one, it's my goal to help you avoid the burnout and lack of direction that, unfortunately, can be all too common in this young industry.

To support what you're learning, I've also compiled end-of-chapter Q&As that are full of real, thoughtful questions I've gotten over the years. In each one I share my unfiltered take on the challenges you'll undoubtedly face as you grow your career. These are available online, and you can download them (for free) at www.changemakeracademy. com/questions.

Finally, as you read through the book, you'll notice a number of exercises, activities, questions, and worksheets. These are absolutely essential to put what you're learning into action. So I recommend downloading them now (again, free) at www.changemakeracademy.com/download able-forms. There are both printable and fillable versions of each form, and the Quick Reference Guide at the end of the book lists them all.

I hope you'll take my advice and grab these resources now. I also hope you'll work through them in order as they'll greatly enhance your learning experience. Even more, they'll help you move from "knowing" to "doing"—the hallmark of every successful professional I've met.

With that said, if you're ready to become the ultimate change maker, let's begin.

CHAPTER 1

OPPOR

TUNITY

HOW TO

Turn **SIX COMMON INDUSTRY** *Challenges* **INTO OPPORTUNITIES FOR** *Success*

Forty years ago, almost no one exercised "for fun."

It wasn't until Dr. Ken Cooper released *The New Aerobics* in 1979 that people started doing cardiovascular exercises like running, cycling, swimming, and skiing as recreational activity. And modern-day health and fitness clubs didn't enter the scene until about thirty years ago. So, if you're working in health and fitness today, or thinking about making a switch, your job is a thoroughly modern innovation.

Compare that to other established professions like law, medicine, clergy, and chemistry, and it becomes clear the health and fitness industry, as we know it today, is *very* young. Like toddler young. Barely walking young. Learning first words young.

That's not necessarily a bad thing. Most children are full of passion and purpose. Their enthusiasm can be measured in decibels. Their energy sparks action. This makes them great experimenters, great learners, great doers. They're the future.

They have their faults, though. Most are impulsive and naive. They make mistakes. They don't think through the consequences of their actions. And they lack the maturity to consider "What do I want most?" instead of "What do I want now?" This makes them first drafts, not final products.

Doesn't this almost perfectly describe the field of health and fitness today?

We're passionate, enthusiastic, even *on fire* for all things food and fitness, health and wholesomeness. Great! We need all that excitement and exuberance. The field is literally creating itself as I write this. Historically, we're on the ground floor of a new movement and a new profession. It's changing fast. And it's our work that'll shape the future.

Before getting carried away, though, those of us working in the field have to recognize that we're *also* inexperienced, impatient, and stubborn. We lack structure and wisdom. We engage in unproductive debates, launch embarrassing products, ignore scientific thinking, and fight for what we think are limited resources.

The good news? This is completely normal.

No one would expect a newly walking one-year-old to complete a ninja warrior course. A four-year-old who just learned about lying to write a dissertation on ethics. Or a six-year-old to do complex math problems after just learning to add. We know they're young and inexperienced; we give them time, and permission, to develop. With support, coaching, and encouragement, they often do. The same should apply for new industries and professions.

Consider chemistry, one of the most mature sciences. Around three thousand years ago, humans started recording and manipulating metals. From there it took one thousand years for Aristotle to propose, incorrectly, that all things are made of four different elements. (There are currently 118.)

Humans later spent another one thousand years trying to turn cheap metals into gold. (Yes, centuries of alchemy.) Finally, oxygen was identified in the 1700s, breaking open our understanding of electrons, protons, atomic mass, and more. Bottom line: chemistry floundered for 2,700 years of infancy and adolescence before humans made modern breakthroughs.

Yet, with maturity, they made them.

Yes, it can feel frustrating to think that many of our questions won't be answered for a long time. Still, it's heartening to know the work we're doing now will lead to future progress. There's a lot to be hopeful about.

And that's what this chapter is about: hope.

It's about recognizing we're a young industry, accepting the obstacles that come along with that, and turning those into personal growth and the advancement of the field.

To help us, this chapter covers the six biggest challenges I see in health and fitness today. Instead of shrinking away from them in embarrassment (*Uh, nothing to see here, I'll just go stand over there*), or getting defensive about them (*No way, that's not true!*), let's find the opportunities in them. In those opportunities, we find learning, growth, and maturity.

CHALLENGE 1

THE *GAP* BETWEEN *Us* AND *Them*

└──→ OPPORTUNITY 1

Close THE *GAP*

Obesity stats are frightening. Lifestyle diseases are on the rise. And health care is about to bust. On the other hand, health and fitness professionals like us have real solutions for all three problems. There are profound opportunities to build a career out of making a difference.

There's just one problem: we've created a big gap between the people who *want to* help (what I'll call group 1) and the people who *need* that help (group 2).

Meet group 1: you, me, our colleagues. We're the small army of health and fitness change makers called to help. Of course, I love this group. We're committed and passionate folks excited to spread the word and change people's lives.

Yet our problem is that we sometimes confuse our *passion* for health and fitness with *actual skill* in helping others improve their own health and fitness.

You see this in sports when a hall of fame athlete tries their hand at coaching without actually developing coaching mastery. Or in business when top salespeople flounder as sales managers.

Indeed, you could exercise like crazy and eat more carrots than a Triple Crown winner. You could earn so many certificates and degrees that you have the entire alphabet after your name. You could achieve a massive personal transformation (like losing one hundred pounds, completing a difficult physical challenge, or reversing a host of lifestyle diseases). You could have a positive attitude, relentless work ethic, and a heart of gold.

But if you *don't* yet have the coaching education or psychological

tools needed to facilitate lasting change in another person, you're just not ready to tackle the hard work of coaching clients.

Sadly, for all its focus on anatomy and physiology, sets and reps, macro- and micronutrients, the health and fitness industry often ignores the *coaching* side of coaching. We look at the *body*, but ignore the *mind*.

That has to change.

For better or worse, this was our legacy. We've all inherited the same rules and ideas. I was no exception. When I started out, I didn't know how to help most people get results, especially those who weren't similar to me. I got frustrated with "difficult clients" or situations that seemed to defy all the rules I depended on. And because I only knew how to help a very small portion of my clients, I worried about the future of my job. I knew I was missing something, but I wasn't sure what.

Maybe you're feeling that way right now. If so, you wouldn't be alone.

In fact, most health and fitness professionals are wondering—at this very moment—why more of their clients and patients aren't getting life-changing results.

They're thinking:

"Maybe I need another certification."

"Maybe I need to go back to school."

"Maybe I should just fire this client so I don't have to deal with this."

"I hope nobody finds out that I don't really know what I'm doing."

And because of that, they're starting to burn out. They're starting to lose their passion. They're starting to give up on their dream.

Meet group 2: our potential clients—the millions of people struggling

with their weight, their health, and their confidence. They're unhappy, not only with parts of their bodies and lives, but with all of us in group 1. And they have the right to be.

They've put their trust in various coaches and poured money into products that haven't worked. The exercise books didn't deliver. The nutrition apps didn't change them. The professionals didn't listen. They're staring down a health crisis.

They're frustrated and feeling hopeless.

Even worse, part of that is our fault. When they asked beginner-type questions, or felt awkward during their first time exercising, we rolled our eyes. (*Newbie!*) When they struggled with things they didn't quite understand, we called them lazy. (*You just don't want it badly enough!*) When they transitioned into middle age, we offered them shiny, airbrushed icons. (*If you'd have taken care of yourself, you'd look more like this!*) And when they looked for help, we told them to change every single thing about themselves and live an entirely different life. (*It's not a diet, it's a lifestyle!*)

But isn't that just telling people they can't be *themselves*? That to eat better, lose weight, or improve their health, they have to become *us*? In my opinion, that's the laziest form of coaching. No wonder it doesn't stick. These folks don't want to be us. They want to be themselves, only healthier.

And so, we have a gap.

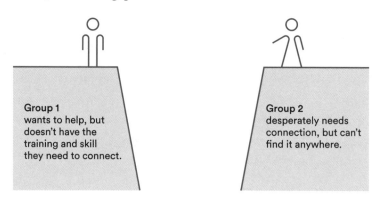

Group 1
wants to help, but
doesn't have the
training and skill
they need to connect.

Group 2
desperately needs
connection, but can't
find it anywhere.

The result? Despite all the attention on health and fitness nowadays, people are still getting fatter, sicker, more sedentary, less mobile, and less functional in their day-to-day lives. They're still getting "preventable" diseases.

That means the health and fitness industry is *still* not improving the health, fitness, and/or quality of life for most of the population.*

Even more, our health and fitness centers have become places where already-healthy and fit people go to hang out with other healthy and fit people to do healthy- and fit-people things. That's fine, of course. If that's who you want to serve, go for it. Let's just be explicit about what's happening: The health and fitness industry is mostly marketing to, and attracting, a very small group of people. While that's a little sad, it also leads to our biggest opportunity: a "blue ocean" opportunity.

In their book *Blue Ocean Strategy*, W. Chan Kim and Renée Mauborgne argue that successful companies often create "blue oceans" where their products and services are so unique, or cater to a largely unserved group, that there isn't much competition for what they do.

This is contrasted with the "red oceans," where companies fight ruthlessly with competitors because they all offer similar products and services to the same people. The analogy is that an ocean full of vicious competition becomes red with blood.

In other words, instead of trying to attract more people "like us" (which is a red ocean because it's a small group and everyone is trying to serve them), we'd be better off trying to attract people "like them" (which is a blue ocean because it's a huge group and no one is adequately serving them).

We'll explore this idea more in Chapter 3.

---

* And not only are we not helping, we might even be doing harm. Consider the opportunity cost, unnecessary injuries, and constant cycle of trading short-term transient changes for long-term healthy behavior. The industry may be wasting people's time, energy, and trust. Eventually, those people give up, worse off and more confused than when they started.

CHALLENGE 2

NOT *UNDERSTANDING* WHAT PEOPLE *Want* AND *Need*

OPPORTUNITY 2

Assume LESS, *Listen* MORE, AND EMPHATHIZE WITH THE PEOPLE *You* HOPE *To Serve*

Everybody has light-bulb moments.

One of my brightest came courtesy of a disgruntled Precision Nutrition client.

Health and fitness coaches often assume that the people who join their programs want to be healthy and fit—maybe to lose weight, lower cholesterol, or move better. I know I always did. **I also assumed that if I could help deliver these physical goals, I'd have another satisfied customer.**

I assumed wrong.

Some years back, I read a review from a former group-coaching client. Someone asked her if she would recommend our program. Here was the gist of her response:

I don't recommend it. I lost some weight, but I never felt like I connected with my coach. I didn't really need much help from her. But if I would have needed help, I'm not sure how much I'd have gotten. So no. I don't recommend it.

Curious where we went wrong, I dug into our database to discover that this client lost over fifty pounds working with us! Yes, *fifty*. In addition, nearly every metric we collected improved—from health, to body composition, to food and nutrition knowledge, to resiliency.

Yet here she was: unhappy and actively *not* recommending our coaching.

I could have chalked up these comments to her being overly picky, to having unreasonable expectations, or to being fundamentally unpleasable. That would have come at a huge cost. Instead, I asked her if she would sit for a paid interview so I could learn more.

What I learned changed our business.

It turns out that losing weight and "getting results," while nice, *wasn't enough*.

Even though she was in a group, she didn't want to *feel* like part of a group. She wanted the *feeling* of a one-on-one relationship with her coach. She wanted someone to reach out daily, someone to get to know her schedule and her children's names, someone who made her feel special, and taken care of, and cared for. And she didn't get that.

We missed a big opportunity to create a meaningful, lasting relationship with this client, and she left dissatisfied.

Of course, if we *had* asked about her goals, she probably wouldn't have said, "I want to feel connected." That's because learning more about clients isn't as straightforward as asking any old question. You have to learn a specific way of asking questions, which I'll share in Chapter 3.

The answers to these questions were invaluable to us. And nowadays we're asking them more than ever. This allows us to better identify the true values of the people we've promised to help. They feel better served and better connected while we feel happier and more satisfied in our work.

I'm confident this can do the same for you.

CHALLENGE 3

NOT DEFINING *Your* PURPOSE

OPPORTUNITY 3

DEFINE *Yours* AND ALIGN IT WITH YOUR *Talents*

In his book *Start with Why*, Simon Sinek shares the idea that most people live their lives by accident—they live as it happens. The antidote, he proposes, is to live life on purpose, to find our "WHY" (the purpose, cause, or belief that inspires us) and use it as a filter to choose the careers, organizations, communities, and relationships that are most likely to lead to fulfillment.

In my experience, most of us working in health and fitness are here because we've had a transformative experience. Maybe, like me, a health and fitness mentor helped reshape your life, and now you want to pay that forward to others. Maybe it's been a part of your life since you were young, and it's been a way to connect with your family or to express yourself. Maybe you lost someone to a preventable disease, and you've committed to helping others avoid that same fate.

Whatever your reason, you must deeply connect with your purpose and explicitly call out the reason you got into this field in the first place. Because work can be tough. Down in the weeds, it can feel like *Groundhog Day*. Wake up, go to work, chip away at your never-ending to-do list, navigate workplace politics, deal with clients, go home, squeeze in some time for self-care, go to bed, repeat.

However, when you have a clear sense of why the day matters, when you know how your daily tasks connect to your reason for doing them, when you recognize how your daily tasks are "moving the needle" on something important to you, things get easier. At worst, this connection helps your day make sense. At best, it keeps you enthusiastic, motivated, and inspired.*

It can't stop there, though.

The magic really happens when you align your purpose with your unique abilities.

Popularized by Dan Sullivan, one of the world's most influential entrepreneurship coaches, the unique ability process defines the things that:

1 you are, or have the potential to be, world class at;

2 you actually enjoy doing;

3 will actually make a difference when you do them.

Imagine a scenario where you have a deeply felt and explicitly stated purpose *and* you're working toward that purpose using your strongest talents, having fun, and making a difference. #livingthedream

Yes, lots of people in health and fitness have strong reasons for why they work in this field. Yet more of us need to explicitly define our purpose (and that takes a little extra work). Once that's defined, we need to discover how to use our unique abilities in the service of that purpose.

In Chapter 2, I'll help you discover both.

---

* One of my good friends does a "Start with Why" exercise with students at the beginning of her workshops. This helps them get centered on why they're there and what they hope to get out of it, which, in turn, helps them stay motivated and inspired even as the fatigue of long days of learning sets in.

CHALLENGE 4

Becoming TOO SPECIALIZED

OPPORTUNITY 4

GENERALIZE *and* EMBRACE THE IDEA *of* THE CASE MANAGER

"I'm looking for a bench-press-only personal trainer, a kale-first nutritionist, and a psoas-only massage therapist," said no one ever. Why not? Because prospective clients—group 2 as described earlier—don't think in terms of specializations.

Quite simply, quite profoundly, clients just want help. They have some sort of pain in their lives—physical, mental, and/or emotional— and they want it to go away.

At the same time, the idea of "staying in your lane" prevents professionals in this field from helping as much as they could. *Personal trainers shouldn't talk about food. Strength coaches shouldn't talk about pain management. Nutritionists shouldn't talk about movement.* This specialty-centric kind of thinking has deepened the divide between the people willing to help and those who need it.

Don't believe me? Then imagine I'm fifty pounds over my ideal weight, my cholesterol and blood sugar are high, I have heartburn, I have pain in my lower back, and I get winded walking across the living room. Imagine it's been like this for a long time, ten years or more, and I'm finally ready to get help. Then, when I reach out, I learn that I'll need:

a physician to treat my cholesterol, blood sugar, and heartburn;

---

a rehab specialist to treat my lower back pain;

---

a nutritionist to help adjust my diet for weight loss;

---

a gym membership; and

---

a personal trainer to help me figure out how to use the gym.

Of course, my insurance only covers a small portion of these fees, none of the specialists work in the same part of town, and none of them know what the other is doing. So, in addition to all the exercising, healthy eating, stress managing, and self-caring I have to make time for, I'll also need to become a project manager overseeing four new part-time employees and one new facility.

Is it any surprise people are struggling?

I know what I'm about to say will be unpopular—especially to those who've developed a deep expertise in a single area, or to those who profit from dividing things into specialties—but it has to be said: in health and fitness, the future belongs to the generalist, not the specialist.

Yes, that was hard to type for a guy who spent twelve years in higher education, each year getting progressively more specialized, and who now runs the industry's top nutrition certification. Yet the writing's on the wall: there's huge opportunity for those professionals who are willing to think of themselves as health and fitness "case managers," "solutions providers," or "concierges."

Of course, there's nothing wrong with being trained as a specialist. There are lots of upsides too. But it can't stop there. **The professional of the future will need to support all aspects of health: movement, nutrition, supplementation, sleep, stress management, and more.**

Do they have to be experts in each area? No. Should they diagnose or prescribe? No. But they'll need the training and expertise to deliver the equivalent of a Cliff's Notes* summary of each topic.

In other words, nutritionists will still focus on nutrition. Trainers on movement. Physicians on diagnosis and treatment. However, each will *also* share resources and insights on other lifestyle-related topics. And they'll tap into their contact lists of—or refer out to—other trusted professionals when they have questions, if someone needs more than they can provide.

This shift is already happening, which is great. But it's happening too slowly—in part because of territorialism and lobbying from professional organizations, but mostly because of old habits and knee-jerk reactions.

For example, in a private Facebook group I'm part of, a personal trainer and lifestyle coach mentioned that his client was recently diagnosed with renal disease, and he was wondering what he could do to support her. He was bombarded with at least fifty comments that sounded like: "You're beyond your scope! You're not a doctor! It's illegal and immoral to help! Run!"

Of course, this trainer shouldn't diagnose or prescribe anything directly for renal disease. But there's a lot of value he could bring to this situation, making himself a crucial part of his client's allied health team.

For example, he could help her *find help*. This is likely a frightening and stressful time for her. The last thing she needs is a trusted coach telling her, "This is out of my scope. Bye." So, while he won't be able to support her medical or dietetic needs, he can help her remain calm, think clearly, and perhaps even help her search for the professionals she requires to move forward. Also, if he feels confident, he could continue to support her exercise, sleep, and stress-management practices, in conjunction with her new health-care team. If he doesn't feel confident, he could help her find someone to take his place. In essence, for a period of

---

* Cole's Notes, for you Canadians.

time, his role may shift from trainer and lifestyle coach to case manager and concierge.*

In the end, if we're to legitimately embrace client-centered coaching (more on this in Chapter 4), the logical next step is to develop a more robust knowledge set and coaching practice (more on this in Chapter 7). No, you shouldn't try to be an expert in everything. But you should learn fluency in all the areas that make for deep health.

Clients aren't interested in perfect squats or nailing their macronutrient ratios. They're interested in living a healthier life.

CHALLENGE 5

GETTING Tangled Up IN Educational OPTIONS

OPPORTUNITY 5

CREATE Your OWN YOU-NIVERSITY

There's a whole buffet of books, workshops, certifications, seminars, websites, and friendly advice available for health and fitness professionals. There's so much information but so little context. And almost no one is tying it all together.

Don't get me wrong: I love education. Like I said, I've done twelve years of higher education (studying medicine, philosophy, psychology, exercise science, and nutritional biochemistry). I've also invested a

---

* You can, of course, provide this kind of service for a fee, if required. While this idea may feel uncommon in health and fitness, case management as a paid service is very common in medicine.

tremendous amount of money in "continuing education" courses both in health sciences and other areas (coaching, change psychology, business, marketing, and so on).

This means I started with a strong foundation determined by the universities I attended. Then I continued my education, delving into the areas I was most interested in, found lacking in my university training, or needed to learn to continue my development as a well-rounded professional.

This strong foundation is what I find missing in a lot of health and fitness professionals today. The majority of their education comes from "continuing education." And that's problematic for two reasons. First, these courses aren't meant to be foundational. They're meant to expand upon an already-strong foundation. No matter how great the courses are, something is always missing. Second, without a strong foundation, professionals aren't really equipped to make good decisions about which course to take next. Sure, following your interests is fun and engaging. However, it's no guarantee you'll learn the things you need to know to be an effective professional.

Consider personal training. With a weekend certificate, anyone can hang up a shingle and start taking clients. After that, the best trainers will commit to a process of lifelong learning. But which courses should they take? When? How can they stack learning on top of learning in a progressive way?

Without a solid foundation or some guidance—what I call context—they're just guessing. Having guessed wrong, many coaches end up chronically busy with courses, heavily invested (financially), without a great education to show for it.

Contrast this with medical training. Physicians have a well-established, multiyear curriculum that includes coursework, clinical rotations, progressively more independent consultation (though still supervised), and context-specific evaluation. That's just to *become* a doctor. After that there are continuing-education requirements to help guide their careers long after medical school is over.

Or take skilled trades. A plumber, for example, is required to attend technical school, get 144 hours of classroom time, and apprentice under a master plumber before they can take their first job. Then, when working as a plumber, they need to collect eight hours of continuing education every year.

While drastically different professions, physicians and plumbers have something critical in common: professional infrastructure based on discrete phases of development. "First you do A. Then you do B, because it builds on what you learned in A. Then comes C, which ties it all together." Schoolchildren don't start with advanced calculus. They start with basic arithmetic and build from there.

The same is true of training clients. You don't randomly give them kettlebell swings, box jumps, and hill sprinting and hope that an elite Olympic performance emerges. As a coach, you offer a progression that goes step-by-step, working systematically toward a specific outcome.

That progressive plan is what's been missing in health coaching, exercise coaching, even—to some degree—nutrition coaching.

This book will help remedy that. Not by proposing governmental regulation or the creation of trade schools (although those could make a difference in some contexts). Rather, by helping you create your own custom curriculum, a personal You-niversity that balances what you need to learn (to be a complete professional) with what you want to learn (to pursue what's interesting and fun).

Not only will this approach help you level up your career, it'll also help you stand out from the sea of amateurs. It's fascinating to look around and see coaches who have PhDs, others who have "read some stuff on the internet," and everything in between. It's also sad to see how this confuses prospective clients. They're not quite sure who's qualified and credible. By creating a solid curriculum for yourself, and articulating what you've done (and why), you'll stand apart. We'll explore this idea more in Chapters 6 and 7.

CHALLENGE 6

NOT PRACTICING *Professionalism*

OPPORTUNITY 6

INTENTIONALLY CULTIVATE *Your* REPUTATION

When most people in health and fitness—especially fitness—hear me use the word "professionalism," they're afraid I'll recommend trading in T-shirts for collared shirts and dropping conversational language for business speak. I'm actually talking about something deeper here: courtesy, integrity, ethics, communication, giving and receiving feedback, dealing with criticism, and the other "soft skills" that earn us our reputation.

You can wear a suit and tie, but your professionalism is lacking if you're constantly late and rude when you do finally show up, if you say one thing and do another, if your business practices are designed only for your personal gain instead of creating value for your prospects and clients.

To be trusted, respected, and seen as professionals, we need to *become* professionals. That means setting a high bar for how we communicate, for how we behave around others, and for how we live (even when others aren't watching). Like it or not, our reputation isn't solely built on the results we get for clients and patients. The rest is determined by how we show up, how we communicate, how we listen, and how we make others feel when they're around us.

We'll dig into professionalism more in Chapter 6.

Again, the health and fitness field is young. And the young often set up false dichotomies. They ask: *Would you rather have a coach who delivers results? Or one who makes you feel good about yourself?*

Both! I'd rather have a coach who delivers results *and* makes me feel good about myself.*

If you want to become the ultimate health and fitness change maker, you'll have to learn to do both. Let others fixate exclusively on muscle physiology, nutrient biochemistry, hormonal pathways, organ systems, macronutrients, and micronutrients.

Yes, learn these subjects too. **But don't miss the biggest opportunity of all—becoming the kind of professional that clients are willing to line up around the block to work with.**

---

* This realization is an inflection point for many. Early in their careers, they believe that if they do the technical side of coaching well, everything else will fall into place. But, once they see evidence to the contrary, they set out to level up their interpersonal skills . . . or they dig in their heels, assuming people are too stupid to see their obvious brilliance. As one colleague said in response to a question about why less-credentialed coaches often get more business: "Have you ever considered, even for a moment, that you may just be an asshole?"

CHALLENGE 1

THE GAP BETWEEN *Us* AND *Them*

→ **OPPORTUNITY 1**

Close THE GAP

CHALLENGE 2

NOT UNDERSTANDING WHAT PEOPLE *Want* AND *Need*

↓

OPPORTUNITY 2

Assume LESS, *Listen* MORE, AND EMPHATHIZE WITH THE PEOPLE *You* HOPE *To Serve*

CHALLENGE 3

NOT DEFINING *Your* PURPOSE

→ **OPPORTUNITY 3** ←

DEFINE *Yours* AND ALIGN IT WITH YOUR *Talents*

CHALLENGE 4

Becoming TOO SPECIALIZED

OPPORTUNITY 4

GENERALIZE *And* EMBRACE
THE IDEA *Of* THE CASE MANAGER

CHALLENGE 5

GETTING *Tangled Up* IN
Educational OPTIONS

OPPORTUNITY 5

CREATE *Your* OWN
YOU-NIVERSITY

CHALLENGE 6

NOT PRACTICING
Professionalism

OPPORTUNITY 6

INTENTIONALLY CULTIVATE
Your REPUTATION

THE HEALTH AND FITNESS INDUSTRY IS young
WITH TIME IT'LL gather THE wisdom IT NEEDS

WE'RE WITNESSING new MOVEMENT
A NEW profession
IT'S CHANGING FAST
our WORK will SHAPE THE FUTURE

close THE GAP BETWEEN THOSE WHO CAN help
AND THOSE WHO most NEED THE help
THIS IS your BLUE OCEAN OPPORTUNITY

assume LESS AND DON'T BUY INTO cliches
LEARN FOR SURE
what YOUR clients ARE AFTER
THEN DELIVER IT

FOR A REWARDING CAREER
explicitly DEFINE YOUR purpose
use YOUR UNIQUE ABILITIES TO serve IT

THE future BELONGS TO THE GENERALIST
SQUATS AND MACROS ARE secondary
change IS WHAT CLIENTS WANT MOST

build A STRONG FOUNDATIONAL CURRICULUM
CONTINUING EDUCATION ONLY WORKS
WHEN you've FIRST BEEN EDUCATED

COURTESY, INTEGRITY
AND COMMUNICATION matter
to be SEEN AS PROFESSIONALS
WE HAVE TO become PROFESSIONALS

CHAPTER 2

CAR

EER

HOW TO

Use Your PURPOSE,

UNIQUE ABILITIES,

AND *VALUES* TO PLOT

Your Career PATH →

Most health and fitness professionals, at least some days, end up feeling like expert witnesses being cross-examined in a courtroom drama. The barrage of questions seems never ending: "How much protein should I eat?" "Why does it hurt when I do *this*?" "Is it okay if I only get five hours of sleep a night?" "Why all the stupid burpees!?!"

However, as good as we are at answering our clients' questions, we're often confounded when trying to answer the following for ourselves:

What's my purpose?

Why do I do what I do?

What are my unique abilities (and inabilities)?

What are my values?

How do my values govern my life?

Not knowing the answers to these questions isn't just frustrating or annoying. It can stall your career, drain your enthusiasm, and leave you considering selling insurance instead of helping people eat, move, and live better.

Now, don't get the wrong idea. One of the health and fitness industry's strengths is that it's full of passionate professionals driven by a soul-stirring mission to help others live healthier, longer, and stronger lives. And, in most cases, this passion comes from an enlivening *origin story*, kinda like the one I shared in the Introduction.

At the same time, I worry that you'll confuse your origin story—no matter how affecting it was—with your purpose. That's because an origin story only provides the initial spark to ignite your career. But the fuel for powering a long, successful, rewarding vocation is something else altogether and includes gaining a much deeper understanding of your:

EXPLICIT PURPOSE
(going beyond clichés like "I want to help people"),

UNIQUE ABILITIES
(putting your one-of-a-kind skills in service of your purpose),

INDIVIDUAL VALUES
(creating professional guardrails to ensure a meaningful life).

I use a six-step process to help team members (and coaching clients) clarify each. By following this process, you'll have a *much* stronger chance of finding value, meaning, happiness, satisfaction, and—ultimately—success in your career and in your life.

Discovering Your Origin Story

In American comics, an origin story describes the circumstances under which superheroes gain their powers. In this book, I'm using the term in the very same way, to describe the circumstances under which health and fitness professionals gain their superpower—their passion for this work.

In my experience, these are the five most common origin stories. Circle the one that best describes you, or add yours in the space below.

I grew up with physical activity and sport.
I've always done health and fitness–related things. I played sports. I connected with friends and family through physical activity or healthy eating. As movement and vitality have been at my core since the beginning, it made sense to continue on with them as a career.

I got mentorship at a pivotal time in my life.
One day, unexpectedly, a health and fitness mentor swooped in and changed, maybe even saved, my life. It was so transformative

that I dedicated myself to paying forward that coaching and mentorship to help others who are struggling.

 I excelled at a particular goal.

For years I worked hard to achieve a particular health and fitness goal, like getting off my medications, losing a lot of weight, or even competing in an athletic event. And I did it! Becoming an exemplar here, I started coaching others to help them achieve the same goal.

 I watched someone suffer.

Someone close to me struggled with a preventable disease. I hated seeing this so I learned how the body works and how exercise, food, sleep, and stress management can help. Then I committed to helping people avoid the same fate I saw unfold in the life of my loved one.

 I fixed my own problems.

I hurt myself, got out of shape, struggled with eating and body issues, or otherwise found myself in the weeds of illness, injury, and suffering. The process of healing myself inspired me to help others. Now I invest my time and energy into helping to heal them too.

If none of the origin stories above describes you, write your own.

 To do this exercise, and all upcoming ones, please download our printable + fillable worksheets at **www.changemakeracademy.com/downloadable-forms**.

In the end, all paths to health and fitness are ultimately good paths because you're here! The benefit of knowing where you've come from is that it can help you decide where to go next.

CAREER STEPS

① Explicitly DEFINE YOUR PURPOSE

② UNCOVER YOUR Unique ABILITIES
   └ AND Unique INABILITIES

③ TUNE INTO Your INDIVIDUAL VALUES

④ USE YOUR Purpose, UNIQUE ABILITIES
   AND INDIVIDUAL VALUES to Choose
   → YOUR PATH

⑤ USE YOUR PURPOSE, Unique ABILITIES
   AND INDIVIDUAL VALUES TO GUIDE
   YOUR DAILY PRACTICE

⑥ REVISE YOUR PURPOSE, Unique
   ABILITIES AND Individual VALUES
   OVER TIME . . .

CAREER STEP 1

Explicitly DEFINE <u>YOUR</u> PURPOSE

While a strong origin story is awesome, it can sometimes lull health and fitness professionals into false confidence, thinking that they've got the whole purpose thing nailed down.

Yeah, yeah, I know all about my purpose. I'm here to help people. What could be more stirring than that?!? So let's move past purpose and onto the tangible career tips.

Not so fast.

In the Introduction, I shared how an influential mentor changed, maybe even saved, my life. In turn, I wanted to pay his mentorship forward and help other people.

But what does "help other people" really mean? "Helping people" could mean working as a paramedic, or a teacher, or a barista, or a volunteer in a shelter. From that perspective, just saying that you want to help people seems vague and particularly *not* purposeful.

Real purpose, the kind that Simon Sinek talks about in his book *Start with Why*, is about finding the cause, belief, or mission that motivates you, and using it as a filter to choose the careers, organizations, communities, and relationships that are most likely to inspire you. I believe that can only be achieved by going deeper, getting specific, and being explicit.

For example, in my career, I always wanted "helping people" at the core of my work. But to discover my real purpose, I had to go beyond that cliché and ask specific questions like:

WHO
do I want to help?

WHY
do I want to help them?

WHAT KIND OF HELP
do I want to provide?

HOW WILL I KNOW
if I've really helped them?

While I started my career as a one-on-one trainer and lifestyle coach, I eventually realized—through questions like this—that I wasn't particularly passionate about helping this group in this way. I saw others who showed up to one-on-one work motivated, inspired, and excited, but I didn't feel the same. For whatever reason, it just wasn't *my* purpose.

After years of early-morning and late-night coaching sessions, repeating mantras and affirmations designed to make me feel more positive and inspired, and trying everything I could to become the kind of person who enjoys one-on-one work, I knew I had to make a change.

Interestingly, that change came when I finally shared my struggles with other coaches and trainers. By opening up and making myself vulnerable—confessing that I *wasn't* living the perfect life; that despite having an extremely successful coaching practice, I was, in fact, struggling—they opened up to me too. And when I saw *their* struggles with coaching, their careers, and their businesses, I realized I wanted to do something about *that*. Helping *them* became all I could think about.

Plus, I realized that I wanted to help the whole industry grow and mature. I saw that it was missing insight, clarity, curriculum, and many of the tools available to other industries. I knew I could bring some of those things here.

These realizations eventually coalesced into a clear purpose statement that I've had for more than a decade now:

When I die, or retire, I'd like to know that my work made a tangible difference in helping health and fitness change makers:

1 see their clients differently,

2 see themselves differently,

3 see their work differently.

In the end, I don't need explicit credit for any of the work I do in this area. It'll be enough to know that I was part of the maturation of the industry.

Having this purpose top of mind—it's posted in my office so I can see it while I'm working—keeps me focused and inspired through the daily grind of meetings, through differences of opinion with teammates, through routine to-dos, and through small annoyances. Even rereading it now, I feel a little shot of adrenaline and a strong desire to do something more, today, to help achieve the goal.

Of course, that's just my purpose; everyone's is different. Take my colleague Jon. A while back, he visited a martial arts studio that advertised it would invest in anyone who was willing to put in the work, attend training, and learn their techniques. But he quickly noticed this wasn't true: LGBTQ members were treated with outright hostility. Jon's purpose came to life. A tireless advocate for inclusiveness, Jon built a fitness, nutrition, and lifestyle coaching business that focused on creating a safe and welcoming environment especially for queer and trans clients. His purpose—much more specific than "help people get healthy"—is clear and gives him roots, not just as a professional, but also as a person. (It also turned into a successful business.)

Another colleague, A'Tondra, was running a coaching business when 2017's Hurricane Harvey hit her community. As she watched the devastation, she commented: "Nutrition is the last thing you want to talk about when you're standing on the roof of your house." When she saw her community rally, she also saw an opportunity to help people build strength for themselves and those around them. So she pivoted her practice and started working with very small and personal groups in hurricane-affected areas. Those who could pay, did. Those who couldn't pay received support anyway, partially funded by those who could. Helping remained at the center of A'Tondra's purpose. But, as she drilled deeper, she got clear about who she really wanted to help, why she wanted to help, and how she wanted to help them. What's more, in her first year of coaching this way, she tripled her income.

Who knows why we're *really* attracted to one person over another, one hobby over another, one career over another? Digging down deep enough, the answer may be "just because." And that's fine. Because when we land there, we've dug deep enough.

My friend James is a great example of this. By day, he's a PhD researcher at a prestigious university. On evenings and weekends, he swaps out his lab coat for a leopard-print singlet, attaches one of those old-timey handlebar mustaches to his upper lip, and gets on stage to bend iron bars, rip telephone books in half, and lift adult women overhead, one in each hand, in strongman exhibitions.

Why is *this* what he spends his free time on? He's shared a few interesting answers with me. But I suspect the real answer is: "Because it's awesome. I don't know why I think it's awesome. I just do." Discovering your "awesome," in a judgment-free and totally accepting way, is another way of identifying your purpose.

Defining Your Purpose

How can you find your purpose? Hear your call? Hone in on both by answering the following questions, either here or in your own notebook or journal. Alternatively, you can download this as a fillable form at www.changemakeracademy.com/downloadable-forms.

QUESTION 1
Why do you want to work in health and fitness in the first place?

Is it your passion? Has it changed your life? Is helping others primary for you? Are you the go-to health and fitness person for your friends and family? What's your origin story?

QUESTION 2
Do you want to work with clients/patients?
Both yes and no are acceptable answers. You can work in health and fitness and never see a client or patient one-on-one. (More on this later.)

If yes, what type of clients do you want to work with?
Men? Women? Athletes? Children? Elderly? Only the motivated? Only people who've failed before? Everyone? No one? (Do you even like working with clients at all?)

If no, what do you gravitate toward instead?
Maybe you'd prefer to organize things or work behind the scenes in a health and fitness business? Maybe you'd like to write, or speak, or podcast, or teach? Run the front desk of a facility? Do the finances? Manage mission-critical projects?

QUESTION 3
Do you really want to help other people?
Does serving, teaching, or taking care of others inspire you? Do you truly want to help people? Or are you driven by something else? Is it external validation and status? (If so, that's okay. You might just want to consider *not* coaching.)

QUESTION 4

Do you want to own or run a business?

If so, do you want to have a small studio or practice? A big facility? Or would you rather work for someone else, such as a well-established health, fitness, or wellness center where you can focus on what you do best and trust your team to do the rest?

QUESTION 5

What relationship do you want with your income?

Are you comfortable with shorter-term contracts? Do you prefer the greater risk and (potential) reward of entrepreneurship? Or do you prefer a consistent, steady wage? Are you shooting for an affluent lifestyle? Or just "enough to live well"? Is money even a factor?

QUESTION 6

What relationship do you want with your work?

Are you looking for flexibility or structure? Full-time or part-time? Do you have children or other responsibilities that you juggle? Do you prefer other people to organize your work, or do you like to direct your own tasks? How much does your work define you as a person?

QUESTION 7

What other skills, talents, and aptitudes do you have?

You probably have lots of non-fitness-related things you can do, or things you enjoy. Maybe you're good with numbers. Or you have a knack for design and creating beautiful, welcoming spaces. Or you love working with animals. Take a complete inventory, even if your skills, talents, and apti-tudes don't necessarily seem relevant right now.

That's a lot to chew on. And not every question here will feel relevant at first. However, spend time with each of them anyway. You never know which question will lead to a new insight.

In the end, while ideas like "find your WHY" and "follow your pas-sion" and "discover your purpose" dominate career conversations nowa-days, they can be meaningless unless you go beyond the buzzwords and consider deeper questions like those above. And this one:

When you die or retire, how will you know whether you've followed your purpose?

For my part, I believe you'll know you've followed your purpose if your work has been meaningful (to you), if it's made a difference (mea-sured by your own metrics of meaning), if it's utilized your strengths, and if it's brought you enjoyment and satisfaction.

CAREER STEP 2

UNCOVER YOUR Unique ABILITIES
↳ AND Unique INABILITIES

If you think of your purpose as WHY you're doing what you do, you can think of your unique abilities as HOW to best live out that purpose, using your one-of-a-kind skills and talents.

While my purpose kept me committed and motivated, there were still some days that ended with me feeling restless and annoyed, like there was a strange, hard-to-reach itch that I just couldn't scratch. This affected not only me but my family. On nights I finished work feeling satisfied, I was a better parent and partner, full of joy, enthusiasm, and playfulness. But when I finished feeling "itchy," I was distracted, short-tempered, and preoccupied.

I remember one day as "the day that broke the camel's back." It was completely dominated by video conferences—one management meeting after another until the day was over. Despite hours of work, I felt like I'd accomplished nothing. It was infuriating. As my workday ended, I paced my office like a caged lion. It took me hours to get over the fact that I was *not* doing the work that mattered to me. Even worse, during those after-work hours, I realized I wasn't the kind of parent or partner I wanted to be.

This was happening far more often than I wanted it to. I wasn't sure what, but *something* needed to change. Somewhat serendipitously, PN's co-founder Phil was in a leadership course that week learning more about the unique abilities concept, and he taught it to me.

Popularized by Dan Sullivan, one of the world's most influential entrepreneurship coaches, and described in the *Unique Ability 2.0* book by Catherine Nomura, Julia Waller, and Shannon Waller, unique abilities are described by:

SUPERIOR SKILL.
You produce outstanding results with your unique ability.
It's so natural you can't help but do this extraordinarily well.
Others notice this skill, rely on it, and value it.

PASSION.
You love to do this, and probably did it in some form long before you got paid for it. (In fact, many people continue to

give their unique ability away for free because they don't recognize how special it is.)

ENERGY.
Using your unique ability gives you a boost of energy. The people around you get energy from you, too, because it's fun and exciting to be around someone who's passionate and talented at what they're doing. Likewise, when you surround yourself with other people living their unique abilities, your days are filled with positivity, dynamism, and creativity.

NEVER-ENDING IMPROVEMENT.
You're already exceptional at this, yet you could do it for the rest of your life and always find new ways to get better and better.*

I've come to think of unique abilities as the things that:

---

1 you are, or have the potential to be, world-class at;

---

2 you really enjoy doing;

---

3 you can make a big difference with, if you use them.

Of course, once I learned about unique abilities, and went through the process to discover mine, it became clear why some workdays ended with me feeling great while others ended with me feeling unsatisfied. Turns out, the "feeling great" days were spent mostly within my unique abilities, using my superpowers. And the "unsatisfied days" were spent outside of them, with kryptonite strapped to my chest.

---

* As one of my well-respected and very experienced colleagues said when reviewing this section: "It took me decades to figure out what my superpower was and it was what people were telling me I was good at for twenty years. I finally listened."

What's more, when I started analyzing my work to figure out how much time I spent in my unique abilities, and how much time I spent outside of them, I realized I was out of balance. While I knew it was unreasonable to expect to spend 100 percent of my time within my unique abilities, it became clear I was spending far more time outside of them than within. And this was hurting me, my family, and even our organization. So I took steps to shift the balance.

Going through this was such a breakthrough that Phil and I ended up using the unique ability process across our organization. Who wouldn't want to spend most of their day doing the things they enjoy, they're world class at, and they can make a difference with? What company wouldn't want the same: a team full of satisfied individuals doing world-class work that makes a difference for the organization?

We accomplished this by following the process I outline in the activity that follows.

Uncovering Your Unique Abilities

If you're ready to discover *your* unique abilities, here's what to do.

STEP 1
Contact five to ten colleagues, friends, and other people you're close to.

These should be people who really get you, who know what makes you shine, who count on you. Ideally, they should come from a cross-section of your life (not all friends or all family or all coworkers, for instance; you want a diversity of opinions, which will actually help reinforce common themes). Ask them if they'd be willing to take a few minutes and create a list with a dozen or so things that come to mind when they think about you. If they're up for it, email them the following questions:

1 What are the talents or abilities or characteristics that describe me?

2 What makes me tick?

3 What do you count on me for?

4 How would you describe my way of doing things?

5 Is there anything that impresses you about who I am?

Make clear that these characteristics don't need to reflect your hobbies, interests, or even work history. Rather, these are the things they've relied on you for or have appreciated about you.

STEP 2

Come up with your own answers.

Independently, make your own list, ideally before you get responses back. Answer the same questions you emailed your trusted list, as well as some others.

1 What are the talents or abilities or characteristics that describe me?

2 What makes me tick?

3 What do people count on me for?

4 What is "my way" of doing things?

5 What makes other people impressed with who I am?

6 What are the things I'm most passionate about?

7 What's important to me?

8 What have been my greatest accomplishments so far?

9 What are my goals—personal, family, career, life?

10 Who do I admire? Why? What can I learn from them?

STEP 3

Identify common themes.

Once everyone's responded, gather the replies. Identify common words, phrases, or themes. Make a list of ten or so that come up most often. Next to each item, write down why you think the person said it about you; specifically write the things you do that might make them say what they said.

STEP 4

Create your unique ability statements.

Take the ten most common themes from Step 3 and turn each into a unique ability statement.

If you'd like an example of what this could look like, check out the box on the next page. It's a one-pager of my own unique ability statements, which I keep posted in my office to remind me of what I should be spending time on.

Keep in mind that this isn't a five-minute compilation. Take your time with it—spend a few hours over several days to get the wording just right—because it's important. Think of it as an official document that clearly expresses your superpowers, just like how you'd cite your work experience in a resume. You'll review this list often to make sure you're staying in balance.

John Berardi's Unique Abilities

Here are my own unique ability statements, which I have posted visibly in my office.

DELIVERING AND COMMUNICATING INFORMATION.
Both formally (blog posts, books, products, speaking) and in personal communication.

GETTING OTHER COMMUNICATORS OF IDEAS TO A BETTER, MORE THOUGHTFUL, OR MORE RESONANT IDEA.
Both in formal editing and in facilitating communication between people.

FINDING ASSUMPTIONS.
Seeing and calling out all the assumptions, clichés, and shortcuts in people's plans and thoughts, and asking, "What if we didn't do it that way?"

INTENTIONALLY PUTTING MISSION-CRITICAL PROJECTS PAST THE POINT OF NO RETURN.
In a moment of clear thinking, committing to a deadline or powerful external force that compels a team to deliver on a commitment or face massive loss/embarrassment if they don't.

OPERATING WITH HONESTY AND INTEGRITY.
Being the same person across roles. Being willing to tell the truth, even when it's difficult, and being willing to commit to the subsequent conversations that happen as a result.

GAINING PEOPLE'S TRUST AND EMPHASIZING "TOGETHERNESS."
Carefully managing voice and body language; never pretending or elevating. Sharing only an authentic message and orienting the

message to the audience. Making people feel like we're "in it together," that it's not "me vs. them," that I'm going through this too.

ENGAGING IN REFLECTIVE THINKING.
Thinking about things before expounding on something aloud. Keeping silent until qualified or prepared to speak. Being willing to say, "I don't know."

ASSERTING AUTHORITY.
Confidently speaking up in areas I do know about. Relying on my self-assurance and confidence in my own capability.

EXPRESSING APPRECIATION.
Noticing when people do good things and letting them know I feel that way.

DEVISING AND IMPOSING STRUCTURE ON CHAOS.
Putting plans together, short term and long term, to get what we need out of the chaos. Committing to figuring it out whenever something is in our way.

ASKING THOUGHTFUL QUESTIONS.
Asking questions that I'm genuinely curious to know the answers to and that I feel are relevant/interesting to me and to the person I'm asking.

MIRRORING, MIMICKING, AND COPYING SUCCESS.
Before beginning new projects, finding an example or template that represents excellent, high-quality work and then modifying it, shaping it, adapting it to serve our needs.

Remember, these statements come from friends, family, and colleagues. They're not necessarily what I think about myself. Rather, they're what *they* think of me. This is essential because most people (myself included) struggle to identify their unique abilities.

I recently walked into the kitchen as my eight-year-old daughter was working on a craft. I asked what she was up to, and she described the project to me. After asking a bunch of follow-up questions: "Why are you doing it this way? Why not that way? I'm wondering if this might improve the project?" she looked up and said, "Dad, you know what's really cool about you? I always start projects like this and have an idea of how they should go. Then, I include you in the project, and you always give me ideas to make it better. You're really good at that."

Cute, I know. But also instructive. Before going through the unique ability process, I wouldn't have listed this as one of mine.

In many ways, I've historically undervalued this thing about myself because it's come easy to me and not everyone is receptive to it. Which is why I need friends, family, colleagues—even my eight-year-old—to help uncover my unique abilities. And so do you.

But the unique ability process doesn't end here.

While identifying unique abilities is a big first step, the next is to find ways in which you can better integrate them into your work. To do this at Precision Nutrition, our team members log all the different kinds of tasks they do in a week. Then they place those tasks in one of the following quadrants: unique ability activities, excellent activities, competent activities, and incompetent activities. The following will walk you through that process.

Spending Time in Your Unique Abilities

Keep a running log of all the different kinds of tasks you do in a week.

Once you've identified your unique abilities, give this last step a try. Figure out how much of your week is spent doing tasks within your unique abilities by sorting the tasks from your log into the following quadrants.

UNIQUE ABILITY ACTIVITIES: **Superior skill and passion.** You're awesome at this and love doing it. You lose track of time here.	**EXCELLENT ACTIVITIES:** **Superior skill and no passion.** You're awesome, but don't love it. You're the go-to person, but don't get satisfaction from it.
COMPETENT ACTIVITIES: **Minimum standard and no passion.** You're capable of it, but it gives you some anxiety and you'd rather do other things.	**INCOMPETENT ACTIVITIES:** **Failure and frustration.** You hate it and it stresses you out. Lots of frustration, and it makes your day horrible.

If 80 percent of your time is spent in the unique ability quadrant, everyone's happy. If you're spending much less time in your unique abilities, consider how to slowly transition out of the other quadrants and into your superpowers.

Keep in mind: it's not always comfortable to identify mismatches between how you *are* spending your time and how you *should be* spending your time for happiness and fulfillment. Sometimes these mismatches will even suggest that you need massive changes in your life. However, the investment is worth it. Explicitly defining your purpose, and then putting your unique abilities in the service of that purpose, is your most reliable path to career satisfaction and success.

CAREER STEP 3

TUNE INTO *Your* INDIVIDUAL VALUES

When you're on fire with purpose and using your superpowers for good, work can feel pretty amazing. (For an instant jolt of gratitude, contrast that feeling with the feeling of having no purpose and doing work that frustrates you because you're not particularly good at it.)

At the same time, it's easy to get swept away by your passion. It's easy to start working long hours, burning the candle at both ends. Easy to focus exclusively on your mission, ignoring family, friends, and others in your community. Easy to seize every opportunity, forgetting that physical and mental growth comes not during massive efforts, but from the recuperation time between them.

That's where your values come in, providing the guardrails to keep you on track.

Values are the ideals you think are essential for a good life. They're guiding principles you feel proud to live out, beliefs you're willing to fight for. They're (hopefully) how you decide priorities. And, when you use them to decide priorities, you're more likely to live a fulfilled life.

To show you how this works, here are the values that have driven my decision-making for a decade:

FAMILY.
I value spending focused, undistracted time with my wife and our four children. I'm particularly keen on high quality one-on-one time with each, which includes skipping work (and school) some days, taking trips together, and more.

SELF-CARE.
I value spending time each day to keep myself physically, mentally, and emotionally healthy. This includes getting enough sleep, exercising often, eating well, meditating, spending time in nature, reading, enjoying the arts, spending time with counselors, and other activities.

PROFESSIONAL GROWTH.
I value the building and ongoing development of Precision Nutrition, as an organization. I value the development of my teammates within the organization. And I value the growth that comes from trying things, reflecting on what happened, learning, and trying again.

More than just a set of conceptual ideals, I've made these values concrete by turning them into priorities and posting them visibly in my office.

PRIORITY 1
Be an active, present partner to my wife and parent to our four children.

PRIORITY 2
Carve out daily time for self-care (exercise, nutrition, sleep, stress management).

PRIORITY 3
Within my work hours, do everything I can to serve and build the Precision Nutrition brand and community.

With clearly articulated values and posted priorities, my life—while very full—is also straightforward. All opportunities and decisions are informed by the following questions:

"Will this help me become a more present parent or partner?"

"Will this help me with my health, fitness, sleep, and stress management?"

"Will this make a big impact on the growth of Precision Nutrition?"

Everything that's not a "yes" to one of the questions above has to be a "no." Even if it scratches my "I get to take a cool trip" itch, or my "I get to connect with someone I really respect" itch, or my "I get to try something new" itch.

Here's an example: A friend and colleague recently asked me to speak at a renowned symposium in Olympia, Greece. No, not Mr. Olympia, the bodybuilding contest. This is the *real* Olympia, the site of the original Olympic games, where they preserve the ancient ruins and house an international learning academy.

I nearly rushed into saying yes. But when I asked my key questions above, I saw a very different answer. It wasn't going to help me be a better parent or partner, wasn't going to help with my self-care, and wasn't going to grow Precision Nutrition. I shouldn't take this trip.

Yet, in the moment, I really wanted to go! So I looked for loopholes. What if I bring my whole family and we rented a nearby villa? Sadly, still a no. (Our youngest was one year old at the time, and I realized that bringing the whole family halfway around the world wasn't right for us.)

I was sad to turn down the opportunity, of course. But that was the *only sensible choice* once I ran it through the "values and priorities filter."

Your values and priorities are probably different than mine. Maybe you think I'm nuts for turning down the Olympia trip. Perhaps "travel" or "having new experiences" is one of your top values. If so, that's great—but articulate it. Capture it. Get clear about it. The activity on pages 51–53 will show you how.

Tuning In to Your Individual Values

USING EXAMPLES FROM YOUR CAREER AND PERSONAL LIFE, THINK OF THE TIMES YOU FELT HAPPIEST.

What were you doing?

What were you with?

What else was involved that contributed to the feelings of happiness?

NEXT, THINK OF THE TIMES YOU WERE MOST PROUD, AGAIN USING CAREER AND PERSONAL EXAMPLES.

Why were you proud?

Who else shared in your pride?

What else was involved that contributed to the feelings of pride?

How and why did the experience give your life meaning?

NEXT, THINK OF THE TIMES YOU WERE MOST FULFILLED.

What need or desire was fulfilled?

How and why did the experience give your life meaning?

What other factors contributed to your feelings of fulfillment?

FINALLY, THINK OF THE TIMES YOU FELT MOST PHYSICALLY ENERGIZED, AT PEACE, OR FULL OF VITALITY AND "FLOW."

What were you doing?

Who were you with?

What else was involved that contributed to the feelings of energy, peace, and flow?

Based on your experiences with happiness, pride, fulfillment, and embodied cognition, consider which sorts of values drive those feelings. For example, if you feel most energized while writing, painting, or making music, perhaps creativity is one of your core values. Or maybe if you feel most proud, fulfilled, and at peace when helping out at a senior center, one of your core values is service.

Here's a list of values that people commonly associate with:

ACCOUNTABILITY

ACCURACY

ACHIEVEMENT

ADVENTUROUSNESS

ALTRUISM

AMBITION

ASSERTIVENESS

BALANCE

BEING THE BEST

BELONGING

BOLDNESS

CALMNESS

CAREFULNESS

CHALLENGE

CHEERFULNESS

CLEAR-MINDEDNESS

COMMITMENT

COMMUNITY

COMPASSION

COMPETITIVENESS

CONSISTENCY

CONTENTMENT

CONTINUOUS IMPROVEMENT

CONTRIBUTION

CONTROL

COOPERATION

CORRECTNESS

COURAGE

COURTESY

CREATIVITY

CURIOSITY

DECISIVENESS

DEMOCRACY

DEPENDABILITY

DETERMINATION

DEVOUTNESS

DILIGENCE

DISCIPLINE

DISCRETION

DIVERSITY

DYNAMISM

ECONOMY

EFFECTIVENESS

EFFICIENCY

ELEGANCE

EMPATHY

ENJOYMENT

ENTHUSIASM

EQUALITY

EXCELLENCE

EXCITEMENT

EXPERTISE

EXPLORATION

EXPRESSIVENESS

FAIRNESS

FAITH

FAMILY

FIDELITY

FITNESS

FLUENCY

FOCUS

FREEDOM

FUN

GENEROSITY

GOODNESS

GRACE

GROWTH

HAPPINESS

HARD WORK

HEALTH

HELPING SOCIETY	RESOURCEFULNESS
HOLINESS	RESTRAINT
HONESTY	RESULTS
HONOR	RIGOR
HUMILITY	SECURITY
INCLUSION/INCLUSIVITY	SELF-ACTUALIZATION
INDEPENDENCE	SELF-CONTROL
INGENUITY	SELFLESSNESS
INNER HARMONY	SELF-RELIANCE
INNOVATION	SENSITIVITY
INQUISITIVENESS	SERENITY
INSIGHTFULNESS	SERVICE
INTELLECTUAL STATUS	SHREWDNESS
INTELLIGENCE	SIMPLICITY
INTUITION	SOUNDNESS
JOY	SPEED
JUSTICE	SPONTANEITY
LEADERSHIP	STABILITY
LEGACY	STRATEGY
LIFE FLEXIBILITY	STRENGTH
LOVE	STRUCTURE
LOYALTY	SUCCESS
MAKING A DIFFERENCE	SUPPORT
MASTERY	TEAMWORK
MERIT	TEMPERANCE
OBEDIENCE	THANKFULNESS
OPENNESS	THOROUGHNESS
ORDER	THOUGHTFULNESS
ORIGINALITY	TIMELINESS
PATRIOTISM	TOLERANCE
PERFECTION	TRADITIONALISM
PIETY	TRUSTWORTHINESS
POSITIVITY	TRUTH-SEEKING
PRACTICALITY	UNDERSTANDING
PREPAREDNESS	UNIQUENESS
PROFESSIONALISM	UNITY
PRUDENCE	USEFULNESS
QUALITY	VISION
RELIABILITY	VITALITY

As you consider how your experiences dovetail with the values listed here, circle or write down the ones that best describe you. If your list is long, narrow it down to the three to five that feel most resonant.

> ⊕

FROM THERE, REALITY TEST THEM BY ASKING QUESTIONS LIKE:
Would my closest friends, unprompted, say these were the ideals that mean the most to me?

> ⊕

Would I support these ideals even if my choice wasn't popular and it put me in the minority?

> ⊕

Am I prioritizing my work, and my life, according to these values today?

> ⊕

Another great way of knowing if you're on the right track is to test them against each other. For example, if you list adventurousness as your top value, consider whether you'd be willing to go on a once-in-a-lifetime three-month trip even if it meant losing out on a fantastic career opportunity. If not, is adventurousness really your top value?

Coming up with your values (and the priorities that naturally flow from them) is heady work. Yet the payoff is huge. Your values and priorities will become much-needed guardrails for governing your work and your life.

Consider: If life flexibility is one of your values, working defined hours in a clinic every Monday through Saturday probably isn't ideal. If family is a value, then seeing clients between 4 and 9 PM doesn't mesh. If you value being in nature, maybe you don't want to be in a windowless massage room for ten hours a day.

Even more than helping you define the career choices to run away from, your values—along with your purpose and unique abilities—can help you choose the work to run toward.

CAREER STEP 4

USE YOUR *Purpose,* UNIQUE ABILITIES AND INDIVIDUAL VALUES *to Choose* ⟶ YOUR PATH

Meet Sara. At the peak of her career (v1.0) she managed complex software projects at Microsoft. It was a prestigious, well-paid position, and she often worked directly with Bill Gates. Yet it was also hard-driving, stressful, and required long hours plus a single-minded focus.

After years of *not* paying attention to her health, *not* investing time in her own self-care, Sara found Precision Nutrition and signed up for our online client coaching program. During the next year she lost fifty pounds, dramatically improved her health, and found much-needed balance in her life.

Having fallen in love with health and fitness, she made the tough choice to leave Microsoft and pursue a coaching career. Ever the achiever, she went through the Precision Nutrition Level 1 and Level 2 certification programs, signed up to be one of our first interns, did a host of other education and certification programs, and fixed her sights on becoming a Precision Nutrition coach.

Talented and driven, she applied three separate times to join the Precision Nutrition coaching team . . . but she never got the job. (We have a limited number of full-time coaching spots, over one thousand applicants each time a spot opens, and rigorous criteria for ensuring we hire folks whose true unique abilities are in line with what's needed to coach the way we coach.)

The experience was disheartening for Sara. Years later, she still tears up telling the story. Yet she's in a great place now. Instead of working as a coach, Sara v2.0 works at a fantastic women's health and fitness company as a special project manager for the founder, taking the company's biggest, most significant initiatives from concept to completion.

Sara's story illustrates two fundamental mistakes that *so many* people make in health and fitness.

MISTAKE 1:
Thinking that the most visibly defined pathways are the only possible pathways

---

MISTAKE 2:
Not considering purpose, values, *and* unique abilities when choosing a career path*

In Sara's case, after transforming her life, her purpose evolved. Helping people live healthier, more purposeful lives became vital to her, and she couldn't do that at Microsoft. After having her first child, Sara realized her values were changing, too, and family came to the forefront. She knew this would be compromised if she continued working long,

---

* These are mistakes that many health and fitness clients make too. They think the most visibly defined pathways (like losing twenty pounds or getting six-pack abs) are the only possible pathways. And they fail to consider their purpose, values, and unique abilities when choosing an action plan (i.e., does a middle-aged teacher who spends his free time doing musical theater, looking for a solution for aching knees and type 2 diabetes, really need to sign up for a Tough Mudder?).

stressful hours at Microsoft. So Sara made the best decision for herself.

Her only misstep was forgetting to consider her unique abilities when thinking about her next move. Coaching requires a completely different set of skills and talents than project management. That's why, as frustrating as it was that she never got the coaching job, it's probably the best thing.

Unknown to her at the time, not getting the job saved her from getting stuck doing work that would have been unfulfilling. Plus it left open the possibility of doing the work she's ideally suited for, this time in an environment more aligned with her values and purpose.

As I look around the health and fitness industry, I see people (over) simplifying their options like this. In their minds, if you're going to work in health and fitness, your only options are:

personal trainer

strength coach

nutrition coach

naturopath

functional medicine doctor

yoga or Pilates teacher

rehab specialist

group exercise instructor

These are wonderful options, of course. But only if they match *your* purpose and unique abilities. Only if the work requirements match your values.

The bad news? Too many people end up in one of the above jobs and, for them, it's a total dead end. While it's probably in the right ballpark relative to their purpose, most aren't uniquely good at the work, and it doesn't match their values.

The good news? For people new to the field, there are so many career options beyond those above. And, for those already in the field, there's always time to change.

For example, let's say you're passionate about exercise and fitness. Instead of trying to become a personal trainer or strength coach, you could also try:

WRITING
about exercise and fitness in books, magazines, or online publications

SPEAKING
about exercise and fitness at trade shows or conferences

LECTURING
on exercise and fitness at high schools, colleges, or universities

PODCASTING
on exercise and fitness

HOSTING
exercise and fitness programming on TV or on the radio*

Another acceptable option is to keep your hobby a hobby; not everyone who loves health and fitness needs to pursue a career in it.

---

* However, as one of my colleagues pointed out: Seeing people write, speak, or post about health and fitness without much experience or expertise hurts the field as a whole. So, before setting yourself up as an authority, be sure you've done the work, and put in the reps, to develop real expertise. Without it, you'll be doing no one a service, including yourself.

Alternatively, with the right training and unique abilities, you could work in **human resources, finance, business development, marketing, tech, design, or leadership** in a health and fitness company that shares your purpose and values.

You could also pursue **entrepreneurship** and start your own business, whether it's a fitness center, online coaching company, or wearable tech company. Indeed, coaching people directly is only one of many potentially fulfilling options.

Take my colleague Pat. He's a systems thinker with a mind for data and analysis who started out as a personal trainer and strength coach. Realizing that he enjoyed spreadsheets more than squats, but still wanting to work in the field, he began studying quantitative methods in sport science. He now works for an NFL team evaluating training demands and how they relate to athlete health, injury, and performance.

This is where the fun begins.

Let's say you're a natural storyteller, gregarious, and connect better in a one-on-hundreds setting than one-on-one. In this case, it'd make sense for your career to involve speaking engagements and connecting with crowds vs. client-based interactions.

However, let's say all that travel doesn't mesh with your values (spending weekends away from your family is a no-no, and all that air travel compromises your self-care). In that case, you'd look for other ways to use your unique abilities.

Could you confine your speaking to local venues?

Could you work in a corporate setting bringing health and fitness to hundreds of employees at a time?

Or could you arrange a way to bring your family with you and take care of yourself too?

Here's another example. Let's say you're awesome at organization and are exceptionally good at keeping the trains running. You never forget a task and are talented at directing and leading people. Plus, one of your values is to have consistency and predictability in your life (which might mean maintaining predictable and traditional work hours so that you can plan your own leisure time, like weekend hikes with friends or having dinner at home every night).

Putting it all together, maybe your unique abilities and values lead you to going into management, supervising a team of health-care professionals, trainers, or nutritionists.

Choosing Your Career

To help you better align your career choice to your purpose, values, and unique abilities, let's list them again here.

Your purpose:

Your unique abilities:

Your values:

With these in mind, brainstorm some career options that best fit all three:

If your current job is among the career options you brain-stormed above, great! You're on the right path. If you're thinking you need to make a switch, the following chapters have suggestions for ways to get on a new path from square one.

This game can feel tricky at first. Not only is it challenging to figure out what your purpose, unique abilities, and values are, it also takes a lot of thought to find creative career options that satisfy all three. Yet that's the secret behind most of the successful people I know.

No one ever said it would be easy. **But you're not reading this book because you want easy. You're here because you're ready to do what it takes to build a successful career and live a deliberate life.** Discover your purpose, unique abilities, and values—and use them to decide your path—and the chances go way up.[*]

USE YOUR *PURPOSE, Unique ABILITIES* AND *INDIVIDUAL VALUES* TO GUIDE *YOUR DAILY PRACTICE*

I recently received an invitation to speak at a one-hundred-person event in Sydney, Australia. I also got a request to be interviewed by the *New York Times* for a nutrition piece. And both came in during a week in which I'd already committed to creating a new video course for Precision Nutrition.

---

* Remember, though, there's no substitute for hard work, thousands of hours of practice, and a true dedication to your craft. No matter how much your career brings together your stated purpose, unique abilities, and values, you still have to work at it, often when you don't even feel like putting in the effort. The good news is that it'll feel more meaningful if it's in alignment with your purpose, unique abilities, and values.

Knowing what you know about my priorities, unique abilities, and values, if you had to choose between them, what would you do? Would you book the ticket to Sydney, do the interview with the most famous paper in the world, or work on the video course?

My decision-making goes like this:

While I hear Sydney is amazing, I say no to the travel because it takes me away from my family, means less time for self-care, and is a very small audience compared to the 750,000 people I can reach through the Precision Nutrition mailing list.

I say no to the *New York Times* because I've been quoted there before and, unless it's a feature piece they're doing on me or on Precision Nutrition, additional mentions provide very little marginal value.

I say yes to the video project because I get to do what I'm best at (using my unique abilities) in a way that will influence the work and lives of health and fitness change makers (using my purpose) and that will grow the business from the comfort of my home office (again, using my values).

Let me be clear: I'm extremely fortunate and grateful to have these opportunities. Earlier in my career I wouldn't have believed it if you told me I'd one day turn down paid trips around the world and interviews with the *New York Times*. However, the real lesson isn't to turn down travel or interviews. It's to figure out what *you* need to find purpose, meaning, and enjoyment in your work. And to stay true to those things, rather than getting swept up by every cool invitation that's not consistent with what you're here to accomplish.

This is one of the most overlooked benefits of articulating your purpose, unique abilities, and values. Knowing them makes almost *every-*

thing easier. It becomes super clear what to say yes and no to. It makes your work more fun. It makes your career more meaningful. It gives you the freedom to develop your unique abilities even more. And it's always evolving—just as you are.*

Making Wise Daily Decisions

While you need to consider your purpose, unique abilities, and values to "zoom out" and make wise, big-picture-perspective career decisions, the same thinking is valuable for zooming *in* and making daily, seemingly pedestrian, work decisions.

To this end, write down a few of the different opportunities you've been asked to choose from lately.

Now evaluate whether those opportunities are in alignment with your purpose, unique abilities, and values. If they all are, rock on! If not, how can you go out and create new opportunities that are in better alignment?

---

* The only caveat here is this: It's often easy to convince ourselves that opportunity X doesn't align with our values when, in reality, we're just scared or uncomfortable trying something new. So make sure to differentiate between saying no because something conflicts with your values and saying no because you're intimidated by the work involved in something you know is worth doing.

REVISE YOUR PURPOSE, Unique ABILITIES AND Individual VALUES OVER TIME . . .

At Precision Nutrition we often use the saying: "Forever, for now." It means that, yes, we feel confident in the thing we just decided. It's the final decision for now. However, it's also subject to revision based on new insights, experiences, learning, and feedback.

Forever for now is a really good way of looking at this six-step career process too. During your first pass through the process, it'll feel like a linear thing with a beginning, middle, and end. However, it can't stop there. Circumstances, time, experience, and insight will have you re-thinking your purpose, your unique abilities, and your values. That's normal. Optimal even.

So view this process as a cycle, not a one-and-done thing. The minute you stop cycling back and refining your thinking—in any aspect of your life—is the minute you stop growing.

Likewise, don't feel pressure to get each step "perfect" or to quickly nail it down. (The idea of career quick fixes is just as unrealistic as nutrition and exercise quick fixes.) So take your time, do the best you can with what you've got at each step, and keep doing refinements over time.

In the beginning of your career, this probably means thinking *a lot* about your purpose, unique abilities, and values. And revisiting whatever you land on every few months. That's because you don't yet know what you're good at, what you'll find meaning in, or how to articulate that gut feeling forcing you to take action. That's normal and expected. Seriously. In an industry that inaccurately valorizes youth and overnight success, it's easy to forget the fact that you can't possibly be an expert (on any particular subject, or even on yourself) without trial, error, learning, and experience.

Revisiting Your Purpose, Unique Abilities, and Values over Time

To make sure you're regularly reevaluating, I'd highly recommend opening your calendar and choosing a date three months from now to schedule an hour or two for your next review. Record it below.

Day and time for my three-month review:

Later in your career, after years of trial and error, and after a host of formative experiences, you'll have more self-awareness, more industry awareness, and will know better what's important to you, which are your superpowers, and what you should be doing with your life.

This process isn't just for newbies. Yes, newbies will need to spend more time with it and revisit it more often, asking key questions every few months. However, even folks mid- or late career need to refine their understanding of their work. By reevaluating the process every year or two, you'll either discover renewed enthusiasm about your purpose, superpowers, and values, or you'll learn that you've changed and have to adjust your career strategy accordingly. One of my colleagues is a great example of this. After her adult children moved out, she became an "empty nester," which triggered her to reconsider her purpose and values, as well as what she'll put her energy into going forward.

You probably already use this revisiting process in other areas of your life. If you're an avid exerciser, you've probably adjusted your mode of exercise, or your philosophy on how to exercise, over time, as you've gathered more experience, lived in a changing body or daily routine, and learned from new teachers. Your nutrition ideas have probably changed, too, for the same reasons.

If you treat your career with the same sense of adventure, openness, and growth-mindedness, even if you don't nail the perfect purpose, unique abilities, and values the first time through, you'll get closer and closer with each iteration.

Q&A with JB: Career

To support what you're learning, I've compiled end-of-chapter Q&As that are full of real, thoughtful questions I've gotten over the years. In each one I share my unfiltered take on the challenges you'll undoubtedly face as you grow your career.

⊕ You can check out all the Change Maker Q&As at **www.changemakeracademy.com/questions**.

This chapter's questions include:

Q: I'm excited about getting into the health and fitness industry. I feel like my purpose is here and my unique abilities will allow me to make a difference. But it does feel really crowded, like a lot of people want to be involved. Should I be worried about competition? (Answer: ~350 words)

Q: Earlier, you talked about using your purpose, unique abilities, and values to help determine what to say yes to and what to say no to. Is that true for every stage of your career? (Answer: ~700 words)

Q: I understand the value in turning down certain opportunities at certain stages in my career. But how can I turn them down without seeming ungrateful, disappointing the people who might be counting on me to say yes, or ruining future opportunities? (Answer: ~650 words)

Q: It sounds a lot like you're saying that passion should drive one's career. I've heard that's not a good idea and you need to be more practical. What do you say to that? (Answer: ~150 words)

WORDS OF WISDOM: CAREER

(AS interesting AS IT MIGHT BE)
DON'T CONFUSE your ORIGIN story
WITH your PURPOSE

Ask YOURSELF
WHEN I DIE OR retire, HOW WILL I KNOW
I've FOLLOWED MY purpose?

Purpose = WHY
UNIQUE ABILITIES = HOW

UNIQUE Abilities
WHAT you're GOOD AT
WHAT you ENJOY DOING

MOST PEOPLE struggle TO
IDENTITY THEIR unique ABILITIES
Get help FINDING YOURS

It's easy TO GET SWEPT AWAY BY PASSION
YOUR VALUES provide the GUARDRAILS
to KEEP YOU ON TRACK

Write down YOUR VALUES, sure
MORE IMPORTANTLY REALITY TEST THEM
so YOU KNOW they're TRUE

DON'T OVERSIMPLIFY your options
THERE ARE SO MANY HEALTH AND FITNESS
paths TO CHOOSE FROM

Adventure, OPENNESS AND GROWTH-MINDEDNESS
WILL HELP YOU GET CLOSER to your
PURPOSE + unique ABILITIES + VALUES

THE minute YOU STOP CYCLING BACK
(AND refining YOUR CAREER THINKING)
IS THE minute YOU STOP GROWING

STRONG PERSONAL MISSION (AND VALUES)
+ HIGH competency (UNIQUE abilities)
+ System FOR EXECUTION (YOUR operating
SYSTEM) = PERSONAL AND CAREER satisfaction

CHAPTER 3
CLIE

NTS

HOW TO

Know WHAT YOUR CLIENTS REALLY WANT AND DELIVER IT *Every Time*

Once upon a time, McDonald's—in an attempt to boost revenue from a flagging line of business—set out to improve their milkshake sales.

As most companies do, they segmented their market by product (i.e., milkshakes vs. hamburgers) and by demographics (i.e., people who buy milkshakes vs. people who buy hamburgers). From there they surveyed large groups who buy milkshakes, asking lots of questions about the thick beverages. Finally, they gathered small groups who buy milkshakes and had them taste and rate different ones.

From the feedback they got, they changed their milkshakes. Yet sales didn't improve.

Disappointed but unfazed, McDonald's tried a totally different approach. They hired an innovative (and, at the time, controversial) team of Harvard researchers to help them figure out the "job" that people "hire" milkshakes to do. Weird concept, I know. But stick with me; it'll all make sense.

To discover the "job to be done," the research team spent days at McDonald's locations, recording *who* bought milkshakes, *when* they bought them, *where* they drank them. They didn't ask questions. They just watched and documented actual behavior, learning that over 40 percent of milkshakes were sold "to go," in the morning, to people commuting to work.

Later they returned to McDonald's and interviewed this large group of milkshake-buying commuters to figure out what "job" they "hired" the milkshake to do. Their summary:

Milkshake commuters were facing a long, boring drive and needed something to keep their nondriving hand busy, an activity to make the commute more interesting.

 They weren't yet hungry but knew they'd be hungry by 10 AM. So they wanted something to eat or drink that would keep hunger at bay until noon.

 They were in a hurry, wearing work clothes, and they had (at most) one free hand.

So, instead of getting a muffin or breakfast sandwich, they chose a milkshake because it's less messy, more filling, and (here's a fascinating insight) trying to suck a thick liquid through a tiny straw gave them something to do during their boring drive. Understanding this was the "job," McDonald's created a milkshake that was thicker (lasts longer, more satisfying) and added chunks of fruit (to make it "more interesting" and, no doubt, create a health halo: "Look, fruit. It's healthy!").

Snickers has taken a similar approach by looking for the "job to be done."

Even if you've never eaten a Snickers, you know their classic tagline: "It satisfies." For more than thirty years, Mars has poured their energy into convincing us that Snickers isn't a "candy bar" but—much like the McDonald's milkshake—an easy-to-grab, not-messy meal alternative.

Their 1980s ad nails the job perfectly: "I got deadlines to meet. I can't let something like hunger get in the way. Snickers fills me up until I can grab a meal. It cuts the hunger. Lets me take care of business." As does their more recent campaign: "You're not you when you're hungry."

The Mars company arrived at these insights in the same way McDonald's did. They hired the same Harvard researchers to hang out in convenience stores and airport terminals to watch people buy Snickers. Then, as soon as someone bought a Snickers bar and walked out of the store, the team would interview them using a particular framework (which I'll share in this chapter).

What they learned was that Snickers customers were mostly young men, hungry (in that "if I don't get food soon, I'm gonna be angry" way), and in a hurry.

Also—and this is crucial—most of the people who bought Snickers *didn't* consider any other candy bars. For them it wasn't a choice between Snickers and Milky Way; they were choosing between Snickers and other cheap, hunger-satisfying, on-the-go snacks like sandwiches, burritos, or beef jerky. Based on this insight, and by convincing people Snickers isn't a candy bar at all but a satisfying meal replacement, Mars turned Snickers into the world's number-one-selling candy bar.

McDonald's milkshakes and Snickers bars have become iconic and recognized worldwide, not because they're necessarily tastier or cheaper than their competitors, but because they were developed and marketed based on deeper, often nonintuitive, insights about the "job" they've been "hired" to do by their customers.

So, milkshakes and candy bars . . . how do they relate to health and fitness? Well, they don't. And yes, a milkshake sounds like a terribly *un*healthy breakfast. But the principle of searching for the "job to be done" does. That's because the health and fitness industry has been historically bad at identifying the "job" people are "hiring" our products and services to do. The result? We end up making (and marketing) things with a kindergarten-simple view of customers and then complain that they don't seem to understand what we're offering or why it's important.

It's time we leveled up.

It's time to think more deeply about the people we've chosen to serve, our clients and customers, and what they're looking for when they reach out to us. Time invested here pays huge dividends by helping you make and market the things people will line up for, tell their friends about, and buy over and over again.

THE *Job* TO BE *DONE:*
HOW *INDUSTRY* GETS IT *Wrong*

As mentioned in Chapter 1, I once read a review from a former coaching client. Someone asked her if she would recommend our program, and she responded with something like:

I don't recommend it. I lost some weight, but I never felt like I connected with my coach. I didn't really need much help from her. But if I would have needed help, I'm not sure how much I'd have gotten.

You might remember the somewhat ironic nature of this comment: She ended up losing over fifty pounds working with us, improving on nearly every measure collected. Yet she was unhappy, and I wanted to know why. So I offered to pay for an hour of her time and interview her.*

Until that point, I believed that clients would be happy if they lost weight and kept it off, if they improved health markers, and/or if they improved their quality of life, especially if they'd tried and failed using other programs before. All of these were checked off for this client.

However, there was a completely different (and legitimate) reason she didn't recommend us: She didn't feel like anyone cared. She didn't feel heard or understood. Losing weight, while nice, *wasn't enough.*** She wanted her coach to be with her every step of the way and her coach wasn't.

Yes, our team won the battle with fat and preventable disease. But we lost the big one—having a lasting meaningful relationship with our client, one where she felt she got her money's worth, one where she raved about how we changed her life. And why did we lose? Because we

---

* You'll often learn a lot more from these "failures" than from your raving fans. It'll hurt your ego, and maybe your wallet, but learning how and why you went wrong with real honesty is one of the best investments you can make. Think about it as a "preventing future screwups tax."

** Recent research suggests that when women seek health information, they tend to look for emotional and social support (i.e., you're gonna be okay and we can help), whereas men tend to look more for informational support (i.e., here's some stuff you need to know).

made too many assumptions. Instead of knowing, we guessed. Instead of asking questions, we bought into clichés.

Today, thankfully, Precision Nutrition does much better. But I see this same problem *everywhere* in health and fitness. It's the reason why magazine covers haven't changed in thirty years; men's magazines continue to drone on about "torching fat" and "rock-hard abs" while women's magazines talk about "long, lean muscles" and "shapely thighs."

These "insights" are the product of a surface-level understanding of clients and customers, like the initial McDonald's approach. This approach rarely works because people's true motivations are often hidden so deep that *they* don't even know what their motivations are until someone strategically uncovers them.

One of my favorite examples of this comes from a discussion with a Precision Nutrition Coaching for Women client. Within a few weeks of joining our coaching group, she was randomly selected to be interviewed. (As we do with all in-depth conversations like this, we paid her for her time.)

During the interview she talked a lot about how she "needed to lose weight" and "realized it was time." As we asked more about "Why now?" she couldn't share any additional insights. However, when we asked about what was happening in her life around the time she hired us, lightning flashed. She mentioned something, in passing, about taking her teenage son for a driving test. While this seemed like an irrelevant detail to her, we knew it could be a critical one.

We learned that her son was a competitive swimmer, and she'd spent the last ten years shuttling him around before school, after school, on weekends. She'd spent thousands of hours in service of his goals: driving to and from, and watching, practices and meets, reading books and messing around on her phone while waiting.

One week after taking him for his driving test, Precision Nutrition Coaching appeared in her Facebook feed, and she signed up. The timing wasn't a coincidence. She'd been wanting to get coaching for years. But it was only after this "trigger"—after her son got his license and no longer needed so much of her care—that she seriously considered taking better care of herself.*

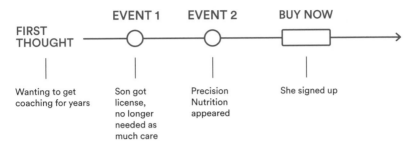

FIRST THOUGHT	EVENT 1	EVENT 2	BUY NOW
Wanting to get coaching for years	Son got license, no longer needed as much care	Precision Nutrition appeared	She signed up

Interestingly, she didn't notice the connection. Which means surveys, focus groups, and direct questions wouldn't have uncovered it. Only by assuming less, asking strategic questions, and listening deeply could we figure out the real reason she signed up when she did. This led to some big, strategy-changing questions for our marketing and advertising team:

What percent of our clients are "hiring" coaching after a significant "trigger" event?
(Answer: A big percentage.)

What kinds of "trigger" events could lead someone to "hire" a coaching program?
(Answers: Getting a scary medical diagnosis, a youngest child starting school, a child getting their driver's license, a child moving away for the first time, separating from a spouse or partner, losing a job, retirement, the loss of someone you're providing care for, and more.)

What if we started proactively reaching out to people most likely to have a "trigger" event?
(Answer: Our advertising costs go down while conversions go up.)

* One of my colleagues told me he lives for these moments in his practice: "I learn the most by listening for small details. They're the most honest and give the biggest clues as to why people behave the way they do."

Sure, folks may want to "lose weight" or "get a flat stomach," but those aren't the real answers to the questions: "Why'd you sign up for *this* program?" "Why *now*?" Those answers come from a deeper place that's informed by a holistic picture of their lives. And, as we'll discuss below, knowing those answers will help shape both your product offerings and your advertising choices.

Of course, it takes mindfulness, even a little moxie, to discard industry clichés and look for the deeper reason people do what they do. But it's worth it.

Learning more about the jobs people are hiring for means standing out from the shouting headlines, no longer needing pressure tactics or hard selling, and attracting clients who feel calm and confident in your ability to meet their needs.

THE *Job* TO BE DONE: HOW YOU CAN GET IT *Right*

While there are many ways to learn more about your prospects and clients—and we use a host of them including informal surveys on Facebook, more extensive surveys using SurveyMonkey, in-person focus groups, thinking aloud sessions, and more—our favorite, and most insightful, tool is the Jobs to Be Done (JTBD) framework.

JTBD is an interview-and-analysis technique that seeks to uncover the "jobs" that people "hire" products and services to do. While it feels odd to think that something like a drill can be "hired" to do a job and "fired" if it doesn't do that job, this is an accurate representation of why people buy things. After all, no one really wants a one-quarter-inch drill bit. They want a one-quarter-inch hole. So they "hire" the drill bit to do the "job" of boring out the hole.

A "job to be done" is not a product, service, or specific solution. It's the "higher purpose" for which a customer buys products, services, and solutions.

Consider why people "hire" trainers. Is it because they're desperate to put heavy barbells across their backs and squat up and down more often? Probably not. So why do most trainers fetishize program design and exercise selection? Why doesn't some portion of their coaching address the deeper needs of clients, usually related to feeling better in their bodies, to reducing both physical and psychic pain? Because they don't exactly understand the job to be done.*

Likewise, consider why people "hire" physicians. Is it because they want to be on meds or go under the knife? Probably not. So why, then, do most physicians rush through appointments, make it rain prescriptions, and shuttle people to pre-op? Why doesn't some portion of their doctoring address the deeper needs of patients, usually related to feeling less fragile, to more gracefully accepting their mortality? Because they, too, don't exactly understand the job to be done.**

The JTBD framework is so valuable because it helps remind us that people don't buy services or products; they hire relevant solutions at different times to get a wide array of jobs done.***

The Jobs to Be Done framework was created by Harvard Business School professor Clay Christensen. Bob Moesta, one of Christensen's colleagues from Harvard, shared it with us, and it changed our business. Within one year, after doing dozens of interviews with prospects and clients, and adapting both our product offerings and our marketing/advertising in response to those interviews, our revenue increased by 50 percent.

---

* Don't get defensive, trainers! Of course, program design and exercise selection are important. I'm not saying it's either one or the other; I'm saying it's both. Learn how to create great programming and how to connect with the deeper needs of your clients.

** Don't get defensive, doctors! Of course systemic limitations, patient compliance, and other factors play into this. At the same time, there might be small opportunities to consider and respond to the deeper needs of your patients. If so, lean into those.

*** "I'm a problem solver." That's how one of my colleagues describes his work when talking to prospective clients and patients.

Sounds good, right? Even better, you can do it yourself. Here's how to use it in your own business.

The Jobs to Be Done Framework

STEP 1

Begin with clear questions that you need answered, such as:

Why do people *hire* my product or service?

Why do people *fire* my product or service?

How are people *struggling* with my product or service?

Where are my *opportunities* to improve my product or service?

STEP 2

Identify people in each of the relevant buying stages, such as:

those who expressed interest *but didn't buy* your product/ service

those who *did buy* your product/service

those who *bought and are actively using* the product/service

those who *bought but aren't actively using* the product/ service those who *bought but then later returned* your product/ service

You could also look for people at various stages such as:

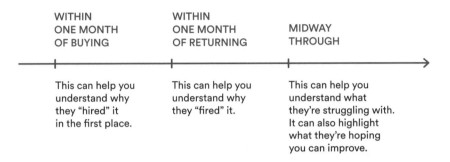

WITHIN ONE MONTH OF BUYING	WITHIN ONE MONTH OF RETURNING	MIDWAY THROUGH
This can help you understand why they "hired" it in the first place.	This can help you understand why they "fired" it.	This can help you understand what they're struggling with. It can also highlight what they're hoping you can improve.

It's also extremely useful to interview **prospects who expressed interest in your product or service but didn't buy,** or who went on to buy something else.

STEP 3
Once you've identified your groups, conduct structured interviews.

To understand the point of sale, ask:

When did you buy the product?

Where were you?

What time of day was it (daytime/nighttime)?

Was anyone else with you at the time?

How did you buy the product?

To find their first thought about purchasing, ask:

When did you first start looking for something to solve your problem?

Where were you?

Were you with someone? What did they say?

What triggered you to think about this?

To discover what else they considered when weighing their options, ask:

Tell me about how you looked for a product to solve your problem.

What kinds of solutions did you try? Or not try? Why or why not?

To uncover the emotions associated with the purchase, ask:

What was the conversation like when you talked about buying the product with your <spouse/friend/parents>?

Before you bought, did you imagine what life would be like with the product? Where were you when you were thinking this?

Did you have any anxiety about buying? Did you hear something about the product that made you nervous? What was it? Why did it make you nervous?

Of course, these are sample questions that should be modified based on whether you're interviewing someone hiring your program, firing your program, or in the midst of experiencing your program. In the case of hiring or firing, what's most important initially is that the interview accesses their memory of events surrounding the action. That's why we start by asking about "when," even though we already know exactly when they purchased or dropped out.

From there you might ask, "And where were you when you did this? Were you with anyone? Do you remember what the weather was like?" Again, you're not necessarily interested in the specific details but in activating their memory and exploring events adjacent to the action. This helps uncover the emotional forces in their decision-making. These are forces that people usually don't mention because they seem unrelated or uninteresting. However, they provide the best insights for product refinement and/or improved marketing and advertising.

Once the interviews—which you've recorded so you can go back to them again—are completed, it's time to organize what you heard into two popular Jobs to Be Done organizational frameworks: **the Timeline** and **the Forces**. These two frameworks help you contextualize the answers you heard. You can then turn the answers into useful stories that help you understand what your clients and prospects are thinking and feeling when they interact with you and your products/services.

STEP 4

THE TIMELINE helps you understand clients' decision-making, giving you a sense for the thoughts and events that brought them to hiring, using, or firing what you've created.

PASSIVE LOOKING	ACTIVE LOOKING	DECIDING	CONSUMING (YAY OR NAY)
I'm not putting in any real energy, but I start noticing options.	I'm investing energy and time into finding a solution.	I've narrowed my options to two or three. I understand my criteria.	I've used it for a while and I understand if it does the job or not.

FIRST THOUGHT	EVENT ONE	EVENT TWO	BUY NOW
What I have might not be working anymore.	I've had enough. This needs to get solved.	If I don't get this solved by a certain time, it's not going to be good.	I've paid money. There is no going back. I've committed.

Organize your interviewees' answers into individual timelines as follows.

 To do this exercise, and all upcoming ones, please download our printable + fillable worksheets at **www.changemakeracademy.com/downloadable-forms**.

STEP 5

THE FORCES helps you map out the feelings that lead a customer toward hiring or firing your thing vs. the forces that lead them away from hiring or firing your thing.

PROGRESS-MAKING FORCES

Push of the situation

Pull of the new idea

EXISTING BEHAVIOR

NEW BEHAVIOR

Allegiance to current behavior

Anxiety of new solution

PROGRESS-HINDERING FORCES

Map out the individual forces that led your interviewees to their decisions.

STEP 6
Look for common themes among your timeline and forces diagrams.

What nudged people to make their decision?

Who did they see as "the competition"?

Which anxieties did they have to overcome to purchase?

How did what they *thought* they were buying match up to what they *actually got*?

STEP 7
Ask yourself new questions.

How can I talk about my business in a way that resonates more with how *my customers* talk about their needs, challenges, and concerns?

How can I reach out to people in places I've never considered before?

How can I see my customers' trajectory and anticipate where they're heading?

At Precision Nutrition we typically interview about ten people at each stage of their customer journey. For example, to better understand Precision Nutrition Coaching for Men, we interviewed:

MEN WHO DIDN'T BUY
Within one month of registration, we interviewed **ten men who expressed interest but didn't buy** coaching.

MEN WHO DID BUY
Within one month of registration, we interviewed **ten men who bought** coaching.

MEN ACTIVELY USING COACHING
Midway through the program, we interviewed **ten men actively using** coaching.

MEN NOT ACTIVELY USING COACHING
Midway through the program, we interviewed **ten men not actively using** coaching.

MEN WHO DROPPED OUT
Within one month of leaving, we interviewed **ten men who dropped out of** coaching.

Listening carefully to their stories, we constructed a timeline for each individual (the events and thoughts that took them from first idea to buying to consuming or not) and examined the forces at work throughout (the things that pushed them toward buying and away from buying).

Next, we looked at all the individual timelines and forces next to each other and searched for common themes. We looked for what nudged them to make their decision, for whom they thought of as "the competition," and for which anxieties they had to overcome to purchase. Also, once they purchased, we looked for what they *thought* they were buying and compared that to what they felt they were *actually getting* once they used the product or service.

Once you're finally able to see yourself "through customers' eyes," you can ask better questions like:

How can I talk about my business in a way that resonates more with how *my customers* talk about their needs, challenges, and concerns?
(This might make your products and services more attractive or feel like they're in better alignment with customer needs. Do this right and they'll think: *Wow, this company understands exactly what I'm looking for!*)

How can I reach out to people in places I've never considered before?
(This could help open up new markets. For example, if prospects generally sign up for services like yours after a significant "trigger" event—like having a child, getting a scary medical diagnosis, ending a relationship, or moving to a new area—why not market to folks who've experienced such an event?)

How can I see my customers' trajectory and anticipate where they're heading?
(This could help you develop new products. For example, if you notice people struggling after a twelve-week weight-loss program, you might create a maintenance program designed to help graduates preserve most of their weight loss and come to terms with any rebound weight gain.)

In the end, knowing what clients *really* want means you don't assume you know what they want. It means you don't copy others because you assume *they* know what clients want. It means you don't even ask your clients what they want. Instead, it means using the inquisitiveness of a detective and the compassion of a counselor to ask the right questions, listen intently, and think deeply. If you do all three, you're more likely to unlock their deepest emotional reasons for taking action. In these you'll see your biggest opportunities in coaching, product development, sales, or marketing. And you'll easily set yourself apart from everyone else in the industry.

THE *Job* TO BE *DONE:*
INSIGHTS *FROM* PRECISION NUTRITION'S *Research*

Using the Jobs to Be Done framework, our team at Precision Nutrition has benefited immensely from deep insights about the people who sign up for our products and services, and those who don't. Here, I'll share a few of these insights.

Keep in mind that these "user stories" may not describe *your* clients or the people you want to work with. Which means, like many of the stories in this book, they're illustrations and examples, not prescriptions. It also means that you'll need to gather the same kinds of insights with your people, in your business. To do so, I recommend the approach outlined earlier. Also, if you'd like more information (and specific direction) on using the Jobs to Be Done framework, check out the work of Chris Spiek and Bob Moesta at jobstobedone.org.

User story #1: "It's not my first rodeo."
PRODUCT: PRECISION NUTRITION COACHING

One of the most important insights we got from the JTBD process was that almost none of the people who express interest in, and eventually sign up for, Precision Nutrition Coaching are trying to "get in shape" or "get healthy" for the first time.

Based on extensive interviews—and follow-up surveys—we learned that the average prospect has tried *five* health and fitness interventions, with varying degrees of success, before considering our yearlong, practice-based coaching program.

In general, before they discovered us, our male clients tried a wide range of options like workout DVDs (P90X, Insanity, etc.), fitness books (*The Abs Diet*, *Body for Life*, etc.), gym options (CrossFit, Orangetheory Fitness, etc.), and personal training. Women tried options like calorie management and prepackaged food (Weight Watchers, Jenny Craig, etc.), diet books (*The China Study*, *Skinny Bitch*, etc.), boot camps, and detoxes. While this knowledge may seem like a no-brainer, it helped us in several ways.

To begin, it helped shape our paid advertising. For example, we immediately ran a series of ads that spoke directly to this experience. The copy for those ads read something like this:

> {Body for Life/Weight Watchers/P90X/Etc.} failed?
> **Try something different this time.**
> [Learn more about Precision Nutrition]

> Gained the weight back? Again?
> **Here's how to keep it off for good.**
> [Discover Precision Nutrition]

(In some cases the ads were animated with a host of common diet and fitness approaches, appearing in succession, followed by some of the copy above.)

Beyond paid advertising, we started publishing free articles and videos that spoke to the experience. We shared our clients' stories and histories. Showed how our practice-based, research-proven program is different from the things they tried before. And demonstrated how our program has been able to help people who've been unsuccessful in the past, even those who lost hope that any intervention could work for them.

Finally, we revised our coaching curriculum to respect the fact that each successive diet/fitness experiment eroded our clients' self-confidence and self-efficacy. This meant including content:

highlighting their resiliency (*if you've tried to get in shape five times already, you're not a failure, you're tenacious*)

---

comparing and contrasting what they've done before with what they're doing now (*yes, this might feel slower, but has fast and frantic ever worked for you in the past?*)

---

continually reminding them that success is possible (*I know it feels frustrating now but take a look at {person Y}, who was in the same boat as you and ended up achieving these remarkable results.*)

Now think about your clients and patients. Are they in the same situation, having tried multiple interventions without lasting success? If so, how might you put this insight to work for you?

User story #2: "Help me become 'that guy.'"
PRODUCT: PRECISION NUTRITION COACHING FOR MEN

As we dug deeper into our interviews with coaching clients, looking separately at our male and female clients, we found new insights specific to each group. One of our biggest men's coaching insights can be summarized by "Steve's" story. (Steve isn't one specific person but a composite based on interviews with dozens of guys.)

Steve is overweight (or at a normal weight but carrying excess body fat). He's not really focused on doing anything about it at the moment. Maybe he's not aware of how out of shape he is or maybe he simply doesn't care. He's, what we call, *liveably overweight/unfit*. He can live with it. Which means he has no drive to change his body. Yet.

One day something happens that pulls his health, and his body image, into focus. This *trigger* is typically an injury, a medical diagnosis, a brush with mortality, an employment change, or a relationship change. In other words, Steve got dumped, changed jobs, injured his leg, or went to the doctor who gave him some potentially scary news.

Steve decides he has to change his image. Because, in his mind, *health* = *image*. Steve looks at a guy who's in shape and thinks, "That guy doesn't have relationship problems." Or, "That guy can't have diabetes." Or, "That guy is in control of his life."

Interestingly, if Steve has recently been diagnosed as prediabetic, he doesn't think: "I gotta find the workout that cures diabetes." Curing his diabetes does nothing for his image. Instead, Steve wants to look like a fit, healthy guy. And he hopes that once he looks like "that guy," the diabetes (and associated ego pain) will go away.

Once Steve's had his *health-to-image focusing event*, he does something to try to improve his body image. In our research, Steve is likely to try P90X, join CrossFit, or hire a personal trainer, all in an attempt to become more like "that guy" who obviously has a better life than Steve.

Steve may try one thing, or multiple things, to improve his image. And then, at some point, Steve experiences *fitness failure*. This happens in either one of two ways.

FAILURE TYPE 1:
Steve gets poor results from his fitness attempt(s) and doesn't change his image (or health) in any measurable way.

FAILURE TYPE 2:
Steve gets some results from his fitness attempt(s) but he's not where he expected to be. He's aiming for 100 percent awesome. But right now he's just at 70 percent and is stuck.

At this point, Steve thinks: *Why isn't this working for me? What am I missing?* The answer, he discovers from an extensive search of articles, forums, podcasts, and books is *nutrition*. So Steve starts searching for nutrition-related information on the internet . . . where he finds Precision Nutrition.

This is the story of how Steve finds his way to Precision Nutrition Coaching for Men.

One additional point about Steve, based on our research: If he's married, he's going to seek permission from his partner to sign up. Indeed, the married men we talked to struggled with the idea of "selling" their partners on joining our program for three reasons: time commitment, money, and/or feeling like they need their partners to buy into the diet changes too.

To give you an example, here's what Steve may hear in his head before he approaches his partner to talk about Precision Nutrition:

TIME COMMITMENT:
"But you're so busy already; how long is this program really going to take?"

MONEY:
"Can we really afford this, Steve?"

BUY-IN:
"Do we have to change everything and shop and eat differently? I don't know about this. . . ."

In the end, we summarize this—surprisingly typical—job to be done as:

"Help me become 'that guy.' The man I want to look and feel like."

And we've created a formula describing this experience:

Liveably overweight/unfit guy + Health-to-image focusing event + Failed fitness attempt(s) + Search = Sign up for PN Coaching

Aside from this being an interesting story, we've used this knowledge to directly inform our advertising, marketing, product creation, and men's coaching curriculum. For example:

ADVERTISING:
We've created ads speaking to guys just like Steve, who realize now that "exercise, alone, isn't enough" and who've experienced something that's triggered a deeper desire for change.

MARKETING:
We've written articles featuring dozens of "guys like Steve," who've experienced what Steve has but who've gone on to achieve remarkable results with our help.

PRODUCT CREATION AND CURRICULUM:
Precision Nutrition Coaching used to be marketed as a single coaching program for men and women. After some of our Jobs to Be Done insights, we started promoting two separate programs with two different sets of lessons and practices, tailored more closely to what we learned in our interviews with men and women.

If you work with men, does this story sound familiar? Do you have a group of "Steves" in your practice? If so, how might you put this insight to work for you?

User story #3: "Help me separate eating from feeling."
PRODUCT: PRECISION NUTRITION COACHING FOR WOMEN

One of our biggest women's coaching insights can be summarized by Julie's story. (Again, Julie isn't one specific person but a composite based on interviews with dozens of women.)

Julie is stuck in a cycle, or a loop. Two loops, actually. But this first one is a tricky one. In this first loop, Julie feels a strong negative emotion like loneliness, anxiety, depression, or stress. To cope with that feeling, Julie turns to food, which helps her (temporarily) feel better. However, coupled with too little exercise and other lifestyle factors, this emotional eating leads to weight gain.

After gaining weight, Julie wants to make a change so she tries something to lose it (Weight Watchers, tracking calories with MyFitnessPal, fasting, cleanses, diet plans, etc.).

Unfortunately, after either 1) not seeing results, or 2) seeing results but gaining the weight back, Julie feels another strong negative emotion like frustration or hopelessness and starts eating emotionally again. The cycle repeats and Julie starts to think: "I know what to do, so why isn't it working? Why can't I do this?"

To summarize this first loop:

Julie feels lonely, anxious, depressed, or stressed → Julie eats → Julie gains weight → Julie attempts something to lose weight → Julie fails to lose or keep it off → Julie repeats loop.

Interestingly, as Julie is going through this first cycle of feeling, eating, feeling, eating, she's also wrapped up in another loop. In the second loop, Julie is "learning" what works for her and what doesn't. Every time there's a failed weight-loss attempt (or she gains the weight back) she builds up a set of ideas about what's "right for her" and what's not.

The stuff Julie "learns" here may or may not have anything to do with success. In other words, in this second loop, Julie is learning things and making assumptions based on those things. She may be learning useful things or simply developing superstitions, but she's not really in a position to know the difference between the two.

From this, Julie comes up with a script like:

I tried Weight Watchers, and counting calories isn't going to work for me. Instead, I need to _____. So, if I hear "counting calories" again, I won't sign up.

Or:

I tried Jenny Craig, and those little packaged meals aren't going to work for me. I need to eat my food. So, if I hear "packaged meals," I'm out. If I hear "eating real food," I'm in.

As Julie goes through her two concurrent cycles, she's *passively searching* for more information and possible solutions to her weight problem. At some point, she hears about Precision Nutrition by:

seeing a post on social media,

hearing about us from someone at her gym,

searching for a key topic like "intermittent fasting,"

reading a guest post we write for another website.

As soon as she discovers our ideas, Julie switches from passive search to *active search*. In the most common scenario, as Julie is investigating Precision Nutrition, a woman she identifies with—a friend, family member, colleague, or social media connection—recommends us, demonstrates success with us (in the form of a review or photos), or talks about working with us. This *social proof* leads Julie to believe that our program could work for her.

As Julie digs deeper into Precision Nutrition, she has a *simplifying moment*, a moment where she learns the answer to the question she's been subconsciously thinking about all along: "I know what to do . . . so why isn't it working/why can't I do it?"

This moment could take place when reading a Precision Nutrition article, taking a free course, watching one of our videos on social media, etc. And it usually comes when she learns:

Less, not more.

Slower, not faster.

She doesn't have to do it alone.

Nutrition over exercise.

Holistic focus vs. weight focus.

Mind over diet.

Connection with others is vital.

Through this discovery, she learns that Precision Nutrition is different. Not only that, it makes sense to her. She thinks: "Of course! This is why I've had a frustrating time losing weight." After her simplifying moment, Julie begins to *check off the criteria* she learned previously.
"PN seems like it . . ."

is sustainable over quick

will hold me accountable vs. provide cheap solutions

encourages whole foods over supplements or packaged foods

prioritizes nutrition over exercise

involves giving up control or handing over control even over getting in control

From there, Julie becomes a prime candidate for joining coaching. In the end, we summarize this job to be done as:

Help me separate eating from feeling. In a way that's sustainable.

And we've created a formula describing this experience:

Loop 1 (feeling, eating, feeling, eating) + Loop 2 (learnings and superstitions) + Search + Social proof + Simplifying moment + Checking off criteria = Sign up for PN Coaching

Again, we've used this knowledge to inform our advertising, marketing, product creation, and women's coaching curriculum. And you can too. Consider your female clients, if you work with women. Can you use these insights in your practice?

Remember that these are just a few user stories based on our research with clients who've signed up for our programs. This means they may not necessarily be useful in the context of your business. To really put the JTBD process to work for you, you'll need to do your own research, as described on pages 82–90.

Also remember that this kind of research doesn't represent every type of client that's signed up for our products and programs, although it does represent the majority of them.

Finally, keep in mind that we've done this kind of research with each of our six programs and with each segment (people who didn't buy, people who bought, people who are actively using the program, people who aren't actively using the program, people who dropped out).

Yes, it's been a time-consuming process (6 products × 5 segments per product × 10 people per segment × 2 hours per interview = 600 hours of interviews). However, before you think "I don't have time for this!" consider that we've done them over several years, and you can too.

You only need to commit to doing something every week, even if it's just one interview. By the end of three months you'd have enough information to more deeply understand an entire customer or client segment. The payoff for this investment? Over a few years, you'll have a gold mine of insights that *almost no one else, anywhere*, will have.

This will help you finally discover what your clients really want, which has obvious marketing and advertising benefits. While everyone else is just promising surface solutions (*Torch body fat now!*), you'll be able to promise something bigger that resonates with their unspoken needs as well as who they are on a deep level (*Gain strength, confidence, and the ability to get what you want out of life*).

Even more, it'll help you *deliver* what your clients really want, adapting your products and services, or creating new ones, based on what you learned from speaking with your target audience. No more guessing, assuming, or following someone else's lead. Maybe instead of just offering meal plans, you'll learn that meal plans plus nutrition coaching are the way to go. Maybe instead of just offering diagnostic and prescription services, you'll learn that health coaching is necessary too.

Making time to do this kind of discovery—and being open to the humbling, yet powerful, insights it produces—has changed our company. By asking new questions we learned *with certainty* what our clients are after. Nowadays they feel better served and better connected, they stay longer, and we feel happier and more satisfied in our work. I'm confident this approach can do the same for you.

Q&A with JB: Clients

To support what you're learning, I've compiled end-of-chapter Q&As that are full of real, thoughtful questions I've gotten over the years. In each one I share my unfiltered take on the challenges you'll undoubtedly face as you grow your career.

⊕ You can check out all the Change Maker Q&As at **www.changemakeracademy.com/questions**.

This chapter's questions include:

Q: The ideas in this chapter are mostly qualitative and I'm more of a quantitative person. Don't you collect measurable data when planning your marketing, advertising, and products? (Answer: ~275 words)

Q: You mentioned a technique called "thinking aloud." What's that, and how does it work? (Answer: ~425 words)

Q: My business is relatively new, I don't have many clients yet, and I only offer one service. I'd love to get deeper insights but don't really feel like I have the time, am not sure I can afford to pay people for interviews, and wonder if what I learn will be useful. What should I do? (Answer: ~350 words)

PEOPLE'S TRUE motivations ARE OFTEN HIDDEN
EVEN THEY don't always KNOW WHAT THEY WANT

Learning WHAT PEOPLE really WANT CAN
INFORM YOUR ADVERTISING, Marketing,
CURRICULUM, AND THE PRODUCTS YOU OFFER

Asking THE RIGHT questions
UNLOCKS PEOPLE'S EMOTIONAL FORCES
WHICH brings THE BIGGEST insights

PEOPLE DON'T buy PRODUCTS
OR SERVICES. THEY HIRE SOLUTIONS
TO GET varying JOBS done

People WILL HIRE you BECAUSE
THEY THINK you CAN HELP GET
THE job DONE

THE JOB ISN'T USUALLY
WHAT you THINK IT IS

TO DISCOVER THE job
Ask THE RIGHT QUESTIONS
Listen INTENTLY
Think DEEPLY

BE PREPARED TO BE humbled
BE OPEN TO new insights

BE willing TO CHANGE ANYTHING
TO BETTER serve YOUR PEOPLE

CHAPTER 4

COAC

HING

HOW TO

Master **MOTIVATION,**

Build **RELATIONSHIPS,**

AND **BECOME**

Client-Centered

Ask most people what their idea of a health and fitness coach looks like, and I bet they picture some sort of comic-book extreme.

A yelling, red-faced, make-you-hurt drill sergeant who shames you into another set of push-ups or bullies you into bingeing on beets. Or a slap-you-on-the-butt cheerleader who rah-rahs you into box jumping onto the roof and chasing it with a green smoothie. (See also: An evidence-based physician who doesn't understand what it's like to fear the weigh scale. A nutritionist whose only food crayon is "leafy green." Or a yoga teacher who can twist like a pretzel but would never condescend to eat one.)

You know what? They may not be *that* far off base.

For a number of reasons, many coaches unconsciously fall into those caricatures (perhaps influenced by popular portrayals of trainers on shows like *The Biggest Loser*). Now, I have nothing against drill sergeants or cheerleaders *when they're actual drill sergeants and cheerleaders.* However, when health and fitness coaches act like drill sergeants and cheerleaders, that's when things go awry.

The world's best health and fitness change makers think differently about their relationship with clients.

Traditionally, in coach-client relationships—doctor-patient relationships, too—professionals act like they're preordained to have all the knowledge and power. Clients are there to be passive, pliable recipients: *I'll tell you what to do; you go out and do it.**

In today's environment, it's a surefire way to fail.

Another less common, but also somewhat dangerous, approach in health and fitness coaching is: Client as best buddy. While this might sound like a good situation, it's not. In this scenario, the coach tries to "motivate" the client by being "nice," spends a lot of time talking about

---

* This is a logical holdover of medical paternalism, a set of attitudes and practices common until the end of the twentieth century. With medical paternalism, physicians believed diseases were nothing more than a collection of symptoms and that patient history (and preferences) didn't matter in providing care. Since the patient was irrelevant in the medical encounter, physicians often undermined their autonomy by making decisions for them, sometimes against their will.

the client's non-health-related personal problems, and may even tell the client way more about the coach's own life issues than the client should know. The result? Coaches can become enmeshed in something close to a friendship (or even more inappropriately, a romantic relationship) with the client. This makes it hard to set a clear direction, focus on the task at hand, offer difficult feedback, or "disappoint" the client (for instance, by taking time to go on vacation or not being available 24/7).

Thankfully, there's a better approach. Instead of seeing the relationship as "teacher-student" or "boss-employee" or "sergeant-trooper"—or even as "buddy-buddy"—today's most effective coaches see themselves more like professional guides.

Their job isn't to lecture about what they know, judge performance, give directives, or become a BFF. It's to collaborate with clients to co-create their program and then walk side by side with them, nudging them down paths they should see, pointing out potholes and missteps they should avoid, and asking them where they want to go next.

Sometimes clients know a lot about the area they're exploring. In this case, the coach is just there to open the client's eyes to new things. Other times, when clients are brand-new to the environment, the coach's work is a little more involved. At times, coaches may even need to offer uncomfortable feedback, prod their client into acknowledging unpalatable truths, or highlight cognitive dissonance (e.g., the difference between what someone says they want and what they're actually doing).

Sure, from time to time, coaches might need to step in front to lead, or behind to push. But, most of the time, the best coaches are right there, next to clients, side by side.

A simple way to remember this? Instead of being a *sage on the stage*, opt for being a *guide on the side*. Think less about who *you* are and what *you* know. Think more about who your clients are and what they need, including:

how they see the world,

what they want from the coaching process,

which stage of change they're currently in,

why they react to change the way they do, and

how you can best help facilitate change.

You've heard the saying: "You can lead a horse to water but can't make it drink." That describes how far most coaches are willing to go in helping clients change. *I've told Drew what to do a million times, given him at-home workouts, told him to cut back on alcohol, and he just won't do it.*

For coaches, it's seriously frustrating. Plus, it lends itself to blaming clients for not following orders. But imagine what it's like for clients, who really do want to look, feel, or perform better but can't figure out how, within the context of their real lives. Then, on top of that, they have this coach giving orders without much sensitivity to the things getting in the way.

Change makers look at the process differently.

They think: "No, you can't make the horse drink. But you can make it very, very thirsty."

Seven Game-Changing Coaching Principles

Most professionals spend their first few years immersed in the science of health and fitness, from muscle physiology to nutrient biochemistry. They learn about energy systems, organ systems, macronutrients, and micronutrients. If they're lucky, they're also taught how to translate that into useful recommendations.

It's a good start, if it were only a *start*. Unfortunately, it's where most education *ends*. Many newly minted professionals never learn how to deal with the real health issues, psychological barriers, and frustrations of working with real people.

If you're planning on being a professor or researcher, you could always stop at the science. However, if you'd like to become an elite change maker, you have to go one step further by also studying, and developing mastery in, the best practices of coaching and change psychology. The following principles will give you the blueprint to do that.

And by the way, many of these principles will work for your business development too. A client might want to lose weight, and you might want to grow your business; the focus is different but the path to mastery is the same.

THE SUPER SEVEN
COACHING PRINCIPLES

① *Become* MORE **CLIENT-CENTERED,** LESS **COACH-CENTERED**

② *Ask* GOOD **QUESTIONS** TO *Practice* **ACTIVE, COMPASSIONATE** LISTENING

③ FOCUS ON *What's* **AWESOME,** NOT *What's* **AWFUL**

④ *Set* THE RIGHT KINDS OF *Goals*

⑤ *Establish* THE RIGHT **PRACTICES** TO REACH **THOSE** *Goals*

⑥ ALWAYS **CONFIDENCE** *Test*

⑦ *Speak* IN A WAY THAT MAKES *People* MORE *Likely* TO **CHANGE**

Become MORE CLIENT-CENTERED, LESS COACH-CENTERED

Think back to a time in your life when you've had a problem or a challenge, when there was something you wanted to fix or change but didn't know how. What did that feel like? Did you start out motivated and confident? Or did you feel something else?

Now consider what it would feel like to reach out to someone for advice and, instead of considering your unique situation, they incorrectly diagnosed your problem and made a bunch of haphazard recommendations. What would *that* feel like?

Let's say you're having stomach pain. You go see a doctor and, within the first thirty seconds, no greeting or anything, the doctor says: "Ah, pain right there? It's stomach cancer. We'll treat it with radiation. Make an appointment at the front desk."

After freaking out, you'd probably think that the doctor was a jerk and that the diagnosis wasn't credible because the doc never asked questions, did diagnostics, took a family history, or anything.

Same goes for most other things, right? When you have car trouble, you don't want a mechanic to flippantly say, "It must be the transmission." When you have computer trouble, you don't want the help desk to answer the phone with, "It must be the RAM." You want people to *hear* you to *help* you. And it's not just because you want to be heard, but because you have some essential information that the other person *needs* in order to draw an accurate conclusion.

In my experience, when someone has an answer before hearing and deeply understanding the problem, it's probably not the right answer. (And, even if they get lucky and come up with a technically correct answer, it usually isn't a helpful one.)

Now, let's take the same principle and apply it to *you*—and how you work with people.

Do you make the same mistake as the doctor, the mechanic, and computer expert above? Are your answers sometimes too flippant? Are you sometimes too focused on *your* knowledge, expertise, and authority (what I call "coach-centered") instead of focusing on the lives and embodied experiences of your clients (what I call "client-centered")?

That's normal, especially at the beginning of our careers. Because we spend so much time learning facts about anatomy, physiology, biochemistry, and biomechanics, it's easy for us to fetishize our knowledge and accidentally prioritize it when sitting with living, breathing humans. This leads to interactions that are all about us, our information, our authority, and our reputation. It makes the whole process feel "top-down," like sergeant-trooper, boss-employee, or guru-disciple.

Think about it: If we're too concerned with "having the right answer" or "looking smart" or "retaining our authority," we're not thinking enough about what the client needs, what they already know about their body, what their real challenges are, and which dreams inspire them.* When we're too concerned with our reputation, we're less willing to humble ourselves in front of clients and ask the deep questions required to help us understand their lives.

Here's one way to think of it. Sure, you're an expert on the body. But your client is the world's number-one expert on his or her own life. Therefore, great coaching can only happen when a coach integrates his or her own expertise with the necessary expertise of the client.

This is the essence of client-centeredness. This is part of what will make you a successful coach.**

---

* Young coaches are often guilty of this, perhaps because they're trying to hide some of the insecurity they feel about their lack of experience. Yet information dumps, overconfidence, and bluster aren't the solution. The solution is openness, curiosity, authentic dialogue, and putting the client first.

** The other part, discussed later in the book, is based on helping clients become more self-aware and make better decisions. If you provide value in this way, you automatically promote yourself to a higher role in the relationship and become viewed as a highly valued consultant vs. a dime-a-dozen taskmaster.

Decades of research in teaching, counseling, and coaching have confirmed what we found to be true with more than 150,000 Precision Nutrition Coaching clients. The client-centered approach cuts down on some of your biggest obstacles: client ambivalence and resistance. Plus, rather than building *you* up, it builds the client. As their dignity, self-determination, self-efficacy, and self-expertise increase, you'll see better, more sustainable results.

(Just don't make the mistake of pretending you're less educated or expert than you really are. While clients want to feel like a collaborator in their own process, they also want to feel like their coach is knowledgeable and experienced. No doubt, it's a difficult tightrope to walk. But it's important. You're doing it right if you're constantly assessing each client to see if a little more expert direction is needed at that moment, or a little more collaboration is needed, and adjusting accordingly.)

Here's an example of the difference.

Coach-centered approach

If a client comes to you with a question that you think you have a slam-dunk answer for, it's easy to feel like a kid in a classroom. "I know this! I know this!" For example, someone's not losing weight, you look at their food journal, and boom! "Replace that potato with veggies and you're all set!"

The problem is that, without a discussion, you don't know enough about why the potato is in their diet in the first place. Nor, without the client's input, do you know whether they'll even want to remove it (or if they'd prefer to remove something else from a different meal).

Client-centered approach

Instead of blurting out your knee-jerk solution, this is a perfect time to ask questions about your client's exercise, overall eating patterns, which foods they can (and can't) live without, what's convenient and easy to eat, and so on.

Once you learn more about the client, you can discuss how, for their goals, they might be eating more carbs, or calories, than optimal. Then, finally, you can ask how *they* might adjust their diet to make the necessary improvements. One of my favorite ways to open the discussion is: "I have a few ideas on what to do next here, but I'd love to hear yours first."

COACH-CENTERED VS. CLIENT-CENTERED

Coach-centered individuals focus on themselves, their authority, and their own knowledge.	Client-centered individuals integrate their knowledge with their client's goals, needs, preferences.

COACHING PRINCIPLE 2

Ask GOOD QUESTIONS TO Practice ACTIVE, COMPASSIONATE LISTENING

A few years back, my wife, Amanda, and I were living with her parents while renovating a house about two hours away. During the week, after working a full day, we'd drive two hours to the new home, work on it for a few hours, and drive two hours back. Then, on weekends, we'd drive to the house in the morning, spend the entire day there, and drive back at night. It was exhausting. For the first few weeks, I didn't work out at all. And I didn't like the feeling.

Now, when I say I had close to zero time to work out, that's accurate. But since it wasn't exactly zero time, I was determined to make something work. So I reached out to a friend who's an excellent coach.

He listened carefully to my story, asked a bunch of questions, and summarized with this: "Here's what I'm hearing. Tell me if I've got it. You have almost no time to exercise but want to do something, even if it's not 'perfect.' You'd prefer to do it first thing in the morning before your day starts. It has to be really short. And you don't mind doing it in your bedroom with only body weight."

He nailed it and went on to create a four-day-per-week circuit training workout that: a) lasted only ten minutes, b) I could do in the morning, immediately after waking up, c) required no equipment, and d) I could do right next to the bed.

Notice what he did there.

First, he listened to my story. Then he asked questions until he thought he understood. Rather than *assuming* he understood, he summarized what he heard out loud so I could correct him if necessary. Only then did he make his recommendations (which turned out to be really creative and exactly what I wanted). *That's* client-centered.

Imagine a scenario where he didn't practice compassionate listening, where he didn't ask lots of questions, where he didn't seek clarity. Imagine if, instead of focusing on my needs, he made it all about himself, his expectations, his expertise. He might have tried to convince me to go to a gym or to persuade me to "just try" four forty-five-minute workouts. He might have said my program demands were unreasonable. Tried to guilt-trip me into making time for more exercise. Or tried to chastise me for making excuses.

But what would that have accomplished? I couldn't have followed a more intensive program at the time. If he had prescribed one anyway, it would have been frustrating. I would have resented him for pushing his agenda on me without respecting my limitations. He would have resented me for not trying hard enough.

Thankfully, it didn't go in that direction. Instead, for the months we renovated that home, I maintained my fitness with those ten-minute circuit workouts, a healthy eating plan, and all the extra physical activity that came from doing the renovations themselves. About six months later, when the house was completed and we'd finally moved in, we outfitted it with a sweet home gym.

Guess who I hired to design my first workout program?

The point here is that the world's best professionals are willing to do everything it takes to understand their clients, which starts with asking great questions and then deeply, actively listening to the answers without any agenda of their own.

This brings us to *high-quality listening*, a critical part of client-centered coaching.

We've all heard this, of course. Maybe you've even heard the adage that we were given two ears and one mouth so we would listen twice as much as we speak.

However, many of us struggle with listening because we feel that we have to be "the expert" and that experts teach, talk, and give next actions. That's precisely why letting go of being "the expert" helps us become better listeners.

It also helps with another thing: becoming students of our clients. When we take our ego needs out of the equation, we can better learn (and understand) what they're thinking, appreciate their current habits, discover what's holding them back, and find ways to inspire better and healthier choices.

Of course, I'm not saying that teaching, talking, and giving next actions are bad things. What I'm saying is: **They're only valuable—in a coaching context—after we've invested the time to truly listen to and understand our clients.**

However, I cringe when people tell coaches to "listen better" and leave it there. That's because I don't think you can become a more active, compassionate listener without learning to ask better questions. Good questions unlock the insights worth listening to. And you can use them in a variety of ways, in almost every scenario, to empower clients to:

share personal information,

gain clarity in their own thinking,

say things out loud for the first time,

actively engage in change talk, and

begin solving their own problems.

Plus, they help extend the adage above. Because, instead of listening twice as much as you speak, I recommend listening at least four times as much. In fact, one way to level up your coaching immediately is to spend about 80 percent of your time asking questions and listening and 20 percent of your time guiding or giving instructions.

Here are a few examples of the kinds of questions we use every day at Precision Nutrition, questions designed to improve our listening skills, to better hone into client needs, and pave the way for giving advice without triggering client resistance.

COMPASSIONATE LISTENING QUESTIONS

QUESTION TYPE	EXAMPLE QUESTIONS
Exploring questions	What things are important to you, and how does exercise and eating fit into this? What sort of things would you like to accomplish in your life? If things were better with your eating/exercise, what specifically would be different? What have you tried? What worked and what didn't?
Imagining questions	Imagine you can X (your goal). Describe your experience. Imagine you are already doing more of X. What would that feel like? Imagine that you have the body and health you desire. What exactly did it take for you to achieve it? If you weren't constrained by reality—let's imagine for a minute that absolutely anything is possible—what might you . . . ?

QUESTION TYPE	EXAMPLE QUESTIONS
Solution-focused questions	In the past, when were you successful with this, even just a little bit? How could we do more of that? Where in your life have you been successful with something like this? Did you learn any lessons that we can apply here? Where is the problem not happening? When are things even a little bit better?
Change-evoking questions	In what ways does this concern you? If you decide to make a change, what makes you think you could do it? How would you like things to be different? How would things be better if you changed? What concerns you about your current exercise and eating patterns?

QUESTION TYPE	EXAMPLE QUESTIONS
Statements that act like questions to validate feelings	I get the sense that you may be struggling with . . . It seems to me like you're feeling . . .
Readiness-assessment questions	If you decide to change, on a scale of 1–10, how confident are you that you could change, when 1 represents not at all confident and 10 equals extremely confident? If you wanted to change, what would be the tiniest possible step toward that? The *absolute smallest*, easiest thing you could try? Tell me what else is going on for you right now in your life. What else do you have on your plate besides this? Let's get a sense of what you're working with.

QUESTION TYPE	EXAMPLE QUESTIONS
Planning questions	So, given all this, what do you think you could do next? What's next for you? If nothing changes, what do you see happening in five years? If you decide to change, what will it be like? How would you like things to be different?
Advice-giving questions	Would it be okay if I shared some of my experiences with you? In my work with clients/patients, I've found that . . .
Statements that get people thinking	I wonder what it would be like if you . . . I wonder if we could try . . . I'm curious about whether . . .

COACHING PRINCIPLE 3

FOCUS ON *What's AWESOME,* NOT *What's AWFUL*

Watch popular portrayals of TV trainers and fitness coaches, and you'll get the idea that telling people how much they suck is motivating.

What's that in your hand? A donut? Typical. Get off your butt and let's see some push-ups, you pathetic unmotivated blob of goo!

These coaches are always on the lookout for awfulness, stalking, ready to pounce on it with good ol' fashioned "tough love."

In real life, most of us would never speak to clients in this cartoonish and extreme way. However, whether we realize it or not, whether it sounds nicer on the surface or not, most of us do our own "awfulness-based coaching." And that makes sense. When it comes to helping people, logic tells us: This person has a problem. You have a solution. Put the two together and results follow.

I think that's why the entire health and fitness field is full of assessments and a subsequent "weakness" obsession. Glutes aren't turned on? Fix it with this exercise. Diet's broken? Fix it with this menu. Blood has too much cholesterol? Fix it with this supplement. Again, no matter how nice we dress up our language, coaches spend a lot of time looking for flaws and rushing in to fix them.

There are three problems with this.

First, most clients who can afford health and fitness coaching are decidedly *not* screwups in most areas of their lives. If they can afford you, chances are they're outperforming you in at least one area: professionally. In other words, there's a good chance that the person you're condescending to about their inadequate protein intake spends the rest of their day performing surgery, running a successful business, or teaching at a university. This is good to know because the skills they use to be successful at work can also be used in the service of their health and fitness goals. (Great problem solver at work? Awesome, let's apply that to your breakfast issue!)

Second, no one—especially people who are winning in other areas of their lives—enjoys being *made to feel* like a screwup. It's demoralizing and demotivating. It kills relationships and results.

Third, coaching using a deficit model—i.e., a core assumption that your clients are fundamentally flawed, defective, and lacking—means that your clients will never be, or feel, or do *good enough*. Sure, they'll "make improvements"—maybe. But the *core belief* (which many of your clients will share) is that they are basically broken. Think about how disempowering and discouraging that belief is. If they're so screwed up, why bother? Might as well just lie down (with poor posture) and suck ice cream through a straw while waiting for death.

That's why shifting from coach-centered to client-centered means thinking less about awfulness (what the client's bad at) and more about awesomeness (what the client's good at). With awesomeness-based coaching, you specifically ask yourself: "Where is this client winning outside of health and fitness?" And, "What skills are they using to win at that?" (Don't know where they're winning or how? Ask them.) Then you look for the following:

AWESOMENESS-BASED COACHING PROMPTS

SKILLS:
What do they already know how to do?

KNOWLEDGE:
What information do they already know?

EXPERTISE/EXPERIENCE:
What have they already done? (In particular, what have they already done well?)

INTERESTS:
What do they like to do? What do they enjoy?

TALENTS:
What are they naturally good at?

NO-PROBLEM TIMES:
When does the problem they often face *not* happen?[*]

Once you understand where clients are awesome, give them the kinds of tasks that interest them or that use their talents. Or help them work toward a goal that inspires or excites them. Use their awesomeness to shape their goals, to solve health and fitness challenges they keep coming up against, or to come up with next actions.

COACHING PRINCIPLE 4

Set THE RIGHT KINDS OF Goals

"What are your health and fitness goals?" It's a question asked by professionals all over the world. And it seems like an easy question to answer. Just rattle off how many pounds you want to lose, what pant size you want to wear, what you want your blood sugar numbers to be, or how much you want to deadlift and you're on your way.

Unfortunately "outcome goals" like these can actively sabotage progress. That's because they focus us on things that are out of our control while, simultaneously, distracting us from the things we should be thinking about instead: our behaviors (which are within our control).

At Precision Nutrition, we spent decades looking at goal setting and at how health and fitness coaches set goals with their clients. We

---

* For example, if a client occasionally binge eats, perhaps you could look for clues on how to not binge eat by examining their no-binge times vs. binge times and noting the differences.

concluded that coaches and their clients repeatedly commit the same three errors when it comes to establishing goals. The good news? It's relatively easy to turn these "bad" goals into "good" ones. You can do it with this three-step process.

SETTING THE RIGHT KINDS OF GOALS

STEP 1
Turn "outcome goals" into "behavior goals"

What are "outcome goals" and "behavior goals"?	An "outcome goal" is something you want to happen, such as losing a certain amount of weight, or running a certain time in a 5K. A "behavior goal" is an action that you'd *do* or *practice* to move toward that outcome, such as putting down your fork between bites, or practicing your running technique three to four times a week.
Why not outcome goals?	While there's nothing wrong with wanting an outcome like a lower body weight, we often can't control outcomes because they're affected by so many outside factors.
Why behavior goals?	Behavior goals, on the other hand, allow us to focus on (and practice) the things we can control—actions, not end results.

What it looks like in practice	A client wants the outcome of "losing twenty pounds." However, to lose twenty pounds, they'll have to do certain behaviors like exercise regularly, better control calories, manage stress, and sleep well. So you turn those into goals. For example, you might spend two weeks with the behavior goal of exercising four times each week for the next two weeks. Then, another two weeks with the behavior goal of eating slowly and until satisfied, not stuffed. Then, another two weeks with the behavior goal of taking a five-minute break twice a day to do a mind-body scan. And another two weeks with the behavior goal of practicing a sleep-promoting calm-down routine starting thirty minutes before bed. Notice how the goal is now an action, not an outcome.
Remember	There's nothing wrong with having a desired outcome. But the outcome is for you, the coach, to think about (and track). Your clients, on the other hand, should be thinking about (and tracking) the behaviors/practices that will lead to that outcome.

STEP 2
Turn "avoid goals" into "approach goals"

What are "avoid goals" and "approach goals"?	An "avoid goal" is something you don't want—something that pushes you away from your current pain, like "I don't want to be out of shape" or "I don't want to be on diabetes medication." An "approach goal" is something you *do* want—something that *pulls* you toward a better, more inspiring future, like "I want to feel confident and strong" or "I want to live pain free."
Why not "avoid goals"?	"Avoid goals"—don't smoke, stop eating junk food—are psychologically counterproductive because telling someone to stop something almost guarantees they'll keep doing it. In addition, a flat-out "don't" reinforces the feeling of failure when someone messes up.
Why "approach goals"?	"Approach goals," on the other hand, give clients something else to do when old habits might have otherwise kicked in. Plus they're about helping people feel good, successful, and inspired to keep on their journey.

What it looks like in practice	Instead of "no junk food," try focusing attention on eating more cut-up fruits and vegetables. Instead of "no soda," try focusing attention on drinking a glass of water with at least three meals each day. Instead of "no stress-eating," try focusing attention on stress-relieving activities to do instead of eating.
Remember	Writing down a habit you want to stop isn't enough. The key is to find a replacement your client can lean on when the old habit could kick in. For bonus points, write down why the new action is good for you. For example, "no soda" can be turned into "tea break," with the following: "Tea is calming, it has antioxidants, and there are lots of flavors I can try. I can even drink it in the mug my daughter made in pottery class."

STEP 3

Turn "performance goals" into "mastery goals"

What are "performance goals" and "mastery goals"?	"Performance goals" are a lot like outcome goals, but they're usually associated with external validation—wanting to win a competition for the prize money or wanting to beat a record time. You're shooting for a specific performance, particularly one that will give you kudos, applause, and/or something good to post on social media. "Mastery goals" are about learning, skill development, and the intrinsic value of becoming excellent at something, or understanding something deeply.

Why not performance goals?	These have limitations because so many things can influence performance like tough conditions or just feeling bad on race day. They can push you to achieve your best, of course. But they're demotivating if you don't achieve them.
Why mastery goals?	Mastery is about the process of continued skill development, which almost always leads to better performance in the long run. Mastery also allows you to focus on the joy of learning, which is gratifying no matter what others think or what time the clock says.
What it looks like in practice	Say your client wants to set a half-marathon personal record. Well, that's both an outcome and a performance goal. To help them transform it into a mastery goal, you might consider working on running with a smooth, efficient stride and better controlling breathing. This could involve watching video of the client running, identifying technique elements to improve, and turning those into behavior goals.
Remember	Again, you can begin by writing down the performance objective. But don't stop there. Continue by listing the skills required to help achieve that objective. Then turn those skills into a series of behaviors. This process makes the goal about progression, not performance.

I worked with two-division UFC champ Georges St-Pierre for a decade. He's a case study in mastery. For example, back at UFC 111 in New Jersey, the crowd saw GSP completely dominate his opponent Dan Hardy for five grueling rounds and twenty-five minutes of fighting.

What the crowd didn't see was that Georges was dissatisfied. When given the opportunity, he failed to submit his opponent and the fight went to a decision. Immediately after, at midnight, following a long day and a long fight, while twenty people waited in a private room to take him to a big party in his honor, Georges spent an hour working on submissions with his grappling coach, so he'd get it right next time.

Another example comes from former client Jahvid Best, an elite NFL running back who retired from football and started competing as a sprinter. When asked about his track and field goals, he replied simply: "To master the technique of sprinting." He didn't talk about winning a competition or going to the Olympics. He didn't even talk about his 100m times. He talked about *mastering his craft*. And, yes, he did go on to compete at the 2016 Olympics.

If behavior goals, approach goals, and mastery goals are what propel the world's best athletes, shouldn't you be using them with your clients too?[*]

COACHING PRINCIPLE 5

Establish THE RIGHT PRACTICES TO REACH THOSE *Goals*

When our daughter started gymnastics—at eighteen months old—I got the chance to look at coaching in a whole new way. On the one end of

---

[*] By the way, "mastering the craft" applies to you too. You can set yourself up for success by outlining the behaviors you'll need to work on in order to develop your coaching skills, coaching practice, and business.

the gym were these toddlers in my daughter's class, with little bodies and big heads, bobbing around, barely able to run in a straight line. On the other end of the gym were the "older girls," six- and seven-year-olds doing mind-boggling aerials, flipping around over high bars, and doing crazy stunts on a balance beam.

I became fascinated with the process. How does a good coach take that clumsy toddler and turn her into a graceful gymnast? I decided to find out for myself. I signed up for private lessons with the gym's head coach and we established a few outcome goals for me: walking handstands and a competent backflip.

However, as mentioned above, outcome goals are insufficient on their own. That's because "do a backflip" isn't a reasonable instruction. As a coach, you can't just demonstrate a flip and then tell your athlete to copy you. They'll surely fail, maybe even get hurt. That's why teaching a backflip means breaking the complex movement down into smaller, simpler movements, teaching your athlete those in a logical progression, and then adding them together over time.

So that's what my coach and I worked on. We broke down handstands and backflips into smaller movement units (skills). Then we came up with specific things I could practice to build up those skills, which would eventually lead me to trying my first walking handstands and backflips.

As I went through my own skill development, I watched our daughter go through hers. They taught her to do back handsprings by starting with 1) back bridges from the floor, then 2) falling into back bridges, then 3) kicking over with one leg from a back bridge, then 4) kicking over with both legs from a back bridge, then 5) doing that with an octagonal tube that guided her smoothly over, and so on until, months later, she got her back handspring. Next, back handsprings on a balance beam.

This idea of progression isn't unique to sports. The best piano teachers use it to help people eventually play Rachmaninoff. The best yoga teachers use it to help people eventually do inversions. And the best language teachers use it to eventually help people become fluent. On some level these teachers realize that accomplishing advanced outcome goals is never done through heroic single efforts. **Rather, outcome goals are accomplished through the mastery of a series of basic skills. And those basic skills are accomplished through regular practice.**

Here's how I teach coaches and clients to visualize the process.

From Goal to Action Worksheet

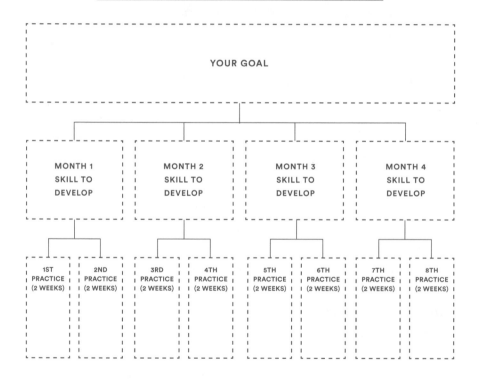

Let's now translate this into a common health and fitness example: weight loss.

Say a client has an outcome goal to lose weight. Sure, write that down on a piece of paper as the desired outcome. But don't stop there. Your next job is to help them come up with behavior goals to accomplish the outcome, one of which might be: *Eat better consistently.*

That's a great start, but it's still more of a goal than a skill. It's sorta like the back handspring in that it needs to be broken down into smaller chunks. So you have to ask yourself: Which skills are required to eat better consistently? At Precision Nutrition, we identified that *better awareness of hunger and appetite* is the primary skill for making progress in this area. (There are others, of course. But we always start with this one as it's fundamental.)

Yet that's still not totally actionable, so we break it down into practices like *eat slowly at each meal* (for the first two weeks) and *eat until satisfied instead of stuffed* (for the second two weeks). Both naturally lead to better hunger and appetite awareness.

There are also secondary skills, like learning to get back on track when you forget to eat slowly or catch yourself rushing. A related skill involves bringing oneself back to awareness, staying calm, and returning to slow bites, without panicking or getting self-critical.

As you can see, the whole point here is that daily practices (eating slowly at each meal, eating until satisfied instead of stuffed) lead to new skills (better hunger and appetite awareness). New skills are the only way to reach behavior goals (eating better consistently). And accomplishing behavior goals is the path to producing our desired outcomes (weight loss).

Here's what that looks like on our worksheet.

TRANSLATING GOALS INTO SKILLS
AND PRACTICES

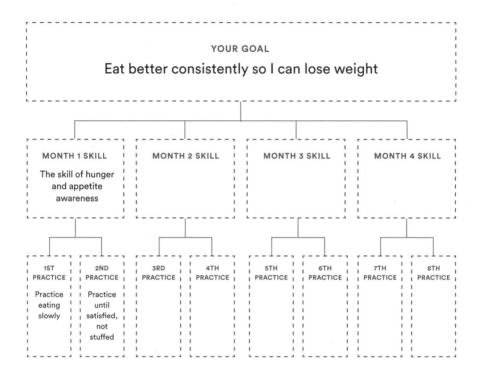

This is just one example. The cool part? The practices-skills-goals model can be applied to every area of coaching. And it's fairly simple to comprehend. Break goals down into the skills required to accomplish those goals. And break skills down into daily practices that help develop those skills.

To create the best daily practices, you can use Precision Nutrition's **5S Formula:**

PRECISION NUTRITION'S 5S FORMULA FOR GOALS

SIMPLE:

The best practices are small daily actions that can be done in the context of real life. If you ask your client, "On a scale of 0–10, how confident do you feel you could do this practice every day for the next two weeks?" the answer should be a 9 or 10. Anything lower and the practice is too challenging or intimidating.

SEGMENTAL:

Most goals are too big, or complicated, to try for in one go. Most skills are the same way. So break them down into defined and organized segments.

SEQUENTIAL:

Breaking things down into segments is great. But you also have to practice those segments in the right order. If you do "thing four" before "thing one" you're less likely to succeed. So have clients start with thing one, then do thing two, then thing three, and so on. Do the right things in the right order and success is a reliable outcome.

STRATEGIC:

Think this process sounds slow? Fact is, if your practices are strategic, the whole process goes quicker. That's because strategic practice addresses the thing that's in your way *right now*. Focus on that one thing—and only that thing—and a difficult process becomes easier and faster.

SUPPORTED:

Practices work best when they're supported by some form of teaching, coaching, mentorship, and accountability.

That moment I watched our daughter in gymnastics, it triggered a whole new area of exploration—to learn about how people learn. What I discovered has completely transformed how I think about coaching (and learning new skills).

It's even opened up a new world for my own fitness as I started competing in Masters-level track and field after twenty-five years off. At nearly fifty years old, if I approached this goal haphazardly, I risked getting hurt, not performing well, not having any fun. So, instead, I followed the practices-skills-goals model. It's kept me relatively injury free for five years now, my times are dropping every year, and I've even medaled at the Canadian national championships.

Oh, and as for my backflip? Nailed it.

COACHING PRINCIPLE 6

ALWAYS *CONFIDENCE Test*

If you had a lifestyle prescription that you knew, with 100 percent certainty, would transform someone's entire life if they were to follow it for a full ninety days . . . but you also knew that—even with the best of intentions—they could only follow it for ten days . . . would you still offer it?

Really think about that. I bet you've been guilty of it at some point in your career, just as I've been. We've written "perfect" diet, workout, or lifestyle plans for people when we knew they'd never be able to follow them.

It's the dilemma health and fitness professionals face every day. Yet it's not just health and fitness clients who struggle. It's well-known in medicine that, on average, patients prescribed life-saving medication will take it less than 40 percent of the time. That's why, when people talk about clients wanting "a magic pill," I often joke, "That's nice, but they wouldn't even take it half the time."

There is, however, a surefire way to increase that percentage: confidence testing.

Before deciding on a course of action or recommendation, simply ask a client: On a scale of 0 to 10—where zero is "no chance at all" and 10 is "of course, even a trained monkey can do that"—how confident are you that you can do Practice *X* every day for the next two weeks? If a client gives you a 9 or a 10, proceed with the practice. If they score an 8 or lower, work with them to "shrink the change." This means coming up with different practices until they're confident enough to give you an honest 9 or 10.

Coach-centered relationships are about instructions. *Do these exercises. Eat this food. Take this medication.* The outcome of this kind of coaching is predictable: low compliance. Sure, a few people will do what you say because you act like the boss. Most won't. And it's not just because they don't like being bossed around, but because you never bothered to ask whether they thought they could do it in the first place.

A coach-centered instructor thinks: "This practice is easy. My client should have no problem following it." A client-centered one thinks: "Once my client and I come up with the next practice that feels right for them, we'll make sure it's something they feel confident they can do for a few weeks."

Even if a practice seems easy to you (*Eating only one extra vegetable a day? That's a joke!*) remember that *coaching isn't about you.* If all your client can do is muster up the confidence to eat one extra veggie a day, even if it's just the parsley garnish, so be it.

Having positive experiences with health and fitness—experiences where they don't feel like a total failure—will lead to more confidence and bigger challenges down the road. Besides, what's the alternative? Asking them to eat five extra veggies, knowing they won't? And then what? Chastising them for being weak even though you knew they wouldn't do it in the first place?

Taking on too much is always a problem—for all of us. When I decided to learn to play the guitar, I came up with ambitious practice schedules (an hour a day!) that I'd never be able to follow. And it paralyzed me. I waited for months until "things got less busy" to get started. Of course, things never got less busy.

That's when, frustrated, I changed the expectations. I told myself that I had to play just five minutes a day, and I'd do it when I was putting my daughter to sleep for the night because she loves music. Sure, five minutes a day wouldn't build my skills at the same rate as an hour a day. But I was doing zero minutes! Surely, five was better than zero. The funny thing is that, many nights, once I got the guitar in my hand, I ended up playing for an hour or more.

Don't we all do this, in some way, in our lives? We get too ambitious in the beginning. Then, when we fall short of those ambitions, we practice "all or nothing thinking." We think: "Well, I can't go to the gym, so I might as well do nothing," when fifty air squats and some stretching is better than nothing. We think: "Well, I blew it with this meal, so I might as well eat whatever I want and start over next Monday," when getting right back on track with the next meal is a better option.

The irony here is that "all or nothing" doesn't get us "all," it usually gets us "nothing." Which is why I like to practice "always something" instead. This means committing to less than I'm capable of on my best day, but something I'm sure I can do on my worst.

When I decided to learn guitar, if I would have confidence tested my one-hour-a-day goal, I would have quickly realized it was too much. And I wouldn't have spent months "not-starting." I would have simply adjusted the expectation down until I got a 9 or 10 on the confidence scale and begun the scaled-back practice the very next day.

COACHING PRINCIPLE 7

Speak IN A WAY THAT MAKES People MORE Likely TO CHANGE

Some days I think the most profound thing I ever learned in health and fitness is that the most passionate coaches, folks with hearts of gold and beautiful intentions, are often the worst offenders in terms of ruining the change process and making clients *less* likely to change.

This blew my mind. I mean, I knew that some approaches were less effective than others. But I assumed that a well-intentioned coach's efforts would, at worst, have no effect.

It never dawned on me that passion *itself* could be moving people further away from their goals. Now I see it every day: caring, devoted, committed coaches speaking to clients in all the wrong ways and talking them out of change.

Early in my career, I was meeting with a renowned athlete to talk nutrition. We started with a review of her last three days of eating, which she recorded in advance.* As she talked me through it, I couldn't help but make my "I'm concerned" frowny face. Maybe you have one of those too? It's the one that says, *Wow, this is pretty terrible. With some better choices here, not only can we turn your performance around, we'll fix your health too*, without you actually saying it.

Her immediate defensiveness was palpable—and understandable. Here I was, a young but passionate upstart, mentally judging a three-time

---

* Back then we used a standardized three-day diet record in which the client would weigh/measure and log everything they've eaten for three representative days of the week. Nowadays, to make it easier for folks, I just ask them to take pictures of the food they eat instead.

Olympic gold medalist because she'd eaten a few fast-food meals and wasn't getting enough protein.

On its face, it was kind of laughable. I mean, how much better did she need to be?!? She'd already won the biggest, baddest competition on the planet *three times*. But, in my passion for "correct" living and eating, I couldn't help but judge her for "falling short" of my expectations.

While the words I said were pleasant enough, my energy said something different. After getting red in the face, she proceeded to list all the good and plausible reasons for why she wasn't getting enough protein and why she ate fast food a few times that week.

I'd lost her trust. And the more I contorted myself to offer suggestions for improvement, the more she argued in favor of McDonald's and Subway and low-protein breakfasts. *Couldn't I see?!? There were no other options. She did the absolute best she could, given her circumstances.* Whether that was true or not was irrelevant. I had backed her into a corner, turning a change moment into a moment of resistance.

When we want *so badly* to help clients, we often find ourselves preaching, lecturing, pushing, cajoling, and prodding. When on the receiving end of all that *pressure*, clients do what humans do: they push back. That's why the more we argue for change, the more clients will argue against it. Paradoxically, it's only when we relax, when we allow for non-change, that our clients become more ready, willing, and able to do it.

But how do you relax and allow for non-change? Check out the following coaching scenarios. They'll show you how to use questions and curiosity to facilitate the change process, not sabotage it.

FOUR COACHING SCENARIOS

SCENARIO 1
The Change Talk Wedge

When someone is expressing ambivalence about change, you start by reflecting on why they *might not* decide to change. It sounds weird but often leads to proposing their own solutions.

[Your client is ambivalent or resisting change. Don't condescend or patronize. Be sincere and compassionate.]

> YOU: "Wow, it sounds like you have a lot on your plate. I can see how tough it is to schedule exercise time."

> OR

> "I know it can be hard to resist those homemade brownies. They're so good."

[Tap into your own busy-ness or love of brownies to offer genuine empathy. Then wait. Be quiet and patient. Let your client speak first. When they do begin talking, they'll likely start telling you why they should change. **This is "change talk," and it's a great step. It means they're not arguing against change, but for it.**]

> CLIENT: "Yeah, I do have a lot going on. But I really should get to the gym. I know I'll feel better."

> OR

> "Honestly, I don't think I need three brownies. I'd probably be happy with just one."

[Once you hear them suggesting change on their own, you're getting somewhere. Using their language, simply reflect and gently imply a next action in the form of a question. Look inquisitive.]

YOU: "It sounds like you'd feel better if you went to the gym?"

OR

"It sounds like maybe one brownie would be enough for you?"

[Now wait again. They may be silent for a bit. Eventually they'll likely keep talking about what they want and how they can achieve it. Let them lead the discussion. Once you feel like they're ready for a next action, go there.]

[Your client shares a few ideas for what she wants.]

YOU: "Given all this, what do you think you'll do next?"

[Notice how you're not playing expert or guru. You're simply using questions to lead them through an articulation of the challenge, then to arguing for change, and then to their own solutions.]

SCENARIO 2
The Continuum

You can use this after listening for change talk. This can help your client move up the continuum of behaviors from worse to better without taking an "all or nothing" approach.

[The client has decided, through Scenario 1, that they want to eat less fast food. But they're not confident that they can give up fast food totally.]

YOU: "Okay, so it sounds like you want to eat less fast food, but eliminating fast food entirely feels like too much, which makes sense. What could you do to just move a tiny bit toward your goal instead of all the way? What would that look like?"

[Notice how you're suggesting the possibility of a third option between "all" or "nothing." And empowering them to come up with the option themselves.

At this point, clients often propose something smaller than "no fast food ever" but something still too difficult to do consistently.]

CLIENT: "Well, what if I went cold turkey and ate no fast food for the next two weeks?"

[Although you haven't confidence tested yet, you have a gut feeling that the change is too big. So you might shrink it a little and see how they feel about it.]

YOU: "Okay, no fast food for the next two weeks. You know, I think that's awesome. But that feels like a pretty big challenge. What about no fast food for just a few days this week? Say, three of the days? Or maybe some days you pick another thing from the menu that's slightly better? What do you think?"

CLIENT: "I can totally do that, Coach—9 out of 10 on the confidence scale! I'll make Monday through Thursday my 'no fast food' days. Or if I go to [insert fast-food restaurant], I'll get the chicken wrap and a salad."

[(This sounds promising!)
At this point you layer in some accountability. And you make a fun "what did you eat instead" game out of it.]

YOU: "That's a great idea. I'm wondering how I can help?

Would you text me at the end of each day to let me know you were successful? Even better, send me a picture of the meal you chose to eat instead!"

SCENARIO 3
The Crazy Questions

If someone is struggling with ambivalence, resistance, and change, it can be really effective to ask some unconventional questions they may not expect.

YOU: "For starters, it sounds like [reiterate what they just said about their understanding of the problem they're struggling with]. So I'm going to ask you two crazy questions. I know it'll sound really weird, but humor me."

CLIENT: [Raises eyebrows]

YOU: "Question #1: What is *good* about the nightly gallon of ice cream? In other words, how does it help you or make you feel better in some way?"

"And question #2: What is *bad* about giving up the nightly gallon of ice cream? In other words, what will be the biggest bummer in that? What might you have to lose?"

[Notice how you're probing for more information about what purpose the "bad habit" serves in their life. And why they might be so attached to it.

At this point, you should be listening closely. They may talk about stresses in life, pressures, and the reasons why they find comfort in the things that are ultimately unhealthy for them. Let them get it all out without judgment.

Now you normalize and empathize, first arguing ever so slightly in favor of *not* changing. This helps prevent you from judging the behavior and causing them to push back against you even though they want to change in the first place.]

YOU: "Wow, yeah, it sounds like there's lots going on there for you. I think I'd want to eat ice cream in that situation too!"

CLIENT: "Thanks for saying that. But I really should find a better way to deal with this."

[(See how they proposed change, not you?)

This is where you can negotiate the next action, confidence test, and plan for the client to check in with a photo that shows them walking instead of eating ice cream.]

YOU: "Well, tell you what. There's no rush to do this. When you're ready, do you feel confident that you could try going for a walk instead of eating the ice cream—at least a few nights for the next two weeks? Or maybe you have the ice cream— but after a walk?"

SCENARIO 4
The Self-Solution

As discussed above, when we help clients develop their own solutions, they're much more likely to feel confident in them and follow through. That's what this option helps with.

[After exploring change and learning about a client's struggles, it's time to affirm, validate, hear, and normalize.]

YOU: "I totally hear you and understand what you're experiencing. It's quite normal. Lots of people feel that too."

[Here you leave some space for the client to respond. Whether they do or they don't is fine. Now it's time to see how the client might solve their own problem.]

YOU: "It sounds like you already have a good sense of the key issues. Knowing this, if you were the coach, what would you recommend?"

[If you feel like they'd be resistant to self-coaching, you can add to it:]

YOU: "Of course, I have some ideas here. But I'd like to hear yours first."

[Let them work through some concepts. Don't be afraid to ask follow-up questions or help shape the recommendations.]

YOU: "Great ideas. I'm wondering, on a scale of 0 to 10, how confident are you that you can do each of them for the next two weeks?"

[They'll rank the ideas. Listen for the ones that score a 9 or 10. If none do, help shape up solutions that they feel really confident they can do.]

YOU: "Awesome, it sounds like we have a winner here. At this point do you mind checking back with me in a few days to share how it's going? What day and time is best for you?"

[Set a time for follow-up and hold them accountable to it.]

In the end, notice how each scenario demonstrates the power of good questions, compassionate listening, and change-oriented dialogue. Always remember this: When a coach argues for change, clients argue against it. So don't argue *for* change! Instead, get clients arguing for it *themselves*. Bonus points if you help them propose their own solutions too.

YOUR MISSION

NO CLIENT LEFT Behind

Mary Kate is a well-known strength coach who's worked with some of the world's most elite athletes, top coaches, and top programs. Most of the coaches she's collaborated with were disciplinarians. *Do this. Don't do that. Gimme another. I don't care if you're tired.*

Once she learned and started practicing the coaching techniques I outlined above, her success skyrocketed. She told me she wished she had a time machine to go back and work with all the people she failed to help over the years.

Many people who learn and use these coaching principles feel that way. They stay up at night thinking about the people they left behind—the ones they desperately wanted to help but couldn't. They think about "difficult" clients and realize that they weren't difficult at all—they were people with real problems, roadblocks, and frustrations. The "issues" were the coach's own because they simply didn't (yet) have the coaching skills needed to help these folks. Even more, they start to realize that, in some cases, their coaching was making clients *less* likely to change.

If you've found yourself in this situation before, try not to dwell on it too much. Or at least find a way to be compassionate with yourself. Now that you know better, you'll do better.

Coaching is a two-way relationship. If clients are resisting something, that something is probably *you*. However, with a new kind of commitment, your coaching life will change. That commitment: Take 100 percent responsibility for your advice and your client's ability to follow it. Lead the horse to water. And make it very thirsty.

Q&A with JB: Coaching

To support what you're learning, I've compiled end-of-chapter Q&As that are full of real, thoughtful questions I've gotten over the years. In each one I share my unfiltered take on the challenges you'll undoubtedly face as you grow your career.

⊕ You can check out all the Change Maker Q&As at **www.changemakeracademy.com/questions**.

This chapter's questions include:

Q: You outlined seven coaching principles, and they all sound important. I'm feeling a little overwhelmed with what to do next. What do you recommend? (Answer: ~200 words)

Q: I find accountability to be a big part of why people hire coaches, but I think they also get frustrated when things don't go their way. How do I balance holding clients accountable without sounding like I'm nagging or bothering them? (Answer: ~200 words)

Q: Clients are always giving me this vague goal of wanting to lose weight, which is great. But now that I know I'm supposed to ask more questions, where do I go from here? (Answer: ~300 words)

Q: What do you do when clients resist nearly everything you suggest? (Answer: ~200 words)

Q: Okay, let's talk results. How do you track them? (Answer: ~225 words)

Q: Got any tips for clients who seem impatient or frustrated by plateaus? (Answer: ~175 words)

Q: I have a handful of clients who are just plain lazy. They simply don't want to put in the work no matter what I try and how easy I make it for them. Now what? (Answer: ~575 words)

Q: Sometimes my clients have elaborate, and incorrect, theories on what works for them and what they should do next. How do I deal with that? (Answer: ~450 words)

Q: So you took a shot at the cheerleader types of coaches. I pride myself on being motivating and positive, and people tell me they like it. So you're saying I shouldn't be like that? (Answer: ~200 words)

Q: You want me to be silent sometimes? I'm supposed to have answers. (Answer: ~425 words)

Q: I'm very frustrated by people coming in and saying they want to try something they've seen on TV. Any advice? (Answer: ~200 words)

Q: My clients swear they're "doing everything right" but I have my doubts. What can I do to challenge them without seeming adversarial? (Answer: ~125 words)

Instead of BEING A SAGE ON THE STAGE
BE A GUIDE ON THE SIDE

SURE, you're AN EXPERT ON THE body BUT
your CLIENTS ARE THE experts ON THEIR LIVES

Follow THE 80/20 rule OF COACHING
EIGHTY percent OF THE TIME
Ask QUESTIONS AND listen
TWENTY percent OF THE TIME
DIRECT AND GIVE guidance

LESS awfulness (WHAT THE CLIENT'S BAD AT)
MORE awesomeness (WHAT THEY'RE GREAT AT)

WANT TO REACH a goal?
BREAK the goal DOWN INTO SKILLS
BREAK the skills DOWN INTO PRACTICES

Always CONFIDENCE TEST
IT DOESN'T MATTER WHAT you THINK IS EASY
WHAT MATTERS IS WHAT your CLIENT THINKS

ALL OR NOTHING DOESN'T get us ALL
IT USUALLY gets us NOTHING
TRY ALWAYS SOMETHING INSTEAD

THE HARDER we WORK TO FORCE change
THE LESS LIKELY someone IS
TO actually CHANGE

CHAPTER 5

BUSI

NESS

HOW TO

Build Your **SYSTEMS,**

Get **CLIENTS,**

AND *Make* **MONEY**

"Business" is a tricky word. Ask one hundred professionals what the word means and you'll get one hundred answers. Some think business is just sales and marketing. Others think it's budgets and accounting. Some think it's leadership and organizational structure. Others think it's systems and standardization.

This idea that people have different, sometimes conflicting, business notions makes complete sense. *Fortune* 100 CEOs *should* think differently than small-business owners, interns, startup entrepreneurs, or solopreneurs. Sadly though, many health and fitness professionals, including some leading their own companies, don't think much about business at all.

Let's fix that in this chapter.

In it, I'll unpack the five most important business skills you'll need to:

figure out what's worth spending time on, and a process for making sure you do;

attract new clients and customers, faster than you can imagine;

support your fast-growing client list, while personalizing each individual's experience;

recruit new team members, people excited to support your mission;

help your team do great work, better than you could have done alone.

Yet these five skills aren't just for professionals who want to own a business, or those who already do. They're for *every* employee, solopreneur, entrepreneur, and business owner.

They're also the most important skills I've had to build over the last fifteen years as I transitioned from employee to solopreneur to entrepreneur to board member to investor. I didn't even know I'd need many of them until I did (like the need to attract and hire talented people *plus* organize them in a way that allows everyone to do their best work).

As you read through these, some skills will feel more relevant than others, depending on where you're at in your career. Yet I highly recommend reviewing them anyway—consider this chapter a crystal ball that will allow you to look into your own future and be prepared for what's to come.

THE FIVE MOST IMPORTANT BUSINESS SKILLS

1 Ruthless Prioritization

2 Marketing and Sales

3 Building Systems

4 Hiring Team Members

5 Organizing Teams

SKILL 1

RUTHLESS *PRIORITIZATION*

RELEVANCY RATING:

EMPLOYEE		
SOLOPRENEUR		
BUSINESS OWNER		

When it comes to building a great career, your first priority is to learn how to prioritize.

Whether we're talking about your professional projects or your social life, recreational activities or entertainment choices, there will always be more options than you have the resources to pursue. Let's say you've started a new business and have identified "attracting new clients" as your big opportunity. That's great. But how will you go about attracting them? With print or online ads? An expensive marketing campaign? Asking for referrals? Appearing on TV? Something else?

With limited time, attention, and money, it'll be difficult to try everything that could work. (And impossible to do it all well.) This means you'll have to decide which one or two things to try, choosing based on cost, time requirements, skills needed, and probability of success. From there you'll have to prioritize those one or two things even over the long list of other things that feel important but can't be invested in right now. You'll know you're doing this right if you occasionally experience regret and the fear of missing out: *Shouldn't I also be doing* X, Y, *and* Z?

It's this idea of doing X *even over* Y that makes prioritization so important yet difficult. Because it means constantly saying no to a host of good opportunities to make room for the few great opportunities truly worth doing now. I remember, early in my career, I dreamed of a day when I had access to more resources, when I didn't have to prioritize so ruthlessly, when I could do everything that felt important. Then I started consulting with companies like Apple, Equinox, and Nike and learned an important lesson.

After a board meeting in which an Apple executive talked about his big frustrations with resource constraints, it hit me. If executives at the biggest companies in the world still complain about resource constraints, those limitations must never go away. So, instead of dreaming of a day without constraints, or complaining about not having enough resources, I'd be better served to get really good at prioritizing as a way to use my resources more effectively.

This applies whether you're the co-founder of a company, an executive at that company, an employee of that executive, or an independent contractor. We *all* have never-ending lists of things we *could* do. Facing these long lists can feel frustrating and demoralizing if there's no criteria for figuring out what's important to do next.

Some folks try to handle this problem by thinking in terms of efficiency. They look for ways to get more done in less time. However, even if you're busy knocking off to-dos at an alarming pace, you won't be accomplishing anything important if those to-dos aren't worth doing. All your time, energy, talent, and unique abilities will be wasted.

Of course, efficiency *is* important. It's always great to use resources well and to get more done with the same amount of time, money, and team members. However, if I had to *prioritize* between efficiency and effectiveness, I'd pick effectiveness—doing the *right* things—every time. This means getting clear on what's worth doing (and what's not worth doing) and then focusing on that almost exclusively. Later in this chapter I'll share how I do it.

For now, don't ask what you can accomplish in a week, ask what you can accomplish in a year

I was recently asked, "In the early days of Precision Nutrition, what did you focus on? Was it content? Did you have help with that? How involved were you on the business side? Or did you hire help there? How about on the coaching side?" In essence, "While you were small and didn't quite have the resources yet, how did you deal with everything?" Those are prioritization questions.

When we started the company, it was just Phil and me. We did everything, so we had to make hard choices every week. Each Monday we'd start by identifying the most important thing to accomplish that week, defined by its ability to help us grow the business. We'd be ruthless about keeping to that, even if something new, exciting, or distracting came up.

As a result, some weeks were all about working on content. Others marketing. Others finance. Others shipping and logistics. It was a constant balancing act using the theory of constraints as our guide, a process by which you identify the most important limiting factor standing in the way of your goals and then improve that thing until it's no longer the bottleneck or weak link in the chain.

Using this methodology, the weekly priorities often changed. But what remained constant was this: We always had one task sitting on the throne of the Kingdom of To-Do. Even more, everything that didn't make the To-Do list became our de facto To-*Not*-Do list. Often that list contained great ideas. But, sometimes frustratingly, they'd have to wait. This *even over* that.

This practice takes discipline because it's easy to feel anxious and impatient within any given week. Indeed, many weeks I was riddled with anxiety, thinking, *I'll never make a dent in my big goals at this pace!* However, experience taught me I can accomplish *a helluva lot* over the course of a year if my activity is well prioritized and I stay focused on the right work. And counseling taught me how to deal with the impatience, stress, and anxiety I'd often feel before I learned that lesson.*

With all that said, I don't want to imply that we were excellent at prioritization from the start. Neither Phil nor I had any formal business training or any reps at figuring out how to prioritize. We weren't perfect. Yet we continued to try our best. Considering that some weeks we got it wrong and others we did nothing worthwhile at all, we still accomplished a lot in a year. Over the first five years we achieved massive goals that we'd have never dared to set in the early days.

Sure, when you're in the depths of time or resource scarcity, it can feel like no matter how much you want to power through responsibilities, there are always ten thousand other things to do. However, prioritization is a skill. Develop it, using the following strategies, and you'll feel less anxiety and experience an improved ability to do the right work in the most efficient ways.

Strategy #1:
Reframe your definition of productivity

In many work cultures there are implicit social rewards for being busy and for doing more than the next person. But working ninety hours a week and feeling like your brain is in a high-speed blender isn't actually rewarded unless those hours lead to the achievement of big, important goals.

What if we could achieve those big, important goals without the brain blender? What if we could do much less than everyone else but make sure everything is of critical importance and moves the needle

---

* I'm a big advocate of counseling as it's been a part of my life since I was a teenager. While it's still a somewhat taboo subject in some communities, and therefore too few people talk about it, I've learned that most of the people I respect and admire have extensive histories working with counselors. In fact, I think it's so important for personal development, and deep health, that Precision Nutrition sets aside a counseling budget for new team members and strongly encourages them to use it.

in measurable, meaningful ways? By prioritizing effectiveness over efficiency, could we stand out from our peers and accomplish more?

It turns out the answer is yes. Most of the extremely high performers I know take this approach.

EFFECTIVE VS. EFFICIENT

Productivity **IS NOT**:

sleeping less, working more, and hustling harder

multitasking social media on your phone while doing invoices and responding to emails on your desktop

"productivity hacks" that are supposed to make you more efficient but scramble your thinking instead

trying to do everything that could make a difference because you're afraid of missing out

Productivity **IS**:

organizing and prioritizing your time *ruthlessly*

ditching many low-leverage tasks and *replacing them* with a few high-leverage tasks

automating the things that can be automated

focusing the rest of your time on your unique abilities

None of this, of course, means that developing your skills and your business is going to be easier or less work. When you're just starting out, there is no "four-hour work week." This process simply helps you make sure all the hard work you're inevitably going to do has a chance of paying off, instead of just keeping you busy.

Strategy #2:
Free up time for more high-leverage work

In health and fitness we often ask clients to fill out food diaries and training logs. The professional equivalent? A time and activity log. The idea is to keep a record of everything you do during your week, cataloging your tasks and the time it takes to do them.

We ask our students to do this every year, and they're always surprised to see how they're really spending time compared with how they think they're spending it. For example, some find they're on social media or browsing the internet or watching TV more than expected. Others realize they might even be—gasp—exercising more than needed.

You don't need fancy apps or time trackers for this, although you can use them if you want. Your logs could be as simple as keeping the Time Diary on the next few pages.

Your Time Diary

Keep a record of everything you do during your week, cataloging your tasks and the time it takes to do them.

7 AM	:00-10	:10-20	:20-30	:30-40	:40-50	:50-60
8 AM						
9 AM						
10 AM						
11 AM						
12 PM						
1 PM						
2 PM						
3 PM						
4 PM						
5 PM						
6 PM						
7 PM						

After a week or so of recording, divide your work into one of these categories:

1 Low-leverage activities I worked on

> ⊕ To do this exercise, and all upcoming ones, please download our printable + fillable worksheets at **www.changemakeracademy.com/downloadable-forms**.

2 High-leverage activities I worked on

> ⊕

3 High-leverage activities I didn't work on*

> ⊕

Next, look at how much time you're spending on low-leverage activities, the ones that feel urgent or important but don't make a difference in getting clients, keeping them, growing a business, or achieving any goal you've set out to achieve.

Back when I was a full-time personal trainer and lifestyle coach, it was scheduling, invoicing, and answering basic questions about protein and peanut butter that felt annoying, low leverage, and in the way of my bigger goals. If I was busy doing these things, I wasn't working on getting new clients, building systems, or learning more about my craft.

Next ask yourself if there's a way to cut down on the time you're spending on low-leverage things by creating templates for the same emails you send out every week, or using scheduling software, or using an automated billing system.

Are there some you can flat-out eliminate? Is there a way to structure your month so certain tasks can be done in a single chunk on a specific

---

* These are the activities you know are important and will produce a high return but you simply didn't make time for them, so they never made it onto your calendar.

day, rather than having them hang over your head every day or every week?

The goal here isn't necessarily to eliminate low-leverage activities. Some of them are necessary—for now anyway. Rather, the goal is to reduce time spent on them, freeing you up to do more high-leverage tasks, including some of the things you've been procrastinating for much too long now.

Strategy #3:
Schedule time to think

If you've followed steps #1 and #2 above, you'll have bought back some time. Maybe a little, maybe a lot. So what should you do with that time?

If you've been overstressed and overworked for much too long, rest. Seriously. Take a nap, go to the spa, spend time in nature. Invest in recharging your physical and mental batteries because you'll need to be at the top of your game for what comes next.

What does come next? Booking appointments with yourself for thinking about, researching, sanity checking, and getting others' thoughts on the high-leverage work worth tackling right now. This is so important that I'd like you to schedule that time immediately.

Schedule Time for Thinking

On which day of the week can you budget a few hours for thinking?

⊕

How long can you budget for this?

How long can you budget for this?

Now pop open your calendar and make your first appointment with yourself to do it. Which day did you choose?

I get it. When there's so much to do, it can seem like a waste of time to spend a few hours per week thinking. Yet, once you reorient your mind to effectiveness over efficiency, you'll see this is your best opportunity to figure out how *not* to get into the same position again. You'll start considering how to eliminate or automate lower-leverage activities. Plus, you'll begin to discover the high-leverage activities that can remove your biggest limiting factors and get you to your goals.

I spend a half day on this every week. In my calendar, "Thinking" is blocked off from 9 AM until 1 PM every Friday. Of course, during this time I don't just sit in lotus pose and hope ideas start zip-lining from neuron to neuron. I use the time for brainstorming, journaling, mind mapping, interviewing experts, reading, and more. All to help solve current problems or to think up my next set of high-leverage opportunities.

Strategy #4:
Play the to-do tournament to decide what's next

After a while, if you do all this right, you'll likely end up with a too-long list of interesting and high-leverage to-dos. This is a great problem to have, yet it can still turn into an imposing wall of items and deadlines, a grocery list of responsibilities where it doesn't matter which aisle you go down first. However, to-do lists shouldn't operate like grocery lists with each item being treated equally. They should operate more like bracketed sports tournaments where items have to compete for the main prize: your precious time and energy.

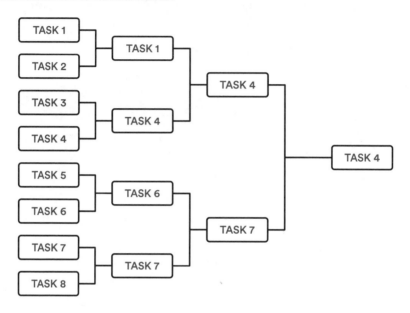

For smaller tasks, daily or weekly tournaments can help you decide what to do for the next few hours, or for the next few days. For larger strategic goals, quarterly or annual tournaments can help make it clear what you should be working on for the entire year, plus they can help you make sure your daily and weekly tournaments are being decided based on your larger goals.

No matter the time scale, if you want to increase your probability of success without committing to working twice as many hours as everyone else—which isn't a guarantee of success either—you need ruthless clarity and prioritization.

As time goes by, more and more opportunities will come flying at you. You'll never have enough resources. Your only competitive advantage is a counterintuitive one: Put rigid constraints on your time, figure out the very few opportunities worth doing, focus on those few unwaveringly, and pass on everything else.

The To-Do Tournament

The tournament bracket method can help you figure out what's worth doing and what to pass on.

To do so, put your ideas and opportunities up against each other using the bracket below or online.

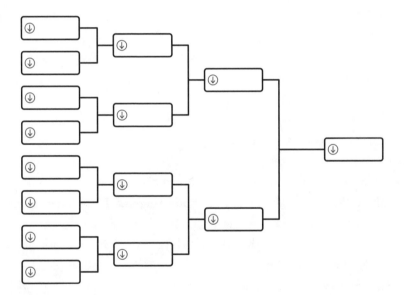

Now, use the theory of constraints—identifying the bottleneck, weak link, or most important limiting factor standing in the way of your next goal—to help inform which activity should win.

One trick that helps me here is to visualize my commitments of time and energy on a zero (no commitments at all) to ten (time and energy are completely maxed out) scale.

Earlier in my career, I'd say yes to far too many things, living in the red zone, right around nine or ten. This meant I was always one unexpected problem or challenge away from overwhelm.

This created difficulties for me personally and professionally. On the personal side, I never had enough mojo for nonwork things like going on fun adventures with friends and family. Heck, even one night out felt like too much to take on. And, on the professional side, should a really meaningful opportunity come up, I would either miss it (because I was too stressed to see its merit) or do it badly (because I didn't have enough time or energy to do it well).

At one point I remember my to-do list included: writing a book, coordinating a multi-center research project, and traveling throughout the US and Canada to give a series of seminars. This on top of my daily Precision Nutrition responsibilities, my self-care, my commitments to friends and family, and helping care for our newborn daughter. I was a hair's width from burnout. Then, in a single week, my wife got the flu and our car broke down. While these should have felt like small, routine disruptions, I felt like they signaled the end of the world.

Of course, everything worked out okay. However, I learned an important lesson that's stuck with me to this very day. I now only commit to the amount of work that puts me in the five or six range.

This offers three important advantages, making it good for business and good for me.

First, it makes me much more selective, forcing me to take on only the highest-impact, most meaningful work and life projects. Second, it leaves me with energy in reserve for personal interests, family time, and more. Finally, it puts me in a position where I can *occasionally* take on additional high-impact, short-term projects because I have energy units in reserve.

To this last point, I'm careful not to do this too often lest I end up back where I started, constantly in the red zone. I accomplish this by doing weekly check-ins with myself (to reevaluate where I am on the time and energy scale) and with my family (to make sure I get an outside view).

FOUR STRATEGIES FOR GETTING BETTER AT PRIORITIZATION

<u>1</u> Reframe your definition of productivity.

<u>2</u> Schedule time to think.

<u>3</u> Free up time for more high leverage work.

<u>4</u> Play the to-do tournament to decide what's next.

SKILL 2

Marketing AND *SALES*

RELEVANCY RATING:

EMPLOYEE		
SOLOPRENEUR		
BUSINESS OWNER		

Many budding entrepreneurs spend a lot of time and money on:

finding the perfect name for their business,

creating the perfect logo, business cards, and letterhead,

protecting their intellectual property via trademarks and copyrights,

finding the very best billing, list management, or scheduling systems,

setting up an optimal tax structure.

Now, I'm not saying these things are unimportant or that you shouldn't think about them. But they shouldn't be your first concern. Precision Nutrition didn't worry about any of them for our first five to seven years. Likewise, we were five years behind on Facebook, Instagram, and Twitter. And we're *still* using an antiquated email management tool that most people replaced back in 2006.

How, then, did we manage to grow a $200+ million business? By focusing our limited resources on the only thing that matters to a new business: Getting customers!

As the saying goes:

Sales solve everything.

I'll always remember a meeting we had about five years after we started our first company. We were at an expensive restaurant in Toronto, conferring with a high-paid accountant. "Your books are a mess!" he told us. "Have you ever seen anything like it?" he asked his assistant, laughing.

During the early years of Precision Nutrition, I heard similar sentiments from well-respected accountants, lawyers, bankers, insurance brokers, and more. Yet I didn't quite feel the shame or embarrassment I think they wanted me to feel. Instead of focusing on intellectual property law or getting the most robust insurance coverage, we focused on *selling things to our ideal clients and customers.* Earning enough to keep going. Profiting enough to grow.

So, when faced with these kinds of comments from other professionals, I've been known to joke: "Yep, we could've taken care of some of these sooner. But we were busy making great products and selling them. Without that we wouldn't be here today, ready to pay your zillion-dollar-an-hour rates. So, by all accounts, I think we made the right choice." They tend to concede the point.

Nowadays we've buttoned down all those other aspects of our business, of course. But only after we'd built a solid foundation and made enough profit to reinvest in these "nice to have" options. While other startups were messing around with lower-value activities, we made it our main goal to keep the main goal—creating great products and making money selling them—the main goal.

There are lots of things that different people will want you to prioritize in your business—and in your life. Some of them, like protecting intellectual property, or using top-notch systems, are good ideas. But remember that prioritization is about *this* even over *that*. When it comes to business, it's marketing and sales pretty much over *everything* else. Because, without income, you can't afford to do *anything* else.

So, how do you get good at marketing and sales? You start by knowing the difference between them.

Sales is someone walking into your physical location (or emailing you) to ask about your products and services. Regardless of where they fall on a scale of 0 to 10 in terms of readiness to buy, it's your job to convince them that a) they need what you're selling and b) they should pay for it today. Your mission is to move them from whatever number they're at on the 0 to 10 scale all the way up to a 10. This requires quick relationship building and a lot of persuasion.

Marketing, on the other hand, is identifying your ideal customer early, crafting a compelling offer just for them, and attracting those people to your physical location (or inbox) *already* at an 8 or 9 out of 10 on the readiness-to-buy scale. In essence, great marketing makes selling significantly easier. Which is why we've always put so much emphasis on it at Precision Nutrition. We've even come up with a fancy name for how we do it. We call it our Tripod Marketing Formula.

THE TRIPOD MARKETING FORMULA

1 Know what people want.

2 Do something awesome to deliver it.

3 Tell everyone about it.

Tripod Leg #1: Know what people want

People passionate about health and fitness—experienced hobbyists and professionals alike—often assume they know what people really want when it comes to coaching: to "look good naked," to improve their blood panels, to get better at their sport. And while that's likely part of why they hire us, it's probably not the full story.

As mentioned in Chapter 3, the best way to find out what's really important to people is to study them. In Precision Nutrition's case, one negative review of our coaching program made me realize that we needed to learn more about what our clients really wanted. So we spent months doing client interviews and exit surveys with people who left our programs.

This was a turning point for us. When we learned for sure what our clients were seeking, business took off. Our clients felt better served, and we felt more satisfied in our work. To this end, I encourage you to become an "anthropologist" of your clients (or potential clients) using the methods I outlined in Chapter 3.

Tripod Leg #2: Do something awesome to deliver it

Through our research, we learned that, no matter what their physical goals were, everyone who hired us for coaching wanted the same thing: They wanted personal attention. They didn't need a lot of it. Rather, they wanted to be pleasantly surprised by personal attention. They wanted to feel cared for and acknowledged *outside the context of a normal coaching interaction.*

It wasn't enough for us to do lifestyle coaching. It wasn't enough to respond quickly and offer guidance when asked for. To give our clients what they truly wanted, we had to find strategic ways to show them we were paying attention—especially at times when they were least expecting it.

This didn't have to be complicated. For instance, we changed our intake questionnaire to make it easier to deliver a personal touch. Previously, when a client joined, they'd fill out a form that asked about everything from their previous exercise and nutrition experience to their personal goals and any injuries or illnesses they had. But armed with this new insight, we added a few questions like:

Do you have any pets? If so, what kind of animal and what's their name?

How will you reward yourself if you achieve your goals? (Will you take a big trip somewhere? Try a new sport or hobby?)

We also ensured that coaches had this important information about their clients close at hand. Every client soon had a "profile" that their coach could see, at a glance, with things like:

their clients' exercise and nutrition history

where they lived

the names of their family members and pets

their hobbies and what they did for fun

their goals and aspirations

how they planned on rewarding themselves once they accomplished their goals

Our coaches could now offer exercise and nutrition help and personalize their interactions with clients in small ways that had a big impact. They started adding simple comments like:

Make sure to stay warm out there; looks like you have a hell of a snowstorm on the way.

Hey, I see it's your birthday coming up. Do you have any plans?

My dog loves these sweet potato doggie treats; I hope you don't mind, but I just sent you and Sparky a box. Let me know what he thinks!

It may not seem like much. But when you're working with an online client, any kind of personal connection—*especially an unexpected sentence or two*—is amplified and appreciated.*

How could you offer unexpected personal attention like this for the people you serve? My favorite way is something popularized by Jonathan Goodman, who wrote the foreword to this book. Here's his strategy, in a nutshell:

Whenever there's an opportunity to do something cool (and quick) for your client, take it. For instance, let's say during one of your sessions, a client mentions he's sick of eating the same thing for breakfast every morning. You can try to give him some suggestions right then. But there's a more thoughtful and personal way to show you care.

After your session is over, make a note for yourself:

Bill hates eating oatmeal every day for breakfast.
Find a couple of recipes and send them his way.

Then, before your next session with Bill, prepare your "gift." It could be a simple link to an article with breakfast ideas. It could be a list of your favorite breakfasts and how to make them. If it's within your

---

* I should also note that forgetting important details is also amplified. I remember hearing from a client who reached out to her previous nutrition coach for help with increasing protein intake. The coach recommended chicken and fish. The only problem? The client was vegan and had mentioned this multiple times. I'm sure her coach wasn't trying to offend her. But that was the result. From this I was reminded that memory isn't always reliable. That's why we built a coaching platform that allows coaches to see all important information while interacting with clients. No remembering necessary.

means, it could be a cookbook or even a Magic Bullet blender. If you like playing chef, maybe you even make him some simple homemade granola, pop it into a Mason jar, and include the recipe. (Very hipster.)

Whatever it is, the next time you have a session with Bill, hand him the gift and say:

Hey, I was thinking about you after our last session, and I thought you'd really like this.

Why is this simple act so powerful?

1 Bill doesn't expect it.
Telling Bill you're going to get him a cookbook or write down your favorite breakfast meal is nice, but it's also an *explicit promise*. If you fulfill that promise, Bill feels good. But if you don't fulfill that promise—if you forget to grab the cookbook or didn't have time to write down your ideas—Bill loses a little bit of trust in you. By writing a note to yourself and surprising Bill the next time you see him, you're delivering something unexpectedly kind, which earns you more points than merely delivering on an expectation.

2 It shows you're paying attention.
Many simply don't have enough people in their lives showing them respect, listening closely to them, and remembering what they shared. By not only listening, but demonstrating that you're listening, you show that you care. This is the unexpected personal attention I mentioned earlier.

3 It shows you don't stop thinking about clients when they're not with you.
And that comes down to how you frame your gift giving:

Hey, I was thinking about you after our last session, and I thought you'd really like this. Who wants to be thought about and cared for, even if they're not around? Everyone.

Tripod Leg #3: Tell everyone about it

Once we figured out what our clients wanted (unexpected personal attention) and simple ways to deliver it awesomely (small, strategic comments and gifts based on new coaching intel), we wanted to tell everyone about our highly effective and surprisingly personal coaching system. The goal quickly became clear: tell our story to more people.

For an online business, that meant getting more people to visit our website. More website traffic (especially if they're legitimate prospects interested in what we offer) means more people signing up for our coaching programs. When more people join our programs, we make more money. When we make more money, we can invest in improving the quality of our service, hiring more team members, and building additional products and services.

But how did we get the ball rolling?

For instance, among our many options, we could have:

written more blog posts and articles targeted specifically to the kinds of people who would be most likely to join our programs;

written guest articles for other blogs and get links back to our website;

improved our referral network and get more affiliates who can send more website traffic;

improved our website's SEO (search engine optimization) and do more targeted ads;

put strategic promoted posts on Facebook targeted to
friends of our clients and customers, linking them to helpful
articles and free courses.

While your business may not be the same as ours, all business realities
are similar: There's only so much time, money, energy, and resources to go
around. Like us, you have to exercise skill number one, ruthless prioritization. You have to pick a path. And have a solid, data-driven rationale for it.

From all the available options, *we* guessed the following approach
would have the highest probability of paying off—promoted posts on
Facebook to friends of our readers, clients, and customers. We chose
this for a few reasons:

1 We already had many Facebook fans: just over one hundred
thousand at the time. That meant we had the potential to
reach millions of friends of friends.

2 Through our interviews and research with clients, we realized
people were more likely to join our coaching programs if a
person they knew had tried it and been successful.

3 We were already getting roughly ten thousand website
visits per week from Facebook; in other words, there was
already an established connection with room to grow.

We spent the next few weeks coming up with a strategy and budget for running promoted posts on Facebook and then rolled it out.
Ka-blam. In just a few weeks, our Facebook traffic went from around
ten thousand visitors per week to just under one hundred thousand per
week. More people visited our website, more people heard about the
awesome things we're doing, and more signed up for our programs.

But let's be clear: Just like there's no best diet, there's no magic marketing method. The tactic that worked for us may not work for you.

Plus, unless you've spent the time to deeply understand your prospects and devoted resources to delivering something awesome, no amount of marketing will matter. Worry about making something valuable that people really want first, *then* figure out which channel to use to sell it.*

When it's time to tell everyone about your awesome product, focus on the one or two methods that best connect you to your audience. Look at data on your clients and the people you want to work with. What does it tell you about where and how to get more people to find you?

Then consider the option that may bring you the most *qualified* leads—in other words, the people most likely to buy your product or service and get benefit from it.

Sheer numbers don't count. Anyone can print a thousand flyers and plaster them all over the neighborhood. And a hundred "Likes" on social media may translate into zero dollars. Instead, ask yourself: *Where is my ideal audience? How can I reach them?* (If you aren't sure who your specific audience is, go back to Tripod Leg #1.)

Gather the data. Look at your current roster (if you have a good group and they represent your ideal client) and ask yourself: *How did these people find out about me?* You may quickly find a pattern (for example, most of your ideal clients might have heard about you from a friend or family member). Once you find a pattern, you can find ways to do more of that. Improve and amplify what's already working.

Important: The Giving vs. Asking ratio

The guiding principle of our marketing strategy has always been what we call the Giving vs. Asking ratio. We want to *give* awesome, free, educational content to our audience at a higher ratio than we *ask* them to buy something. So, rather than promoting our coaching programs directly,

---

* However, as one of my colleagues always reminds me: Often people build something they think is valuable and awesome, but because they didn't spend time to consider how to talk about it or who it helps (and if that person even wants that help), they end up releasing something no one will pay for. So remember parts one and two: Know what people want. Then make something awesome for them (that you know they'll want).

we promoted very high quality, free five-day courses for men and women, teaching them how to eat, move, and live better to improve their health and fitness. This sales funnel looked like this:

Once prospects click on the ad,
they're taken to...

A compelling landing page that persuades them
to sign up for the free course

Once prospects give their name
and email address, they're sent...

Days one through five of the
free five-day course,
on consecutive days, via email

Upon completion of the five-day course,
they receive...

A follow-up message to join
a special presale list that gives them
a discount on coaching

After joining the presale list,
they receive...

Five days of follow-up content
to help them better understand
the coaching program

A few days before our next
coaching program's launch date,
they receive...

A chance to sign up
for coaching

Notice how much free general and product-specific education we've *given* before ever *asking* for something (i.e., to join our program). When calculated out, our Giving vs. Asking ratio across our entire website, and all our programs, is about ten to one.

What Can You Give?

At Precision Nutrition, most of our "gifts" are free articles, courses, and videos. Yours could be different. Capitalize on *your* own unique abilities. For example:

If you're a good writer, write a free article, booklet, or useful handout.

If you have a knack for design, create infographics or workout journals.

If you love to cook or bake, whip up some free protein bars or green drinks.

If you're a performer, make free educational or instructional videos.

What kinds of things could you give to readers, clients, and prospects to increase your exposure, build trust with them, and increase the chance they'll buy from you in the future?

Forget features and benefits; focus on a hopeful future

Many health and fitness pros bristle at the idea of marketing and selling because, when approached by prospects, they get embarrassed and "just don't know what to say." They feel like they need a great pitch that covers all the features and benefits of what they're selling. At the same time, they feel like long, boastful monologues about themselves and their product are unpalatable.

Well, they're right about that last part. Boastful (and boring) monologues *are* unpalatable. That's why I recommend a totally different approach. Because marketing and sales aren't about you, your product, or your service. They're not even about the features or benefits of your product or service. Rather, marketing and sales are about painting a compelling and hopeful future for your prospects.

This cartoon sums it up perfectly:

POTENTIAL CUSTOMER + YOUR PRODUCT = AWESOME PERSON WHO CAN DO RAD THINGS

(This isn't what your business sells.)   (This is.)

Get it? When telling people about your product or service, you shouldn't be talking about *what it is* and *what it does*. Rather, you should be talking about *what they can do with your product*. The first is about you while the second is about them. And that's why people buy things: to help *them* solve some sort of problem in *their* lives. So make sure all your marketing and selling is about the hopeful future they can expect when working with you.

The Hopeful Future

Marketing and sales are about painting a compelling and hopeful future for your prospects. To do that, fill out the following.

Write down who you are and what you do.

Example: My name is John and I run a company called Precision Nutrition that offers coaching for clients, certification for professionals, and coaching software for certified professionals.

Now write down the features of your product or service.

Example: The Precision Nutrition certification includes a) a 600-page definitive textbook covering the art and science of nutrition coaching, b) an online learning portal with videos, lessons, and quizzes, and c) a group forum for interacting with instructors, coaches, and other students.

Now write down the benefits of your product or service.

Example: The Precision Nutrition Certification helps you master the science of nutrition and the art of coaching using a university-level curriculum without having to quit your job and go back to school. Study at your own pace, anywhere, take the quizzes online, and earn a certificate in exercise nutrition.

Now write down the hopeful future people can expect when working with you.

Example: With the Precision Nutrition Certification, you'll master the industry's most effective nutrition coaching system, helping you get life-changing results for yourself and the people who come to you for advice. You'll feel competent and credible in any coaching scenario, with any client. And you'll be able to deliver advice that you know is right, in a way that helps your clients put it into action immediately, without resistance, and without eventually falling off the wagon.

When writing about our coaching programs, we don't talk about habits, sustainable change, or lessons and thought exercises even though these are the cornerstones of our programs. Nor do we talk about workout details, diets, meal plans, or menus.

Instead, we talk about how we help them:

eat better, without dieting or feeling deprived;

get active, no matter what shape they're in now;

ditch the food rules, dropping the fad diets and conflicting advice;

build fitness into their life, without it taking over;

achieve, and maintain, their goals, even when life gets busy.

We tell them how they'll end up:

losing the weight/fat they haven't been able to shed for years;

building physical strength and confidence in their body;

gaining mental confidence, no longer hiding their gifts and talents;

letting go of food confusion, learning what to do, how to do it;

getting off the diet roller coaster once and for all, and never looking back.

To really paint a hopeful future, we help them imagine a life where they can . . .

. . . feel physically and mentally strong, capable of taking on any challenge without worrying that their energy levels or body weight will get in the way;

. . . run around with their kids, or grandkids, without feeling pain, winded, or tired—and they can do it again the next day;

. . . excitedly book a beach vacation without wondering how they'll look (or feel) in a swimsuit, walking along the shore;

. . . have their picture taken without being shocked at how different they actually appear from how they imagine themselves to look;

. . . feel like food is their friend, not their enemy, and never diet again.

Even better, we show them real examples of other people we've helped live this more hopeful future with more than one thousand before-and-after pictures, hundreds of testimonials and quotes, and dozens of feature-length interviews with and stories about our successful clients.

It's okay if you don't have this volume of evidence. Even a handful of compelling success stories is a good start and enough to convince your next handful of clients to give your products and services a try.

Your Elevator Pitch

To help paint a crystal-clear picture of what you do, who you serve, and the hopeful future you can provide people with, it's important to create a brief "elevator pitch" like this.

I help {kind of person}
to {action/benefit}
so that they can {brighter future/more inspiring benefit}.

Here are some examples of what you might come up with:

I help {new moms},
to {get active and eat better},
so that they can {drop their baby weight and feel more energy}.

I help {busy executives},
to {find time in their schedule for healthy habits},
so they can {finally get their health under control}.

I help {people with back pain},
to {move freely again},

so that they can {live their lives without pain and disability}.

I help {young athletes},
to {improve their movement quality},
so that they can {dominate on the playing field and injury-proof themselves}.

I help {women with health challenges},
to {figure out what's going on with their bodies},
so that they can {manage their symptoms and feel in control of their bodies again}.

I help {people in their sixties and seventies},
to {begin a new movement practice},
so they can {walk, jump, run, and play with their grandkids}.

Give it a try:

I help

> ⊥

to

> ⊥

so that they can

> ⊥

Get your first few clients with survey selling

Once you've identified your ideal client, the benefit you can deliver for them, and the hopeful future they can expect in working with you, it's time to go out and look for them. One strategy I've found particularly effective for getting your first few clients is "survey selling."

Begin by creating your survey. (I recommend Google Forms for this as it's free and easy to use, with quick how-to tutorials for beginners.) When creating your survey, start with a title, a compelling description, a few demographic questions. Here's an example of what you might come up with if you were a fitness and nutrition coach:

Tamara's Awesome Coaching Business

I'm looking for ten new moms ages 25–40 who live in Toronto, Canada, and are looking to get active and eat better so they can drop their baby weight and feel more energetic. If this is you, please fill out the form below. All eligible applications will be contacted by phone.

* Required

Gender *

○ Male

○ Female

○ Other: _____

Age *

_____

How committed are you to dropping 10–20 pounds of baby weight, safely and effectively (1 = Meh, I could care less; 10 = I'll eat fire to reach my goal)?

1	2	3	4	5	6	7	8	9	10
○	○	○	○	○	○	○	○	○	○

Phone number *

_____

Here's the formula:

> *I'm looking for {number of people} {gender} ages {age range} who live in {your location} and are looking to {goal}.*
>
> *If this is you, please fill out the form below. All eligible applications will be contacted by phone.*

Once your form is complete, be sure to enable notifications so that you'll be emailed every time a prospective client submits a completed form.

Next, share a link to your survey (on Facebook, Twitter, Instagram, or wherever you prefer) by posting your survey description as follows:

> ****I'm looking for {number of people} {gender} ages {age range} looking to {goal} that live in {location}.****
>
> *I am looking for {gender} who want to:*
> *-{benefit 1}*
> *-{benefit 2}*
> *-{benefit 3}*
>
> *Spots are extremely limited and I'm only looking for {number of people} who are ready to make a change today. To apply, fill out the quick survey below and I'll be in touch if you meet the requirements:*
>
> *===> {link to your Google form}*

The benefits you include will vary but they should speak to the hopeful future I described earlier.

Once you get the message out and people start responding, make sure someone calls them right away to learn more about their goals and expectations and to tell them more about how you work. As discussed in Chapter 4, take a client-centered approach here, asking questions and focusing on who they are and what they need before talking about what you can do, your fees, etc. Ideally you'll get in touch within twenty minutes of them filling out your survey, at the peak of their interest.

If you're able to get in touch with them and you schedule an initial appointment together, fantastic. If not, keep following up, with a friendly check-in, once a week for the first month. If you're still unsuccessful, follow up once a month after that until they become a client or tell you they're not interested in working with you.

This is where most people drop the ball, assuming that if someone hasn't gotten back to them or made an appointment, they're not interested. This is a bad assumption. Sometimes people are busy, need to think more, or have to talk it over with a significant other. By continuing to reach out in a friendly way, you make sure that when they are ready to get started, it's with you.

If you decide to try this method, you'll be up and running with your first post inside of thirty minutes. Most people who try it report getting one to three clients within a day or two. Even if you think it's too simple or couldn't possibly work, try it anyway. People constantly tell me that they would have never expected something like this to work. But it did, exactly how I said it would.

Tell People What You Do

Every year, through our Precision Nutrition Facebook groups, we do a two-week challenge. Our certification students and graduates are encouraged to do something simple (yet, apparently, radical these days). They are asked to talk to people. You know, like, real people. In real life.

Specifically, we ask them to tell one person a day what they do.

That person could be anyone: the barista that frothed the milk on their latte, the cashier at the grocery store, or the lady sitting next to them on their commuter train. The goal is to develop a "script" about what they do, get comfortable talking about it, and maybe even get a new client or a referral. If you're interested in trying it, here's how it works.

The "Tell People What You Do" Challenge

Begin by making sure you can describe what you do without rambling and without boring listeners with irrelevant details. A simple way to do this is to use the statement you created in Your Elevator Pitch on page 186:

I help {kind of person}
to {action/benefit}
so that they can {brighter future/more inspiring benefit}.

Next, pick a person (any person) every day to talk to. You can approach folks however you like to get the conversation started. If you're not sure how to do that without coming off creepy, break the ice with something like this:

Hey!

I'm doing this two-week challenge where I have to tell someone about what I do, and you're who I chose today!

Is that cool?

If they're game, lay the elevator pitch—or something like it—on them. If they seem interested, expand on it. The conversation could end pleasantly but without any real interest on their part and that's okay. You'll still benefit from the practice. However, should they express real interest, keep the conversation going with something like:

Hey, thanks for listening. Mission accomplished on the contest!

Before I roll, you seemed kinda interested in {some aspect of what you talked about} and a really cool resource just popped into my head that I'd love to share.

Could you write down your {email address/phone number/FB page} so I can send it over?

Just so you know, "no" is a fine answer here. After all, we just met.

However, I do think you'll dig it. And I promise not to bug you beyond that.

If they share their contact info, wait a day and follow up with something awesome—a cool article, some recipes, an infographic, an inspiring YouTube video—whatever you think will be helpful and is in line with what you talked about. It doesn't have to be your own content. Just something that's high quality and will be genuinely helpful. Here's how you might follow up.

Hi!

It's {your name}, we met yesterday at {place} and we talked about {topic}.

Wanted to follow up with {the thing I promised}, which I think you'll like.

Here's the link:
{link to the thing here}

No obligation to {watch it, read it, etc.}. I just thought it might help.

If they follow up and thank you for the link, reply with a casual reference to your services.

Thanks for the note!

I'm so glad you liked {the thing you sent}!

I don't know if you, or anyone you know, would be interested in this . . . but I'm running a program that starts in two weeks.

I'll be working with {number of people} {gender} ages {age range} looking to {goal}.

Spots are extremely limited and I'm only looking for {number of people}.

Again, if you or someone you know is interested, let me know by filling out this super-quick survey below.

===> {link to your Google form}

Again, no pressure. Just sharing this in case you, or a friend, might be interested.

So there you have it. A step-by-step guide on how to talk to people and follow up in a non-creepy, not overly pushy kind of way. The point of this exercise is to show you that there are potential clients everywhere. You just need to speak up so they know you're there.

Leverage your existing communities

Many of us belong to one group, or a host of them, either online or in person. These are often unrelated to health and fitness, which—in this case—is a good thing. It gives you the opportunity to share what you do with a new audience.

For example, you might be part of:

a Facebook group for new moms

a Saturday-morning bring-your-dog-and-hike group

an online forum for people who dig classic cars

a faith community where you worship plus participate in community activities together

a weekly online mastermind group of career-change entrepreneurs

If you do it right, as my friend Carolina did, these groups can be an amazing source of new clients. Here's how she did it.

Carolina is from Mexico, but she currently lives just outside of Toronto. When she came to Canada, she joined a Facebook group for Mexican women living abroad. She was genuinely excited to connect to this group and took her time getting to know the members. She responded to people's posts, and posted her own successes and woes living abroad as a Mexican woman. She took note of the tone and "vibe" of this group, and generally just tried to be kind, helpful, and supportive to the other members without talking much about what she does for a living.

After a while, she posted about her coaching work. It was more of a "this is my life story" kind of post, but she also happened to mention that she was an online lifestyle coach and dropped some information about a program she was running that was starting soon. Not long after she posted, Carolina had:

700+ reactions to the original post

180+ comments asking for more information

250+ new "Likes" on her personal coaching Facebook page

80+ brand-new subscriptions to her mailing list

too many private messages to count

Not bad for a free group that she was interested in hanging out with anyway.

How to Leverage Your Existing Communities

To try this method yourself:

JOIN A GROUP. Consider the groups you're currently a member of (online or in person). If you're not a member of any, consider whether there are any groups you'd like to be a part of that would be good candidates for your coaching. (Remember, it's better if they're not health and fitness groups.)

ENGAGE WITH THE GROUP in an authentic, helpful, supportive way. Don't just join groups to make your elevator pitch as this is universally frowned upon. Instead, become a real part of the community and only talk about what you do if it's relevant to the conversations already going on.

OFFER GENUINE HELP. If a health and fitness topic comes up, bingo! Help answer questions. Offer support. Send people helpful links, articles, videos, and other resources. You can be subtle about self-promotion by simply linking back to your website or social media profile. Still, hold back on mentioning your services.

OCCASIONALLY MENTION YOUR SERVICES. After you've built trust and made genuine connections, mention your services. Have your information easily available if people want it, but don't be pushy about it. If you need a ratio to work with, for every ten helpful comments you make, you can slide in one about your coaching.

In the end, as mentioned earlier, when it comes to business, it's marketing and sales pretty much over *everything else*. Because, without income, you can't afford to do *anything else*. But don't let the blizzard of information on these topics overwhelm you.

Marketing is simply:

1 Knowing what people want,

2 Doing something awesome to deliver that thing, and

3 Telling everyone about it.

And sales is simply showing people the compelling and hopeful future they can expect when working with you and creating some urgency around getting started now.

If you're interested in going deeper into marketing, I highly recommend Robert Cialdini's classic book *Influence*. In this book he outlines the six universal principles of persuasion used across industries to get people to say "yes" and shares examples of how you can apply them.

If you'd like to learn more about sales, check out Neil Rackham's *SPIN Selling*. In this book he teaches the art of consultative selling, a highly effective sales process in which the buyers do most of the talking and the sellers do most of the listening.

SKILL 3

BUILDING Systems

RELEVANCY RATING:

EMPLOYEE		
SOLOPRENEUR		
BUSINESS OWNER		

Prioritizing high-leverage tasks is one of the keys to using your resources effectively. However, you still have to do *some* low-leverage tasks. That's where systems come into play. Systems allow you to find redundancies and time wasters in your work and streamline them to free up time for other activities.

For example, let's say you're an exercise and fitness coach, and you know you'll have to answer the same few questions a bazillion times this year:

How many calories should I eat?

How many reps this time?

Is it okay to drink while I'm on vacation?

What workout can I do on my own this week?

Even if you're fast and can put together answers in a few minutes, you'll still spend hundreds of hours every year addressing the same things. That's wasteful because you're usually just providing the same basic info about macronutrients and muscle fibers, multivitamins and metabolism, again and again, only slightly adjusted for each person.

Imagine getting all that time back by having an "answer template" you can copy and paste from, adding small personal touches to ensure your messages don't *feel* copied and pasted. That's a lot of time freed up for higher-leverage, more enjoyable work. That's time you can use on new initiatives to help grow your business instead of spending time in a never-ending loop of repetitive low-leverage tasks.

But how can you create these kinds of systems in simple ways without being a systems engineer or requiring expensive software? Here's an example for those who do a lot of written communications.

Building Your Systems

STEP 1
Create a "General" file

You'll need a list of the communications you use repeatedly. For a standard coaching business, this may include:

information about services and pricing

welcome messages

reminders about upcoming sessions

post-session check-ins

monthly "How's it going?" messages

regular "You're doing great" messages

requests for data like weight, measurements, blood work, etc.

ads and marketing materials

What categories of communications (info about services and pricing, welcome messages, reminders about upcoming sessions, post-session check-ins, etc.) do you use regularly?

Once you have your categories in mind, write the content itself. You'll probably want to do this on your computer so you can save your own templates and paste in content from emails, brochures, or other material you've already written. Depending on the nature of your offerings, and how often you like to check in with clients, there might be a lot of things to document. That's okay; take a few weeks to get this done. Don't rush; do it right.

STEP 2
Create a "Programs" file

Whatever services you offer, you undoubtedly have to deliver them (and communicate about them) over and over. These communications might include:

intake questionnaires

workout plans (weight loss)

workout plans (weight gain)

workout plan FAQs

meal plans (weight loss)

meal plans (weight gain)

meal plan FAQs

meal-planning strategies

supplement guidelines (weight loss)

supplement guidelines (weight gain)

supplement FAQs

body-measurement guidelines

What categories of programs/deliverables (intake questionnaires, workout plans, eating plans, supplement guidelines, etc.) will you be using?

Again, capture these on your computer for easier copy/paste later.

STEP 3

Create an "Emails" file

Go through a couple months' worth of "sent mail" messages and look for patterns. In the seeming hodgepodge of your communications with clients, there are probably repetitions. Typically, coaches send lots of messages about:

nutrition, workouts, and supplements

sleep, and stress management

travel and schedule-change challenges

meal-planning challenges

questions about nutrition basics

general anxieties about life/goals/programs/progress

Which emails are virtually the same? What categories of emails (nutrition/exercise/supplement discussions, sleep/stress-management discussions, travel/schedule discussions, general anxieties about life/goals/progress discussions) could you capture for easy copy/paste later?

In a new document, make a list of your email categories. Under each category heading, paste in your best email on the topic, and tweak/perfect it as necessary.

STEP 4

Create a Master Folder

Save your "General," "Programs," and "Emails" files in one easily accessible folder. Now you have a master database of the most common things you'll need to type out. You can pull from it when it's time to reply to questions, to send programs, or proactively reach out.

STEP 5

Remember to personalize

By the time you pull information from your Master Folder and paste it into a new document, email, or text message, you're 90 percent done. The other 10 percent? Customizing for the specific person.

To do this, start with a friendly greeting and a sentence or two about how they're doing, what they've been up to, etc. Then personalize your standard reply based on their situation. After that, sign and send.

This is just one example of how you can systematize your work, saving hundreds of hours every year. The same can be done for every repetitive thing you do—billing software for invoicing and collecting payments, accounting software for financial record keeping, scheduling software for booking and rearranging appointments, and so on. While some come with a price tag, you can think of this as buying hours back.

Using systems can feel less personal at first. And they'll definitely become less personal if you turn into a copy-and-paste machine that de-values connection. At the same time, these very same systems can also help you deliver a more personal touch. If you spend some of your new-found time on engagement (listening, understanding, customizing, and doing the thoughtful things others won't have time to think of doing), automation will help you deliver more, in better ways, than anyone else.

SKILL 4

HIRING *TEAM Members*

RELEVANCY RATING:

EMPLOYEE		
SOLOPRENEUR		
BUSINESS OWNER		

Solopreneurs and business owners eventually get to the point where the influx of new clients and customers outpaces their ability to keep up, no matter how they prioritize. On the one hand, they feel on their way to achieving big professional goals. On the other, they feel more stressed and anxious than ever. They wonder why, if growth is supposed to be fun, they're not having any.

If you're experiencing this, take heart. This is a *great* problem to have. (Too much business? Come on now!) Even better, these feelings indicate that you've solved the previous limiting factor in your business and are now butting up against a new one: not enough humanpower. This means it's time to make hiring a top priority, at least for a little while, until you address this new constraint.

I know this cycle all too well. When Phil and I started, it was just the two of us. It was a few years before we hired our first full-time coach. It was a few more before we next hired help with product logistics and customer service. Then came someone to help with content. Then web development and design. Precision Nutrition now has close to 150 people working as full-time team members or contractors.

I'll be honest: Over the years I've had a mixed relationship with hiring. So many questions swirled in my head in the early days. *Can we really afford to pay someone to do what I've been doing? What if they can't do it as well? What if they don't care as much? Will they protect our brand reputation or ruin it?*

At the same time, I knew we couldn't go on working the way we were. Our options were to scale back (moving in the opposite direction of our goals), try to work at a burnout pace (which never goes well), or take the risk and bring someone new onto the team. We obviously chose the latter, learning some valuable lessons along the way.

Lesson 1: Don't hire until it hurts

Most people don't consider hiring until they're struggling. The need for help slowly creeps up until they're feeling overwhelmed and disheartened, even though their business is growing. They're making more money but working more hours, too, and things in the business feel like they're held together with duct tape. Left with no other choice, they finally bring on another team member.

This is a common experience. Many solopreneurs take a little too long to make their first hire. Interestingly, many hire too freely after that, especially if the first went well. That's why I encourage folks to "wait until it hurts" not only with their first hire, but with subsequent ones. In other words, *don't* hire when you or someone on your team feels: "I could use a little help over here." Instead, hire when they feel: "This is growing so fast that, if I don't get help, I'm going to split apart!"

This, of course, assumes you and your team have developed Skills #1 and #3: Ruthless Prioritization and Building Systems. It's easy to feel overwhelmed with long to-do lists of meaningless or repetitive tasks and then put in a request for hiring. So I'd add a caveat here. Yes, wait until it hurts to hire. But make sure the hurt is happening because of new clients, customers, and opportunities, not poor prioritization or lack of systems.

Lesson 2: Get clear on exactly what you need and hire for that

A few years back, a group of seven women I know and respect got together to start a women's fitness company. While it seemed like a cool idea to everyone else, I cringed. They shared similar backgrounds, skills, and interests, so six were redundant. They'd be splitting startup revenues among seven people when only one was necessary. This would make it impossible to hire the additional skills required to grow the business. Because of this, I felt the partnership couldn't last. It didn't.

This is one of the reasons my partnership with Phil has been so valuable. When we partnered, we brought totally different—but complementary—backgrounds, experiences, and skills to the table. I came with an extensive background in exercise, nutrition, and lifestyle, plus writing and speaking experience. Phil was a health and fitness enthusiast with a systems design engineering degree and a special interest in business. Between us, we had enough raw materials for deep subject-level expertise, content creation, a digital presence, and business fundamentals. Neither of us was redundant; we were synergistic.

What's good for partnerships is also good for hiring in many cases, but not all. So it's important to get really clear on whether you need:

someone like you but more junior, to help with work overflow

someone like you but more senior, to help level up your business

someone totally different, to bring new skills into your business

Think carefully about exactly what you need. Articulate it clearly. Then go out and try to find that thing in a person. The clearer you are, the better your chances of making the right hire.

Lesson 3: Get some help with recruiting

When hiring for a role at Precision Nutrition, we look for individuals who we think could have a high probability of succeeding in our culture and in the role. But not just one or two. In most cases we start with hundreds of applicants, narrow that group down to dozens of prospects, and further narrow that group down to three "can't lose" candidates.

Contrast this with what most small-business owners do: search their own contact list. This can sometimes work. But it's often a recipe for failure, as individual networks are rarely large enough to produce even one "can't lose" candidate, let alone three. (This is especially true if they're looking for someone totally different, who can bring new skills into the business.)

Working with recruiters, whose job it is to build huge networks of well-qualified and well-vetted candidates, helps to strategically expand your network. It magically puts you one degree of separation from any talent or skill in the world.

But how do you find a recruiter in the first place? If you know someone who works in human resources or recruiting, ask them for guidance. They may know the top recruiters in your area. If you don't know anyone in the industry, begin with an internet search. For example, if I were hiring for a marketing position at Precision Nutrition I'd type in "marketing recruiter Toronto." Or, for an executive position, I'd type in "executive recruiter Toronto."*

From there, narrow your search to firms with a strong track record of placing people in the kinds of positions you're looking to fill. For example, if you're looking to hire help with marketing or programming, choose a recruiter who specializes in placing the kinds of marketers or programmers you're looking for. This gives you access to the biggest networks and

---

* We're a virtual company that works remotely and, therefore, team members can work anywhere. At the same time, I sometimes prefer to start with a local recruiter who has global reach so that reference checks, in-person meetings, etc. are easier.

increases your chances of finding the right person. But don't just take their word for it; ask for references. Talk to people who've been hired through them as well as people who didn't choose them and ask why.

Is this process more time-intensive and expensive than the alternative? Absolutely. However, the cost of hiring the wrong candidate is far higher. In my experience, it's much better to wait a little longer to begin a hiring search, so you can do it right, than to hire haphazardly and get the wrong person.

Lesson 4: Put less stock in interviews, more in assessments

Let me say this without sugarcoating: On their own, interviews suck. Unless someone's belligerent, antagonistic, or mentions how much they hate some aspect of your product or service, interviews will rarely give you clues into a person's fit for your work culture or their ability to do the work you're hiring for (unless, of course, *being interviewed* is part of the job). Yet that's how many small businesses hire: by doing job postings and then interviewing the candidates.

Over the years we've learned a much more rigorous approach. Our goal is to make sure candidates are a good fit for our culture and can actually do the work, so we explore both, as follows:

CULTURE ASSESSMENTS.
We've experimented with many personality and work-style assessments to vet candidates. The Caliper Profile (which ranks people according to more than twenty leadership, interpersonal, problem-solving/decision-making, and personal-organization/time-management dimensions) and the Kolbe Index (which identifies people's natural tendencies for how they take, or don't take, action) are the ones we use most consistently. Even if someone has a stellar resume,

we're unlikely to hire them if their Caliper and Kolbe results don't suggest a good fit for the organization.*

WORK PROJECTS.
If you want to know whether someone can do the work, why not ask them to actually do the work? If their Caliper and Kolbe profiles look good, we either have them help with an actual Precision Nutrition project or create a simulated project for them to help with. (Depending on the scope of the project, we'll either pay them for this or send them a surprise gift.) Then we ask a panel of credible experts to rate their work, especially if we're hiring to add a new capability and don't have an internal team that knows what a great job looks like in this new domain.

Only after these two steps are complete do we interview candidates. Remember, I said interviews, *alone*, suck. However, interviews done to clarify what you've learned through personality and work assessments are useful. Indeed, most of the time we spend in interviews is about exploring, in dialogue, how a candidate's Caliper and Kolbe results might relate to their previous work experiences. And how their work projects can give us insights into their thought processes.

Lesson 5: The hurting doesn't stop once you hire

In Lesson 1 we discussed how it's often best to "wait until it hurts" when considering hiring. The implication is, of course, that hiring will make the hurting stop. Sadly, that's not true in the short term. Hiring actually makes the hurting worse.

---

* Caliper, in particular, offers a valuable service where their in-house experts will review a candidate's results, in the context of your needs and culture, to help you make sense of whether someone is a fit for your organization or not.

Why does it hurt more *after* hiring? Well, hiring requires a lot of organizational "onboarding." The bigger the organization, or the higher the rank, the longer the process. This means the first few months, possibly even years for executive hires, are about teaching "how things work around here."

If you've ever started a new job, you know the feeling. You have to get to know:

THE PEOPLE, how they think, how they work;

THE SYSTEMS, how to log into them, how to use them, how not to break them;

YOUR ROLES AND ACCOUNTABILITIES, what's expected of you, what's not;

THE PRODUCTS, what they offer, what they don't;

THE CUSTOMERS, who they are, what they're looking for.

Finally, once you know *all that*, you can get to the work.

Think of the implications here if you're the one doing the hiring. Just yesterday you were occupying the role yourself. The responsibilities were overwhelming, and you weren't sure you could keep going for too much longer. Now you *still* have to do all that work. And you *also* have to do the work to oversee your new hire's onboarding.

Yes, it can feel disheartening to know that if you wait until it hurts to hire, the hurting continues. At the same time, if your new hire is onboarded well, not only will all the onboarding come to an end eventually, but they'll also soon take over the roles and responsibilities they were hired for. So hang onto that.* Difficult times feel much easier when

---

* Part of successful onboarding relates back to system building. The more effective and thorough your systems are, the easier it is to onboard. Because, while not hiring until it hurts is one thing, it's quite another not to even think about, or plan for, future hires.

you can see light at the end of the tunnel and you're playing an active role in reaching it.

Lesson 6: You don't have to become a manager, executive, or leader

As Precision Nutrition grew, I carried with me a particular narrative. I believed that:

1 as founders hire new people, they have to become managers,

2 as founders hire new managers, they have to become executives, and

3 as founders hire new executives, they have to become leaders.

In other words, I thought Phil and I had to stay "at the top" of our organization, to eventually become C-Something-Os and then eventually become presidents or chairpeople at the highest point of an imaginary Precision Nutrition totem pole.

This made me absolutely miserable. In the early days, I spent my time researching, writing, crunching numbers, and telling stories. As an introvert, I got long stretches of uninterrupted, quiet time for focused work. Then, suddenly, I was in meetings all day, every day. People wanted me to tell them what to work on, to help them prioritize their daily activities, to make decisions, to sync up the team. Workweeks would end and I'd be miserable. I hadn't created a thing. My unique abilities weren't being utilized. I was exhausted from the constant interpersonal work.

This affected my family life too. I didn't have much energy or joy to share with my wife, Amanda, or our children. Finally, in the midst of a depression, I decided to call it quits. I remember writing a list of ways I could escape the scenario. It included many reasonable options like selling my shares of the company to Phil. It also included a host of unreasonable ones, the most chilling of which was, "Drive off a bridge so Amanda and the kids at least get some insurance money."

That last one was a real wake-up call. I found a great counselor to help me through the depression. And I talked with Phil, who suggested a different way to think about my work.

Instead of worrying about having to be a manager or an executive, he encouraged me to go back to doing what I loved. We could hire managers and executives, he told me at my home, the day I shared my struggles with him. In fact, he said, hiring them would probably be much easier than trying to find someone to replace what I do best.

He was right. Now, years later, we have an awesome team of managers and executives, a fantastic group of people who allow me to work within my unique abilities without having to be something I'm not.

Keep this in mind as you consider your hiring plan. You get to make the rules within your company. If you love management and leadership, by all means do what's required to grow in that area and tackle the challenge. If you don't, that's okay too. Build out your team to handle those tasks while you focus on the things that bring you, and the company, the most value.

SIX IMPORTANT HIRING LESSONS

__1__ Don't hire until it hurts

__2__ Get clear on exactly what you need and hire for that

__3__ Get some help with recruiting

__4__ Put less stock in interviews, more in assessments

__5__ The hurting doesn't stop once you hire

__6__ You don't have to become a manager, executive, or leader

SKILL 5

ORGANIZING <u>TEAMS</u>

RELEVANCY RATING:

EMPLOYEE		
SOLOPRENEUR		
BUSINESS OWNER		
CHIEF EXECUTIVE OFFICER		

If you've gotten to this stage, big high-fives! This kind of business development isn't for the fainthearted. However, don't let up just yet. A growing team means a new focus on teamwork.

Unfortunately, most business owners don't think much about teamwork as they begin hiring. This makes sense as most hiring starts as a way for them to get help with necessary, important, but "lower-leverage" activities like answering phones and emails, shipping products, servicing clients, posting on social media, etc. The goal, of course, is to continue to free themselves up for the higher-leverage activities that can grow their business.

This focus on "hiring help" is what's needed in the beginning. However, it can become a problem when the team gets bigger and everyone reports directly to the business owner. Quickly, the owner's time becomes consumed with managing people doing lower-leverage activities. Which means there's no time left (and no one available) to do the high-leverage growth activities.

Phil and I experienced this firsthand when Precision Nutrition grew to about thirty team members. Even though we were growing fast, we were still operating as if we had a small team of "helpers." Everyone reported to either me or Phil, and we were the key decision makers on every project. We were constantly in meetings or having one-on-one conversations with team members.

Bottom line: We were overworked, overstressed, and doing our jobs badly. Team members were left directionless for long stretches of time, and they were starting to lose their enthusiasm as well as their confidence in us. We were all flailing and weren't quite sure why.

I'll never forget one meeting we had during that time. Phil and I were giving a product and marketing presentation, and I could see one of our team members rolling his eyes and shaking his head. Finally, he stood up and blurted out that our data were poorly collected, our conclusions facile. He wasn't quite right, but his criticism did wake us up to something important. Our team members were feeling disconnected and losing sight of our vision.

A few months later, I was listening to a podcast mentioning something called the "Rule of 3 and 10," put forward by Hiroshi Mikitani, founder of Japan's largest e-commerce retailer. Over the years, Mikitani noticed that "everything breaks" at predictable intervals, specifically when companies triple in size. In other words, they break when you grow from one to three employees. They break again when you get to ten, again at thirty, again at one hundred, again at three hundred, and so on. Mikitani's multibillion-dollar company now employs over twelve thousand people so he's seen a lot of breaks.

But what does he mean by "everything breaks"? Simply that the things you were previously doing, and seemed to be working—processes for decision-making, business systems, marketing, sales, accounting, payroll, benefits, infrastructure, scheduling meetings, and leadership structures—become less effective and/or begin to produce unintended consequences.

Mikitani's rule explained clearly why we were struggling. We were expecting the same organizational structures, work processes, and communication systems to serve thirty people just as well as they had served ten people. And they were, predictably, failing.

Further, when the team was small, we could focus nearly all our efforts on what we were putting out into the world. However, as we grew larger, we had to think about how that work got done. Specifically, we had to consider how to most effectively engineer work groups where different people, holding various roles, could effectively collaborate, make decisions, and get things done quickly at a high standard.

I still remember the first time I knew we were making progress in this area. At the end of my workday, I walked out to the end of my driveway to collect the mail. I discovered a revelation! A thick packet had arrived, outlining my family's new PN-sponsored health insurance plan.

This was so awesome, not only because we finally had health care, but because I didn't have to make any decisions about it. Heck, I didn't even know anyone was working on this! Just a few months earlier, there wasn't a single thing I didn't know about; I was involved in every decision. But now, with our new organizational structure, the team was doing awesome things without needing my input at all.

Of course, there are entire disciplines devoted to studying how to organize teams (from functional structures to divisional structures to matrix structures to flat structures) and how to lead those teams (from top-down hierarchies to flatarchies to holacracies). If you're operating a small business, it's probably not necessary for you to go down the rabbit hole just yet. However, if you're over twenty-five team members and growing fast, I highly recommend the classic *Reframing Organizations* by Lee Bolman and Terrence Deal. It shares four key frameworks for understanding organizations and what they need to be successful.

Are you working outside or inside the wall?

Before spending all your time on organizational work, though, it's important to keep some perspective. Many professional managers and executives spend too much time thinking about "how we work together" and too little about the work itself. To this end, I like to think of companies as castles with walls separating the inner workings of the castle from the outside world.

Outside the wall is the content you put out into the world, including your products and services. It's also where your customers live, how they experience your products and services, and how they perceive your company. Things like editorial content, advertising, sales, marketing, and user experience are all *outside the wall* activities.

Inside the wall are your team, your processes, and your policies. It's how you are together and how you work together. Things like leadership, management, human resources, internal communications, values statements, and mission statements are all inside the wall activities.

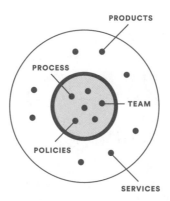

As you grow it's important to make sure you don't take your eyes off what's happening outside the wall, which is very easy to do. I often call this "playing company." It's where a disproportionately high amount of your resources goes into business plans, budgets, spreadsheets, slide decks, meetings, and "sync-ups" while too little goes into understanding customers, serving them well, selling them great products, and curating your reputation.

BALANCING "INSIDE THE WALL" AND "OUTSIDE THE WALL"

To make sure you find the right balance, ask yourself:

How much of my own personal time is being spent on inside the wall vs. outside the wall work?

How many of our team members are doing inside the wall vs. outside the wall work?

How much total time is spent thinking about ourselves and how we work together (inside the wall) vs. our customers and what they're thinking, feeling, and experiencing (outside the wall)?

It's okay for some weeks to be out of balance. However, when teams become so enamored with "working on ourselves" that they chronically neglect "working for the customers," companies fail fast. That's why it's important to always get back into balance. If push comes to shove, and you need to choose one *over* the other, what's going over the wall should win out. Without customers giving you money, there's no castle, no wall, and no one inside it.

Remember, these five business skills are essential for figuring out what's worth spending your time on, attracting new clients and customers, supporting your fast-growing client list, recruiting new team members, and making sure your team can do great work.

Again, while not every skill outlined here will be relevant to you today, consider this chapter a look into your future. Think of it as advanced preparation for what's to come as you develop and grow your business.

Q&A with JB: Business

To support what you're learning, I've compiled end-of-chapter Q&As that are full of real, thoughtful questions I've gotten over the years. In each one I share my unfiltered take on the challenges you'll undoubtedly face as you grow your career.

(↓) You can check out all the Change Maker Q&As at **www.changemakeracademy.com/questions**.

This chapter's questions include:

Q: I love the whole tournament idea to help with prioritization and I'm going to start doing it. I'm just not always sure which to-do should win out over another. Can you help? (Answer: ~300 words)

Q: What if I'm still having trouble? (Answer: ~300 words)

Q: In health and fitness, I see a lot of people with side gigs. Either their coaching is the side gig for another job or they have other side gigs to supplement coaching. Is this a good idea? (Answer: ~175 words)

Q: There seem to be a lot of people making careers out of being internet or social-media famous. Is that a reasonable business model? (Answer: ~150 words)

Q: Are there any other business lessons you've learned over the years? (Answer: ~625 words)

YOUR FIRST objective IS
TO master PRIORITIZATION
THERE ARE ALWAYS MORE
options THAN RESOURCES

PRIORITIZATION MEANS
spending LESS time
ON THINGS THAT CAN BE
AUTOMATED OR eliminated

PRIORITIZATION also MEANS
spending MORE TIME
ON HIGH-LEVERAGE tasks
THAT MOVE THE NEEDLE

IN BUSINESS, prioritize
MARKETING AND SALES
WITHOUT INCOME you
CAN'T AFFORD ANYTHING ELSE

MARKETING summarized:
<u>KNOW</u> **WHAT** people **WANT**
<u>DO</u> **SOMETHING** awesome **TO DELIVER IT**
<u>TELL</u> everyone **ABOUT IT**

Good **SYSTEMS** <u>AND</u> **PRIORITIES**
LET you <u>FOCUS ON</u> **GROWTH**
<u>AS</u> **YOU** grow, **HIRING** <u>BECOMES</u>
<u>A</u> top **PRIORITY**

HIRE thoughtfully:
GET <u>CLEAR</u> **ON WHAT** you **WANT** <u>AND</u> need
<u>THEN</u> **GET** help **FINDING IT**

<u>AS</u> **YOUR TEAM** grows **YOU'LL** <u>NEED TO</u>
agree **ON** <u>HOW</u> **TO WORK** together
THIS <u>BECOMES</u> your **ORG STRUCTURE**

CHAPTER 6

REPUT

ATION

HOW TO
Earn RESPECT
AND *Bring* ELITE
PROFESSIONALISM
TO *Your* WORK

Many who work in health and fitness believe that respect and reputation hinge on two things:

how much you know

---

how authoritatively you demonstrate what you know

In other words, if you have a deep understanding of scientific topics like anatomy, biochemistry, biomechanics, physiology, and research methodology, and you can authoritatively demonstrate that knowledge using scientific terminology, then respect and reputation are yours.

Yet how well do you think this will go over with Mrs. Jones?

Well, Mrs. Jones, it's simple. You're gaining weight because your hypothalamic-pituitary-thyroid axis is dysregulated. While some prefer to take a more somatic approach to treating this, I prefer a psychoendoneuroimmunological one. We'll eventually work on thermodynamics, gut dysbiosis, and pancreatic response to carbohydrates. For now, though, let's start with something more cognitive . . .[*]

Yes, having knowledge is a good and necessary thing, as is being able to share it. However, when you craft a persona based on impressing other professionals—and, make no mistake, the desire to display knowledge is often driven by professional competition, not client service—you risk losing sight of the fact that you're not in a *knowledge*-first business but a *people*-first one.

Remember, our clients aren't the ones holding us to academic standards in our understanding of shoulder mechanics or carbohydrate metabolism. Our peers are. (Or so we imagine.) We're afraid—whether consciously or subconsciously—that if we're caught not knowing something about beta oxidation or tendinosis, we'll be exposed. This prevents us from focusing on what matters.

---

[*] This is an "impress your colleagues" way of saying: "Your hormonal system may be out of balance. However, let's not rush into eating less, exercising more, reducing carbs, and adding probiotic foods just yet. Rather, I'd like to start with stress management. Once that's under control we'll tackle the rest."

Jamaican sprint coach Glen Mills is a guy who hasn't made this mistake. Mills is the longtime (and beloved) coach of the most successful sprinter of all time, eight-time Olympic gold medalist Usain Bolt. He's also the longtime coach of the second-fastest 100m and 200m runner of all time, Yohan Blake. And he's coached athletes to seventy-one world championships and thirty-three Olympic medals.

Even with these accomplishments, "knowledge-focused" track and field people sometimes deride Mills on social media and discussion boards as "an idiot" or as someone who "doesn't know what he's doing" because he either doesn't have a deep understanding of, or doesn't speak well on, a host of academic subjects ranging from the biomechanics of sprinting to the philosophy of coaching.

Let's see. According to a small group of critics, a guy who's helped account for more than one hundred international titles and several world records is, apparently, an idiot who doesn't know what he's doing. Sheesh, I wish I were that kind of idiot!

One of my favorite quotes fits perfectly here: "No matter how beautiful the strategy, you should occasionally look at the results." In the case of Glen Mills, whether his strategy is beautiful or not, there's no questioning his results. And that's what he continues to focus his energy on.

Now, what you know *is* important. For example, if coaches don't understand how potential energy, stored in chemical bonds within our food, can be freed up to help us do work, they're more likely to be fooled by fad diets and miracle-of-the-month supplements. They're also more likely to spread false information to clients. Likewise, functional medicine docs *are* judged on their knowledge of diagnostics and prescription. Manual therapists on their assessment and treatment knowledge. Trainers on their program design and implementation knowledge. And so on.

At the same time, unless you're a full-time researcher or professional philosopher, you're not in a knowing profession; you're in a *doing-stuff-with-people* profession. That means you're accountable for *how you are with people* and *how often those people get results* (as opposed to how much you know, how smart you sound when sharing it, or how elegant your solutions seem on paper).

As the old saying goes, "People don't care what you know until they know that you care." This highlights the fact that you need both "knowing" and "caring" to build your reputation, earn respect, and become an elite change maker. Find the right mix of these "hard skills" and "soft skills" and you'll:

attract clients more easily,

enjoy a steady stream of referrals,

earn the respect of your peers,

be exposed to new opportunities,

meet more interesting people, and

maintain richer and mutually beneficial friendships.

When in doubt, remember this: Reputation is a human factor. It's *what other people think of you.* The sooner you accept that, the sooner you'll realize that human factors are more than touchy-feely psychobabble. Instead, they're tangible, necessary skills that pay huge career dividends.*

How, then, can you build this mix of "hard" and "soft" skills? Here's how I've done it.

---

* If you're the kind of person who values competency over all else—i.e., Dr. House from the television show *House MD* is your professional hero—you might wonder, *Why don't people just reward professionals who are good at their job and quit worrying about relationships!?!* The answer is: *Because they don't.* People want something more than a diagnostic robot. They want competency *and* care. If, after reading this chapter, you still don't see why that's important, you might consider a role in an industry that doesn't involve coaching people.

<u>MY</u> *THREE-PART REPUTATION Formula*

Early in my career, I didn't fully appreciate the need for an ironclad reputation. Yet, today, I'm consistently blown away by the benefits of having one. For example, my weekly newsletter reaches one million people. I've never met most of these folks. However, because of my reputation, when I encourage them to do something interesting or helpful or enlightening, they actually do it. Hundreds of thousands of them! All because they trust me and believe in my intentions.

Likewise, on any given week, I'll get five invitations to give keynote lectures at large events and conferences without any outreach on my part. Think about that! I'm just sitting here, working on something totally unrelated, and, out of the blue, someone sends me an email offering a paid chance to get my message out to 500, 750, 1,000 people.

When I think back to my early days in this industry—when I had to beg for any opportunity, no matter how small; when I was giving free talks to six people in aerobics studios and small breakout rooms—I feel gratitude for the amazing things that are now simply dropped into my lap and a genuine awe for how powerful something as nonquantifiable as "reputation" can really be.

While I do think it's hard to pin down all the factors that help create this kind of professional reputation, I believe my own formula has been made up of these three parts.

Part 1: Earn a set of unimpeachable credentials

Perhaps the *second most difficult part* of building a lasting reputation is earning credentials. Not just one or two, though. I'm talking about an unimpeachable set of them.

For example, in my career I've:

won bodybuilding, powerlifting, and track and field championships

earned a PhD in exercise and nutritional biochemistry and taught at universities

published bestselling books and nearly a dozen peer-reviewed research papers

coached thousands of clients and educated thousands of professionals

worked with dozens of elite Olympic and professional organizations

grown a business with tremendous reach, impact, and financial value

advised Apple, Equinox, Nike, Titleist

Notice how any one of these, on its own, helps establish credibility. However, put together, the list is even stronger. When faced with it, how could anyone reasonably argue that I'm not a credible professional? And *that's* what I mean by unimpeachable credentials. For a visual, imagine walking up to a poker table and you notice one player with a mountain of chips. Without even watching them play, you'd assume that they knew what they were doing when it came to cards.

That's how I visualize this first part of reputation building. Each accomplishment is a chip I can add to my credibility stack. When I was young, I started out with no chips at all. Actually, I probably owed the house money. But, over the last twenty-five years, I've slowly added chips to the stack. Now I'm the guy at the poker table with a stack that's hard to beat.

This, of course, is one of the more difficult parts of building a reputation. It takes a long time and a host of achievements. However, like all things hard-won, earning new credentials—not just degrees and certifications, mind you, but tangible accomplishments relevant to your career goals—is worth the effort because it's so difficult to compete with.

Part 2: Do great work, celebrate others' great work too

There are two benefits to earning credentials. First, the process of earning them provides valuable experiences that, if you're growth-minded, can help you learn to do great work. Second, they act as a shortcut for others, letting them know that you *might* be able to do great work.

Notice the important thing here: *Actually doing great work.*

This is the cornerstone of your reputation: Consistently and reliably doing notable work (and producing great results) in your area of specialty. Absolutely nothing can replace it. No matter your credentials, if you show up and don't produce, you won't get hired again.

As mentioned above, earning credentials is the second most difficult part of building a reputation because consistently doing great work is, for sure, *the most difficult part.* Largely because, before you get to great, you have to spend time being good, before that, fair, and before that, maybe kinda crappy.

No one starts out being "great," no matter how eager, "talented," or committed they are. On the flip side, people can *become* great, even if they're not "talented," simply by putting in the reps and devoting themselves to an ongoing process of mastery—focusing their energy on one thing for a long time, staying disciplined in their daily practice of that thing, avoiding distraction from new things, and using every experience to get better.

No one had great expectations for me when I started out. I was a pencil-necked, introverted kid who could barely communicate with other human beings and was wandering aimlessly down a path of self-destruction. Yet, after my wake-up call and after receiving some critical mentorship, I took my first steps down a new path of self-mastery, en route to becoming a capable communicator, coach, and business leader.

As a byproduct of that journey, I've written (or contributed to) some of the most-read books and articles in the health and fitness industry. I've coached (or contributed to the coaching of) hundreds of thousands of clients who've achieved phenomenal results. I've helped grow one of the biggest businesses in the health and fitness industry and helped advise countless others.

While my credentials are important, the work I just listed is even more important.

Equally important has been my secret reputational weapon: I notice when others are doing similar work and proceed to make a big deal out of that too.

Indeed, whenever I see a great piece of work, I take a few minutes and send the person (or team) responsible a short message saying: *Wow, I loved the thing you did. You're awesome! That is all.*

REACHING OUT WHEN OTHERS HAVE DONE GOOD WORK

Here's an example of a note I sent to recognize good work. My friend Molly is the founder of a company doing fantastic work to empower women to be their strongest, most confident selves (Girls Gone Strong). Although I didn't know her before she released her first product, once she did, I found her email address and sent her this note:

Subject Line:
Hell yeah!

Message:
Wow, I love this:

> *<linked to product page>*
>
> *The product looks awesome.*
>
> *Really great sales page too.*
>
> *It's all beautifully done, thorough, accessible.*
>
> *I can tell a lot of care and attention went into this.*
>
> *High fives!*
>
> *JB*

Since then, I've become an advisor to Girls Gone Strong and have enjoyed countless referrals from her business. Even more, Molly and her partner have become great friends, making time to visit us annually and join us for family vacations.

Phil and I often talk about "catching people doing something right" instead of just "catching people doing something wrong" (not only in our own business but outside our business too). To this end, we're constantly on the lookout for great work.

When we find it, we're quick to send a message saying: *Hey! Caught you! You just did something amazing! You're SO busted!* People remember this because it's so rare and feels so good, especially if it comes from someone whose work they respect.

But I don't just share my praise privately. I also share it publicly on social media, through email broadcasts, and at in-person events. This improves my reputation in two ways. First, the person being praised feels grateful that I both recognized their work in private and was willing to share it publicly with my community, the people who trust me.

Second, the people in my community recognize that I have good taste and high standards, that I'm a curator of great things. This increases my reputation, leading to more affinity and trust.

It's for this same reason I *never* recommend low-quality products or services, even if a friend asks me to. I'd be doing a disservice to the people who know, like, and trust me. I'd diminish my reputation. The person who created the thing would never be challenged to do better or improve their craft. And the entire industry would be that much less professional.

Part 3: Show up as a respectful, trustworthy, and consistent human being

If earning unimpeachable credentials helps you meet the hosts of a dinner party, and doing great work gets you invited to their party, this last step is what earns you an invite to their next one. That's because everyone wants to collaborate with professionals who are credentialed, who do great work, and who are fun to do it with. Now, that doesn't mean nonstop practical jokes and silliness. But it does mean respectful, trustworthy, down-to-earth human interaction.

For example: I don't offer private coaching or mentorship for individuals. However, once in a while, I'll meet a young professional who's so curious, open, growth-minded, and interesting that I'll invite them to a professional gathering or see if they want to have a career chat.

In fact, for a few summers, my children were part of a daily, hourlong learn-to-swim program at an outdoor pool within a local park. As they were all in the pool at the same time, I had a full hour free each evening to do with as I pleased. So I started inviting interesting young mentees to spend that time with me on a park bench, talking, as we watched my children swim.

During these visits we talked business, personal development, relationships, parenting, life, and everything in between. Then, as soon as the children got out of the pool, the session ended. These sessions would come to be known as "The Park Bench Sessions" among a group of local (and not-so-local) entrepreneurs who'd drive as long as two hours to join me on that bench.

Why did they spend their free time in that way? Because they recognized the opportunity for mentorship and the value of personal and professional relationships. Plus, they were willing to go to great lengths for both, sometimes spending five hours to have a one-hour conversation.

Why did I spend my time in that way? Because, eventually, you get to a point in your career where you want to share with young people. You want to help and coach and mentor them. You want to pass on what you've learned so they don't make the same mistakes you made.

But you don't want to share with just anyone. You want to share with people who are respectful, trustworthy, vulnerable, and human. People willing to take your advice, put it into action, and honestly report back on what they did and how it worked out.

Yet we've all met the opposite. Professionals who don't have any real friends, who see every minute as an opportunity to get ahead. For them it's all work, all the time. Everyone's a business contact. Every relationship is a hustle. Even if they're nice, it still feels gross to be around them. They're single-minded and clearly there to pump everyone for whatever they think they need to get to the next step of their career. Then they move on without gratitude, without a second thought.

I remember taking my daughter to an event a few years back. She was five years old at the time, fascinated by the entire experience, and glued to my hip. After my talk, a group rushed the stage to ask questions, take photos, and get books signed. While most were kind, friendly, and respectful of the fact that I had a young child with me, one was not.

He pretended my daughter wasn't there, totally ignoring her. He then drilled me with frenetic questions for fifteen minutes. When my daughter needed attention—after all, she'd just sat through an hour-long adult lecture and another thirty minutes of post-lecture conversation—he got annoyed, talking over her so I'd attend to *his* needs.

Don't be that person.

No mentor worth learning from will bother with you if you're so obviously wrapped up in your own concerns that you can't acknowledge the needs of others around you. Further, if you don't build the capacity to really connect, you won't develop the skills required to be successful with clients and/or team members. Finally, without real human connection, mental and emotional health suffers.

That's why I always try to show up—as a mentor, mentee, colleague, student, or friend—as a human first. These are the qualities I've tried to embody as I've built my reputation.

NINE IMPORTANT QUALITIES TO BUILD YOUR REPUTATION

1 **Respectful** of the other person's time, always checking in to make sure I'm not being too pushy, aggressive, asking for too much, or overstaying my welcome

2 **Grateful** for the fact that they've spent time with me, and showing my gratitude through words (genuine thanks) and actions (gifts, tokens of appreciation, etc.)

3 **Trustworthy** in that I keep private information private, that I make good on what I say I will, and that I follow through on the things I commit to

4 **Open** to learning about the other person by asking them questions about what's going on in their lives, what they're interested in, and why they're sharing certain things with me

5 **Compassionate** about their lives, thinking about how I'd feel if I were in their shoes, and asking them how they're feeling instead of guessing, assuming, or ignoring because I'm not sure

6 **Honest** about what I'm thinking, feeling, and experiencing so they don't have to guess or assume things about me

7 **Curious** about the world, about how people behave, and about what I still have to learn, asking lots of questions but never to trip people up or back them into a corner

8 **Consistent** in that I show up as the same person every time, with every group of people, in all situations

9 **Intentional** in that I tell myself, in advance, how I plan to be in upcoming interactions, what I hope to get out of them, what I hope others get out of the interactions, how I'll know if that's happening, and what I'll do to correct what doesn't meet expectations

While all this might seem like common sense, it's anything but common practice. That's why those who show up as I've described stand out.

JB'S THREE-PART REPUTATION FORMULA

Part 1: Earn a set of unimpeachable credentials.

Part 2: Do great work, celebrate others' great work too.

Part 3: Show up as a respectful, trustworthy, and consistent human being.

Doing these three things has helped me earn respect, grow my reputation, and become a more mature professional. Of course, your path to growing your reputation could look different than mine. That's why the rest of this chapter includes eight foundational principles you can use to build your own reputation and professionalism in a way that feels right for you.

EIGHT REPUTATION PRINCIPLES

① ALL *SKILLS,*
INCLUDING *REPUTATION Skills,*
REQUIRE PATIENT *PRACTICE*

② *FEEDBACK,*
EVEN IF *IT'S DELIVERED*
Unskillfully,
IS A PRECIOUS *GIFT*

③ *Aggressively* HUNT *FEEDBACK,*
EXPOSE Yourself
TO *ALL Growth OPPORTUNITIES*

④ LEARN *TO GIVE*
Great FEEDBACK TOO

⑤ GETTING GOOD AT
CRUCIAL *Conversations*
MAKES *You* THE MOST
Valuable PERSON IN THE ROOM

⑥ *Know* AND ARTICULATE
YOUR *Goal* IN
EVERY SITUATION

⑦ CULTIVATE AND *Invest*
IN WISDOM

⑧ OPERATE WITH UNFLINCHING
INTEGRITY AND *Authenticity*

REPUTATION PRINCIPLE 1

ALL SKILLS, INCLUDING REPUTATION Skills, REQUIRE PATIENT PRACTICE

We all know people whose smile, personality, and social presence provide the energy equivalent of the sun. They exude good vibes and seem to get along with *everyone*. Seeing those folks at work makes it easy to think that "some people have it and others don't." That you're either great with people or you're not. But that's simply not true.

As a lifelong introvert, I spent my early years exhausted and confounded by nearly all social interaction. Even being in public was difficult. I remember when I was a child, visits to the local mall with my mom would require a few hours of recovery in my room alone with the lights out and curtains drawn.

This pattern persisted until my midtwenties, when a friend introduced me to the "pick-up" industry, sending me an e-book by information marketer Eben Pagan, then writing under the pseudonym David DeAngelo and selling products under the company name Double Your Dating.

Though there are definitely creepy, sexist elements to the "pick-up" industry, Eben's use of social psychology research to examine human interaction rituals appealed to my inner nerd. Plus, the promise of his work—*be better with people!*—appealed to my inner recluse.

As I worked through his materials, I gathered new social strategies that made meeting people (both friends and romantic interests) much easier. As someone who assumed I'd be "afflicted" with introversion and social phobia for life, this was a revelation.

Through Pagan's work, I was also turned on to another book, a practice-based handbook outlining thirty days of small daily activities that, if done regularly, promised social mastery. So, every day for a month, I tried something new from the handbook. One day it was to make friendly eye contact with three random strangers. Another was to make small talk with three people I didn't know. And so on. After this month of intentional practice, social interactions became *dramatically* more comfortable, and I was set on a path to actually seek out new social experiences.

But, even more important than specifically learning how to develop my social skills, I finally grasped a life-changing meta principle: the idea that any skill can be built, even a skill I thought impossible for me, if I first believed that I can improve, and then practiced patiently until I do.

Of course, I was first exposed to this idea in the gym. Starting out at five feet nine and 135 pounds, I used daily exercise and good food choices to build seventy pounds of muscle and a national championship body. But this principle didn't become a deep part of my worldview until I transformed from someone shy and introverted, with social phobia, to someone comfortable meeting new people, starting up conversations at events, and speaking in front of audiences.

Now's *your* turn to incorporate it into *your* worldview.

It all starts with a growth mindset

According to Carol Dweck, author of the book *Mindset,* people who successfully build new skills or change old patterns believe that their efforts will actually pay off.

In other words, they believe the most basic abilities can be developed through dedication and hard work. And, because they believe the hard work will be worth it, they see learning as fun, not frustrating. They see criticism as necessary feedback, not soul-crushing judgment. They become bold in the face of challenges rather than cowering in fear. And they look at *everything*—even "bad" things, annoyances, or temporary setbacks—as a path to getting better. This is what Dweck calls a "growth mindset," something she believes is the hallmark of fast-developing people and professionals.

Those with a growth mindset see every experience as a chance to improve their skill. They see challenges and failures as opportunities to ask future-thinking questions, like:

Why did things happen that way?

Could things happen differently?

What if I tried a new way to solve the problem?

What if I put more effort into it, or asked for help?

Who else can help me learn how to do better?

On the other hand, those who believe certain qualities are unchangeable—*Oh, I'm a hardgainer and can't build muscle; No, I'm socially awkward and won't be able to get better*—are practicing a "fixed mindset," according to Dweck. They don't believe in the ability to grow. They don't think practice is worth it. As a result, they see everything but positive feedback as a threat. Eventually a kind of learned helplessness sets in as they start believing "things are what they are" and can't be changed.

Of course, very few people would raise their hand and say, "Yes, this fixed mindset idea describes me completely!" In reality, many people practice a growth mindset in certain areas and a fixed one in others. The key to making progress on any skill is recognizing those areas where you're practicing a growth mindset and those where you're practicing a fixed one. Simply calling out where you'd benefit shifting from fixed to growth will unlock a huge vault of possibilities.

When doing this kind of inventory, be especially careful not to let fixed-mindset symptoms parade around as oversimplification and rationalization. For example, some people rationalize a lack of growth with sentiments like: "Relationship people know how to 'suck up' or 'play the game.' I've got more integrity than that. So I'll stick with being me."

The problem is that "me" isn't a fixed entity. Research shows that people are much less constant, over time, than they think. It's called the "end of history illusion" and it's a phenomenon in which people of all ages believe they have experienced significant personal growth and changes in tastes *up to the present moment*, but will not substantially grow in the future.

A thirty-year-old's impression of how much they'll change in the next ten years feels small compared to a forty-year-old's recollection of how much they actually changed in the last ten years. This happens at every age.

The bottom line is that you *will* change in the future, much more than you expect. Practicing a growth mindset means being in the driver's seat of those changes. It helps you understand that change and skill development are possible. It helps you direct your attention to the areas you most need to improve. And it helps you feel like all the hard work that's about to come is worth doing.

Yet growth happens through daily practice

In Chapter 4 we talked about how your clients can only reliably achieve their goals when they a) engage in the daily practices that b) lead to the development of the essential skills required to c) reach those goals. It's important to know that this applies to *everyone* and *every goal*. Indeed, to develop the reputation skills you'll need to become the ultimate change maker, you'll also need daily practice.

What's fascinating about daily practice is that most of us are on board with it when we're recommending it *to someone else,* like a client. However, when it's recommended *to us,* we frantically search for another way: *Isn't there a life hack for this!?!*

I've seen this thousands of times with the Precision Nutrition Certification program. The Level 1 program, as mentioned earlier, comprehensively covers the art and science of nutrition coaching. And it's delivered in the way you'd expect. There's an authoritative text, a workbook, online learning modules, and quizzes.

The Level 2 program, on the other hand, is completely different. It takes Level 1 graduates through a practice-based program. This means that every day students are asked to practice specific coaching skills with clients, family members, friends, and more. These practices map to multiweek modules that are part of a yearlong curriculum designed to help students become master coaches. This is all accomplished by moving away from cognitive learning and toward embodied doing.

As we all know, clients don't get healthy by learning about health. They get healthy by patiently practicing nutrition and fitness, consistently (and, often, under the guidance of a coach). Likewise, coaches don't develop expertise by learning about coaching. They become experts by patiently practicing excellent coaching, consistently (under the guidance of their own coaches).

Yet some bristle at the idea of taking a dose of their own medicine. Sounding just like the clients who frustrate them with their own impatience, some of our Level 2 students will wonder: *One year . . . why can't it go faster!?!* And: *This program isn't what I thought it'd be . . . it's too slow and I can't see how it'll help me become a better coach!* Or: *I don't have time for any of this practice!* You should hear the distress when we ask them to *actually do their own food journal*!

Don't be like these students!

Instead, do whatever it takes to remind yourself that daily practice is the only way to develop any skill, from learning a language, to playing an instrument, to improving your fitness, to earning a degree, to building your reputation. There are no shortcuts and no hacks.* There's only believing you can get better (growth mindset) and doing the painstaking work of actually getting better (daily practice).

REPUTATION PRINCIPLE 2

FEEDBACK, EVEN IF IT'S DELIVERED Unskillfully, IS A PRECIOUS GIFT

A few years back, Precision Nutrition developed a free online course for health and fitness professionals. When it was finished, our team sent it around to a number of influential colleagues to see if they'd be interested in sharing it with their readers, prospects, and clients.

Mike Boyle—a friend and one of the most respected coaches in the business—was quick to send his feedback, which wasn't particularly flattering. Specifically, he criticized the main image on the landing page, a friendly-looking young personal trainer with a shaved head. He was wearing a blue tank top and his muscular arms were crossed. Mike felt the image perpetuated industry stereotypes, was a huge cliché, and would be rejected by most readers. He essentially told us he'd never promote the course unless we did better.

Understandably, after working hard on the course for nearly six months, team members had a strong knee-jerk reaction. From what I

---

* At Precision Nutrition, we believe the word "hack" essentially means "conceal mediocrity at." Trying to "hack" your nutrition or sleep or exercise means trying to get the benefits without developing skill or mastery. And, as we all know, that's unlikely to happen in health and fitness or anywhere else, including your business.

could see, they felt a mix of ego pain and defensiveness. And some flat-out disagreed with his assessment. They weren't sure what to do next. Should they believe Mike and change the image? Or forget Mike and do what they thought was best?

My response was a little different. Instead of judging Mike's skill in delivering feedback, arguing against his position, or accepting his position blindly, I got curious. I wondered: "Is Mike right, here?" "If so, how did our entire team miss seeing what he's so clearly seeing?" "If not, what is he missing?" Finally, "How could we know, for sure, if his criticism is valid?"

We decided to let our audience settle this. We'd create five different landing pages for the course, each with a different image, and send 20 percent of our audience to each page. From there we'd see which converts the best, in other words, which better compelled visitors to sign up.

Before launching the test, though, I emailed Mike to express deep gratitude for his feedback. Truth is, Mike was the only person who actually stepped up, took time out of his busy schedule, and offered his honest, unfiltered thoughts. Here's an excerpt from what I wrote:

I just wanted to send a quick note to thank you for your feedback on our free course landing page (i.e., the tank-top dude).

Honest, useful feedback is so valuable and, I've found, gets rarer the more "successful" I become. (Unless, of course, I spend too much time on Facebook. Lots of it there. ;-))

Anyway, I shared it with the design team to help them further refine their ideas. I find designers sometimes lean on clichés and we have to push them really hard to think differently about health and fitness images.

With that said, we do a lot of split testing. In fact, based on your feedback, we now have five different images we're testing to see which performs the best in terms of sign-ups.

The attached is our baseline landing page for the course.

But we'll be testing four other versions to see which "wins." (Including tank-top guy, which a percent of our audience will see, but certainly not all.) In my experience, the winner is never the one we bet on. It's always a surprising dark horse candidate.

Anyway, again, wanted to thank you for taking the time to offer your thoughts. Super valuable to us. And super rare. I value it very much.

This wasn't me trying to flatter or "suck up" to Mike. I honestly, genuinely felt grateful for his feedback. My gratitude increased when the split test generated a winning image that none of us would have expected, an image we're still using to this day because the landing page is converting at a percentage that's way above industry standards.

Again, this was only possible by looking past his style and focusing on his substance. By getting curious and asking "What can we learn from feedback?" and "How can we find out if the feedback is right?" and "Should we do something different based on it?" And by sending a grateful and graceful response to Mike to ensure he's willing to share his feedback in the future.

If we saw Mike's feedback as an attack on our skills, talents, or worth, we would have lost a learning opportunity, a business opportunity, and a relationship-building opportunity. Based on our email exchange, Mike *did* share the course with his audience, which sent a lot of prospects our way. Plus he also sent a nice response to me; my reputation was enhanced in his eyes.

Of course, it's easy to talk about receiving feedback well when it's so clearly beneficial. But what if it comes from an ogre boss or a cranky client? Well, personally, I see *all* feedback as valuable. Accepting it well is an essential part of becoming successful. Seeing past style and looking at substance pays huge dividends.

This is true even if someone is so bold as to suggest: "You suck at *X*!" The trick is to remember this acronym: WAIT, which stands for Why Am I Talking? In other words, when someone's giving feedback—of any kind—don't argue, defend, justify, or react. Just quietly receive it. Even better, thank them for it regardless of how it makes you feel in the moment.

RESPONDING TO FEEDBACK

"Thanks for being open enough to sharing this. Can you tell me a little more about why you think that way? I'd like to do better at this in the future and it'd be really helpful to understand what you're seeing and how I might improve."

This is easier if you remember *you're in control*. You don't have to do anything with the feedback. It's not necessarily even valid or true. But deciding its worth, or whether to take action on it, isn't something to do in real time. Your goal is to simply receive all data without blocking transmission. Gather now, process later. You can evaluate what's worth taking action on once you've had the processing time. From there, you can use your growth mindset to learn, adapt, and evolve based on what you think was valuable.

In the end, if you practice this skill, you'll eventually see *everything*—even vitriolic Facebook comments questioning your viability as a human—as an opportunity to help you get better.

REPUTATION PRINCIPLE 3

Aggressively HUNT **FEEDBACK,** **EXPOSE** *Yourself* TO **ALL** *Growth* **OPPORTUNITIES**

On a recent trip, I asked a colleague, "If you were the CEO of a company, would you hire me? If yes, what would you hire me to do?" As we have a long-standing relationship of honest, supportive, helpful feedback, his response was, "Well, I certainly wouldn't hire you to do any kind of management."

Now, I co-founded one of the world's largest nutrition coaching, education, and software companies. I helped it grow from zero dollars to a valuation of over $200 million with no investors or bank loans, and helped grow the team from two people to one hundred.

I could have chosen to get offended or argue about why he's wrong. But that would have denied the truth of his statement. Because management is what I concentrate on the least. I'm mediocre at best. Since I'm not very good at it, and I don't enjoy it, I'm always trying to avoid it. So management *is* a growth opportunity for me. Yet it happens to be one that I'm not going to act on now because, at this stage of my career, I'm focused on a few other, more important ones.

Since I decided to keep my mouth shut (remember: WAIT) he continued on, sharing a few other growth areas for me (that I *have* acted on) and a lot of positive feedback that was equally helpful. Had I gotten offended, argued, or denied the first point, I would have signaled to him that I wasn't actually interested in his feedback. He might have shut his mouth too. And I'd have missed out on all that other useful information he shared, the stuff that came after the first part.

This idea of actively soliciting feedback is what I call "hunting feedback." The fastest learners I know do it aggressively. They're on a mission. They collect more feedback per day, per week, per month, per year than everyone else. And this exposes them to every possible growth opportunity available.

To accomplish this myself, I send standing requests to clients and colleagues, friends and family members, to share their feedback—the good, the bad, and the ugly. I let them know that, although I might not always enjoy criticism in the moment, I want and need it. That I'll be receptive to it. That I'll view it as a gift.

ASKING FOR FEEDBACK

Here's a script for how you might do the same:

Can I ask you to help me with something important?

Growth is really important to me at this point in my life. So I'm asking some of the people I respect and admire to share feedback on how I'm doing—good, bad, or ugly—whenever it pops into their minds.

This is so important to me because, like everyone else, I have blind spots. I have to rely on the folks around me to help me see what I'm missing so I can be a better coach and colleague, friend and family member.

Please know that I want you to be as honest as possible. In exchange, I'll do my best to not respond emotionally or defensively. I consider this feedback a gift, no matter how difficult some of it might be to hear.

Hopefully there will be a nice balance of positive and negative. But it's okay, too, if there isn't.

Is this something you're comfortable doing?

Likewise, I take every opportunity to ask for feedback situationally: after a coaching session, after completing a piece of work, after a difficult conversation, or after a particularly fun day. When that feedback comes, I make good on my promise. I collect this "data" like laboratory notes for later evaluation and try to never argue, defend, or react to it emotionally.

Of course, not all feedback should be weighted equally. Some people are more articulate, thoughtful, or believable than others.* Theirs should be weighted as the most important. At the same time, the more feedback the better. And all feedback should be considered.

This won't always be easy. Most people hide from feedback because there's risk. If it's a particularly sensitive or caustic topic, it can guillotine your ego. And when you're feeling hurt, your more primitive brain centers can take over, overruling higher brain centers. The result: you externalize the hurt, defend against it, attack the person giving it (which prevents your learning, strains your relationship, and guarantees you won't get feedback—so necessary for growth—in the future).

Yet by recognizing that feedback is your only reliable path to growth, by looking at substance over style, by remembering WAIT, and by getting as much feedback as possible, your skill will quickly build in this domain. You'll be in a position to maximize every growth opportunity. Plus your reputation will grow as people start to see you as a mature, seasoned, respectful professional.

---

* I learned this concept from billionaire investor Ray Dalio. When evaluating opinions, he most heavily weights the ideas of those who "have repeatedly and successfully accomplished the thing in question, who have a strong track record with at least three successes, and have great explanations of their approach when asked." In other words, those who are most believable.

LEARN *TO GIVE* *Great* FEEDBACK *TOO*

Learning to hunt feedback brings a host of career-changing benefits. However, if you're not careful, it could come at a cost. Because, when some individuals get really good at *taking* feedback, they get really bad at *giving* it. All about substance over style, they forget that most others aren't yet hunting feedback, they're hiding from it. While others aren't practicing WAIT (Why Am I Talking?), they're opting for DRIP (Deny, Repress, Ignore, Pretend) instead.*

Even if you share the same kind of feedback you personally thrive on, if you're too direct or you offer unsolicited feedback, you could be triggering a judgment war. *They'll judge you* for being mean, unkind, threatening their ego, or lacking tact. And *you'll judge them* for being irrational, fixed minded, and lacking the ability to take feedback well. That's a lose-lose proposition. They don't get the opportunity to hear about how they can improve. And you'll have wasted your time doing something you thought they'd appreciate.

So, as you intentionally set out to grow your reputation, your next goal is to become more adept at sharing your feedback with others in thoughtful, caring, compassionate ways. It's to recognize that most people won't have your feedback-taking skills, and that you'll have to craft your delivery in a way that makes others more likely to receive your comments well.

If this feels like a mismatch, it is. You *are* being asked to do double the work. To do the heavy lifting of turning all the feedback others send to you—no matter how insensitively it's delivered—into something useful. And of turning all the feedback you're sending others into some-

---

* Hat tip to my friend Dr. Krista Scott-Dixon for coining this acronym.

thing that's compassionate and shared sensitively. But that's part of the deal. Earning respect, garnering a rock-solid reputation, and becoming the *ultimate* change maker means doing work others aren't willing to do.

SEVEN STRATEGIES FOR GIVING BETTER FEEDBACK

If you're looking for ways to give better feedback, here are seven strategies I've found helpful.

FEEDBACK STRATEGY	WHY IT'S SO USEFUL
Give feedback when things have calmed down.	Some people hold a false belief that things have to be "worked out" in the heat of the moment, not realizing that this is most often going to worsen the conflict, not solve it. But all feedback—positive, neutral, or negative—should be delivered at a time when emotions are low. This helps both parties feel calm and safe. Even positive feedback can feel disingenuous if it's delivered in the middle of conflict.
Speak slowly and quietly.	Whenever emotions run high, heart rates accelerate, and people speak more quickly and intensely. This leads to emotionally charged, unnaturally fast (and loud) monologues that are never well-received. That's why, when giving feedback, wait until things are calm. Then calm them down even more. Slow your tempo. Speak softly. Even if you feel like you're going too slow, that's better than rushing and being too loud.

Be neutral, curious, and focus on the relationship.	When giving feedback of any kind, deliver it with neutral language and natural curiosity. "I noticed that . . ." or "Can you tell me more about . . ." are better than "You always . . ." Also, make it clear that you care about them and their growth, that your goal is to build the relationship, that they don't have to respond to your feedback right away, and, in most cases, they don't have to do anything with the feedback at all. They're in control.
Be specific and as objective as possible.	Rather than global, general feedback like "You're awesome!" or "That sucked!" give precise, specific, concrete feedback that's situated in a particular time and place, and that describes something that really happened (or didn't). For instance: "When you presented to our team on Tuesday afternoon, I noticed that you discussed Topic X but not Topic Y. From my perspective, including Y would have been useful because Z." "When interacting with Client X just now by the front desk, I noticed that you couldn't find the sign-up sheet. Would it be worth looking at the front desk organization system to see if we can make the process easier?"

Always put your feedback in context.	When sharing constructive feedback, always make it clear that your comments don't represent the sum total of how you feel about the recipient as a team member or as a person. After all, they're in your life because of good things. So make sure you communicate that you like them, respect them, think they're awesome, and are sharing your feedback in that context.
Share lots of positive feedback too.	In most successful romantic partnerships, there's a 20:1 ratio of positive comments to negative when not arguing. But, even when arguing, those couples have a 5:1 ratio of positive to negative. So make sure you're sharing the right balance of positive to negative feedback. Instead of always "catching people doing something wrong," be sure to "catch them doing something right." This makes it easier for them to understand the context above and to take constructive criticism in stride. Positive feedback also gives people a useful "action plan" for what to correct, improve, and/or develop. For instance, "I overheard you chatting with Client *X*, and I noticed your sales communication is really coming along well! In particular it sounds like you've been working on active listening and trying to understand their story in order to tailor our membership offer to what they're seeking. That's really effective! Keep working on that!" Now the recipient knows exactly what they did well, and what they can continue to strengthen too.

Ask for permission.	This might sound obvious but it's often lost: People usually take feedback better when they've asked for it. So start by asking for permission: "Would it be okay if I shared some feedback about *X* with you?"
	With that said, sometimes you'll *have* to share unsolicited feedback. In those cases, consider calling it out: "I wanted to share some unsolicited feedback with you. I totally get that you haven't asked for it and that I'm just showing up with it unannounced. Is now a good time to talk about this? If not, when's better?"

REPUTATION PRINCIPLE 5

GETTING GOOD AT CRUCIAL Conversations MAKES You THE MOST Valuable PERSON IN THE ROOM

As you can probably tell, I'm a big believer in the feedback loop, both as a way to grow personally and professionally and as a way to communicate your maturity and professionalism to others.

Another type of communication that's essential to building a strong reputation is what authors Kerry Patterson, Joseph Grenny, Ron McMillan, and Al Switzler call "crucial conversations" in their book by the same name. A crucial conversation is a discussion between two or more people where stakes are high, opinions vary, and emotions run strong. Examples include:

asking a friend to repay a long overdue loan

talking to a client about their alcohol or drug abuse

giving your boss feedback about their actions or behavior

critiquing a colleague's work

asking clients to keep certain commitments

If your heart beats faster just reading the list, that's normal. Many respond this way because of past experiences with these kinds of dialogues. Whether they've taken the initiative and kicked off crucial conversations themselves, or simply have been in the middle of one, these conversations often end in silence (deny, repress, ignore, pretend), collapse (shame, embarrassment, withdrawal), or hostility (physical or verbal combativeness, aggression, and threat).

Combine these experiences with no obvious path to skill development and it's no wonder some people avoid crucial conversations at all costs.

At the same time, being able to skillfully navigate crucial conversations will take your coaching game, your professional collaboration, and your personal relationships to the next level. Instead of avoiding key issues or bringing them up in a way that creates defensiveness (and, therefore, no real resolution), you'll be able to masterfully navigate situations that others can't see their way out of. You'll become the most valuable communicator in the room, in any room.

I wasn't always good at this. In fact, I've devoted a decade to it because I was *bad*.

Early in my life I fancied myself a "tell it like it is" kinda guy. I said what was on my mind and thought that made me an authentic, no-BS person of high integrity. Turns out I was really just selfish, abrasive, and unkind.

I remember working in a research lab during graduate school. One of my coworkers and I never really saw eye to eye, yet we had to collaborate daily. As I was still in my "telling it like it is" phase, I ended up receiving multiple visits from our human resources director.

Realizing that behaving this way wasn't working for me, I tried to act "nicer." But since I hadn't done any internal work yet, I was just delivering the same kind of message as before. The "niceness" was a mask that felt disingenuous and manipulative.

After a few months of this, another coworker called me aside and leveled with me. "I can tell you've been working hard to try to get along with Linda. But, I have to be honest, it feels phony. Everyone knows you don't like each other. But now, in addition to having obvious resentment for her, 'nicer JB' is just acting inauthentic and contrived."

She went on to recommend *Crucial Conversations*, which completely changed my outlook. As I progressed through the book, I realized that I was spending far too much time blaming others and far too little time searching for the role I might be playing in our difficulties.

For example, previously, leading up to difficult conversations, I'd obsess over what the other person was doing, what they were like, what they might say in response to my words, and how I would "counter" their arguments. I was trying to force things to go my way. This was the exact opposite of the advice in the book, which taught me to lead with curiosity, be open to real conversation, and seek a free flow of information and meaning.

As I began to put into practice these techniques, I learned to stop obsessing over "what to say" and, instead, spend my energy preparing my mind and my heart to listen.

Why is listening so important? Because, in crucial conversations, you need everyone's ideas, theories, feelings, thoughts, and opinions to build what I call "the shared pool of meaning" (*Crucial Conversations* authors call it "the shared pool of information"). The more information (and understanding) we can share, the higher our chances of making the right decisions—and the right compromises—to get everyone most of what they want and need.

To ensure I'm doing enough listening, I now enter all crucial conversations by asking questions. In giving others the chance to talk first, it shows that I care about their perspective, which makes them more likely to care about mine. And the combination of both leads to a deeper and wider shared pool of meaning. Yes, this kind of dialogue takes patience, ego detachment, and lots of extra time. But the alternative takes much longer because it simply doesn't work.

While I never did figure out how to have a great working relationship with Linda, our conflict did light a fire in me to learn how to lead crucial conversations, to respond positively to them when others initiate them, and to mediate crucial conversations between other people.

It's taken me a long time to improve in this area—here's that patient practice thing again—but I've noticed that this kind of communication has helped me grow my personal and professional reputation more than any other. In situations that could otherwise become heated, I've come to be seen as clear thinking, insightful, and wise. Even more, it's led to some of the most rewarding moments of my adult life. Thorny issues that might have otherwise threatened my relationships have led to beautiful moments of deeper clarity and connection with the people I care about most.

To evolve your own crucial conversation game, here are four strategies, adapted from the book.

Change your own motives

Helpers *love* to fix other people. However, the only person you have any control over, and the first person you need to work on, is yourself.

When difficult situations arise, first examine your own personal role in the problems and challenges you encounter. Ask "in what ways, no matter how small, am I responsible?" Knowing how you contributed makes you less likely to project blame, or shame, onto the other person.

Also, as you enter into crucial conversations, make sure you're clear on your real goal. As tensions arise, it's easy to get sucked into wanting to look good or defend against looking bad—or win. But, most often, the goal you most want is to find a mutually beneficial solution that strengthens your relationship with the other person. Ask, "Am I contributing to the shared pool of meaning now or have I lost sight of that goal?"

While it's true that sometimes we are caught in a genuine dilemma with only two bad options, most of the time we have healthy alternatives. So consider replacing "either/or" thinking ("Well, I guess it's either this or that") with "both/and" thinking ("How can we both get this and that"). By looking for "and" solutions, our brains move to higher-level, more complex, integrative thinking. Ask, "Now that I understand exactly what the other person wants, how can I help them get it AND work toward getting what I want myself?" In other words, see if you can play the game so *everyone* wins.

Create a safe space

When things go wrong in crucial conversations, most people assume the *content* of their message is the problem. So they try to explain it differently, or try to water it down, or just stop talking altogether.

However, difficult conversations usually go off track because people don't feel safe and supported. They feel like their position, or their pride, or their livelihood is at risk. However, when your intent is clear, and you're giving off supportive vibes, and you make things safe, you can talk to almost anyone about anything.

To create a safe environment, people need to know that you care about their best interests and goals and that you share some of the same interests. This is called *mutual purpose*. They also need to know that you care about them as individuals. This is called *mutual respect*.

You can let them know both implicitly (with your body language and facial expressions, by listening first, by not interrupting, by showing that you're clearly interested in their thoughts, feelings, and perspectives) and explicitly (by telling them "I want you to know that I care about your interests and goals here; I've thought about them a lot and think I have a sense for what they might be, but I'd love to hear them from your perspective first so I'm sure to get it right . . .").

Keep in mind that no amount of posturing replaces real care. That's why, leading into crucial conversations, your time is better spent thinking about why the people involved—and your relationships with them— are valuable in light of what you're going to say next. By actually caring, and by demonstrating you care, people can relax and can absorb what you're saying. They feel safe.

However, the instant they don't believe you care (and it can happen instantaneously—even with those we have long and loving relationships with), safety breaks down, and silence, collapse, or hostility follows.

Add your perspective

When it's your turn to talk, use the STATE method.

1 First, *Share your facts* instead of your story. For example, say someone is often late. Instead of sharing your interpretation of the fact (that they "don't respect your time"), simply begin by saying that you noticed they're often late.

2 Then, once the fact is out, you can *Tell your story* about the fact. This is when you can share your interpretation, making it clear this is just your interpretation, not necessarily fact.

3 Finally, you can *Ask for their path*, remembering that the goal isn't to prove you're right but to understand their perspective and resolve the situation.

To incorporate all three strategies, you could say something like: "I've noticed you're often late. Now, I'm not sure why that's happening. But it gives me, and others, the impression that you're unreliable or don't care about how your lateness affects them. Am I missing something about what's going on? I'd love to hear things from your perspective."

---

4 When sharing your story, again, remember it's an assumption, not a fact. So *Talk tentatively* and show that you're open to being wrong. Saying things like: "It makes me wonder" and "I get the impression" works better than "It's obvious to me" or "It's clear that."

---

5 Finally, *Encourage testing* by asking them to share their viewpoint, even if it's completely opposite to yours. This helps add to the shared pool of meaning while also demonstrating you want to hear what they have to say. If they're uncommunicative, you can prompt with "Let's say I'm wrong here. Can you help me see things from your point of view?" or "You seem frustrated and I'd like to understand why. Can you help me see your perspective?"

THE STATE METHOD FOR CRUCIAL CONVERSATIONS

Share your facts

Tell your story

Ask for their path

Talk tentatively

Encourage testing

Find the path to action

The ultimate goal of dialogue isn't just to create a healthy climate or even a clear understanding between parties. While both are helpful, they fall short of the real purpose: to get unstuck and take appropriate action.

Without action, all the healthy talk in the world is for nothing and will eventually lead to disappointment and hard feelings.

To take action, always mutually agree on when and how follow-ups will take place. It could be a simple email confirming action by a certain date. It could be a full report in a team meeting. Or it could be a follow-up conversation. Regardless of how or how often you do it, you need follow-up to create ongoing productive action. By collaborating on this (rather than you dictating how it'll happen), the chances of follow-through are much greater.

Also, document your work. Effective teams and healthy relationships are supported by records of the important decisions made and the agreed-upon assignments. These documents are revisited to follow up on both the decisions and commitments. When someone fails to keep a commitment, candidly and directly discuss the issue with them.

Early in my life, despite my "tell it like it is" attitude at the time, and my later "be nicer" approach, I stressed out about having crucial conversations. Going into them, I felt incompetent, intimidated, frustrated, and angry. Coming out of them, I felt defeated and exhausted.

I still vividly remember the first time I had to "fire" someone at Precision Nutrition, one of the ultimate crucial conversations. There were days of agony leading up to it. *What will he say? If I say this, how might he respond? Then what will I say to that?* And on and on. Compared to the dread I felt, the conversation actually went okay. There *was* anger, and tears, from the person I was talking with. And I was less communicative, compassionate, or understanding than I've since learned to be. What I remember most clearly, though, was the aftermath. Immediately I went to bed and slept for twelve hours. It took nearly a week until I felt fully recovered.

If you can believe it, after years more practice, I'm now *thrilled* each time a crucial conversation comes up (although I never relish the idea of letting someone go). That's because crucial conversations have become so rare that it's hard to get practice. And reps are needed to develop an ever-growing mastery at solving problems, improving relationships, growing reputation, and earning the respect of others.

FOUR STRATEGIES FOR HAVING CRUCIAL CONVERSATIONS

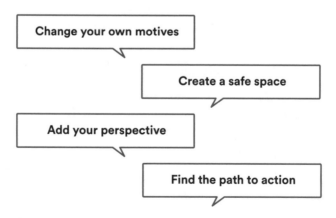

REPUTATION PRINCIPLE 6

Know AND ARTICULATE YOUR *Goal* IN EVERY SITUATION

A few years ago, I was giving a keynote lecture to about five hundred health and fitness professionals. The session went really well until the Q&A, when one audience member stood up and aggressively contradicted a recommendation I gave.

As I've learned to do, I gave him space to share his viewpoint, told him I'd be happy to have a discussion with him after the session, and asked if there were any other questions. Unsatisfied, he got even louder and more aggressive. I told him I could sense his frustration and I could see where he was coming from. I promised to fully hear him out in a few minutes, at the end, and give him as much time as he needed.

After the session was over, we had a surprisingly calm and peaceful discussion (led by some of the crucial conversation strategies described earlier). Later, a colleague asked me how I do it, how I remain calm and confident, never raising my voice, always addressing unprofessionalism professionally. My answer: I keep the goal in mind.

This can feel hard to do. Imagine you're the main event and you're getting attacked—loudly, publicly. Why not use the pulpit to fight back, chest-thump, and exert dominance? Because that's not the goal. It can never be the goal.

Think of it this way: Is my goal to win a fight with a single audience member so clearly trying to draw the attention away from me and toward himself? Of course not! The goal is to demonstrate to the other 499 audience members that I'm a calm, rational professional. That I'm confident, know my stuff, and am compassionate, approachable, and helpful. That I'm someone they want to learn from and do business with.

What else would my goal be at events like this? Arguing, trying to win arguments, or trying to demean others makes the exchanges about me, not the person I'm arguing with. It makes them about my ego. And I'm not there to stroke my own ego. I'm there in a professional capacity to be an ambassador for myself, my business, and (in some ways) the entire field.

Further, there are others watching, observing, evaluating, judging. People are *always* watching, whether it's an audience, your family, colleagues, coworkers, friends, or social media contacts. That's why, regardless of who "wins" any public conflict, both parties lose. It's why one of my mantras comes from "Takeover" by Jay-Z.*

> *A wise man told me don't argue with fools*
> *'Cause people from a distance can't tell who is who.*

So I don't argue. Instead, I thank people for their thoughts and comments. The more disrespectful, combative, or triggering they're trying to be, the more intentional I am about taking a deep breath, reminding myself of the goal, and responding with that in mind.

Knowing Your Goal

Asking "What's my real goal here? What am I trying to accomplish?" will help you avoid distraction and stay focused on what matters. To get started, consider your goal in each of the following scenarios.

When giving a seminar

 To do this exercise, and all upcoming ones, please download our printable + fillable worksheets at **www.changemakeracademy.com/downloadable-forms**.

---

* The wise man he was referring to is likely Mark Twain, who said: "Never argue with a fool; onlookers may not be able to tell the difference," and "Never argue with stupid people; they will drag you down to their level and then beat you with experience."

When interacting on social media

⊕

When writing an article

⊕

When speaking with a client or patient

⊕

When in a staff meeting

⊕

When responding to criticism

⊕

This idea of keeping the goal in mind also extends to every situation in your career and life. From crucial conversations to stage presentations. From social media posts to parenting children. From creating your refund policy to handling unprofessional behavior.

Asking "What's my real goal here? What am I trying to accomplish?" will help you avoid distraction and stay focused on what matters. Practice this and you'll be recognized as the consummate professional, as someone who's unflappable, as someone who keeps the main goal the main goal; your reputation will grow.

CULTIVATE AND *Invest* IN *WISDOM*

Having the self-knowledge to understand your own goals, and the discipline to stick with them in the face of distraction, relies on developing wisdom. While it often feels like an intangible quality, psychologists suggest wisdom is a thinking process that *integrates* knowledge, experience, deep understanding, common sense, and insight.

Observe how wise people operate and you'll see they think in unique ways. For example:

They recognize patterns, noticing how things play out over time.

They seem comfortable with ambiguity and lack of control over life.

They have a tolerance for the uncertainties of life as well as its ups and downs.

They also see the big picture, have a sense of proportion, and know themselves.

But wisdom isn't something you're born with, nor is it a quality that "just happens" for some people. Rather, it's something you commit to, invest in, work on. Wisdom is something you cultivate like a garden: preparing the soil, planting the seeds, watering, weeding, pruning, and clipping. Finally, after a long growing season and a lot of work, you harvest.

How do you cultivate and invest in wisdom? Here are a few ways.

TRY UNFAMILIAR THINGS.

Each time you try something unfamiliar—from visiting a new place, to experiencing a new hobby, to checking out a different form of entertainment, to trying a new skill at work—you open yourself up to learning. Approach it with a growth mindset and *current you* slowly becomes *wiser future you*. Even more, you'll better home in on your purpose, unique abilities, and values. Because experiences teach you which things to do more of and which to do less of.

STRATEGICALLY FACE YOUR FEARS AND DO THE UNCOMFORTABLE.

It's often the things we're afraid of, the things we come up with seemingly good justifications for *not* doing, that help us grow. Or, at the very least, hold the key to helping us handle discomfort in the future. Don't purposelessly expose yourself to real or psychic danger, of course. Instead, look for the fearful things—like starting that book you've been wanting to write, or applying for the new business loan, or asking a colleague for help—that will give you *meaningful growth* rather than just pointless pain or anxiety.

TALK TO PEOPLE WITH DIFFERENT PERSPECTIVES.

Listening closely to people who think differently than you (about social, political, economic, religious, and scientific issues) and have different life experiences (from where they grew up, to the jobs they've held, to the hardships they've faced, to the triumphs they've experienced) can teach you about perspective, kindness, and compassion. You have to really listen, though. And ask: "What's it like to live in their shoes? What would my worldview be if I were them?" You don't have to agree with their conclusions. Yet the more you're able to see the world through multiple lenses and understand why those exist, the wiser you'll be.

PURSUE EDUCATION.

No, you don't have to go back to school. But you do have to learn with intention. Because the more exposed you are to organized and well-researched viewpoints, the more likely you'll be to discern fact from fiction, signal from noise. We'll talk more about this in the next chapter.

READ.

Reading can be done as part of your educational curriculum or purely for pleasure. Whatever the goal, read. Not only does it expose you to the narratives and inner lives of thousands of real and imagined characters, it also gives you the quiet time to absorb, process, and reflect on what you're learning in *your* life and help integrate it into *your* thinking.

SPEND TIME WITH WISE PEOPLE.

Humans are expert mimics. From infancy, we learn everything by copying others. People around us walked, talked, and fed themselves. So we figured out how to walk, talk, and feed ourselves. If wisdom, then, is our new goal, the next step is obvious: Spend time with wise people. Yes, ask them how they think, what frameworks they use to see the world, and why they do what they do. But, most importantly, observe what's behind the words: how they live.

KNOW YOUR (CHANGING) SELF.

While learning from others is clearly important, wisdom also comes from balancing what they offer with what *you* offer.

As mentioned earlier, "self" isn't a fixed thing but an ever-changing one. Yet, at any point in time, each of our selves does have a purpose, unique abilities, and values. Get to know each iteration of your *today self*—expecting, of course, that it'll one day change—to grow ever more comfortable with the wisdom of change.

LEAD WITH A BEGINNER'S MIND.
As you gather experiences, education, and insight, it's easy to rely on pattern recognition, make quick assumptions, and get everything wrong. That's why it's important to enter new situations like a beginner: wide-eyed, open, and curious. Ask questions, listen closely, and confirm that your understanding is correct before assuming you know exactly what's going on and what to do about it.

REVIEW CAUSE AND EFFECT OFTEN.
Nothing feels more frustrating and foolish than making the same mistakes, over and over and over, without learning anything or even seeing what's happening. Wisdom is able to see patterns and links between inputs and outputs, rather than insisting that something *should* work, even though it demonstrably hasn't. However, it's hard to see this without making space to reflect, and without purposely looking for how things might be connected.

SLOW DOWN.
When you act (or react) too quickly, you don't have time to engage all the parts of your brain. Especially the parts that store your accumulating knowledge, experience, understanding, common sense, and insight. To develop this skill, practice meditation, mindfulness, or even counting to ten. Respond too quickly and emotionally in high-stakes situations and it's like you've never cultivated wisdom at all.

Practice these things, cultivate your wisdom, and you'll begin to see through the matrix. You'll start noticing patterns and seeing the big picture while others get bogged down in the details. You'll remain calm in the face of both challenges and opportunities while others swing from soul-crushing despair to irrational optimism. And you'll be able to help others do the same.

And here's one final reason why wisdom is so important.

We live in what's been called "the information age," which means that most people now have access to the kind of information (i.e., facts and figures, procedures and processes) that people of the past never would have even known about.

Just a few hundred years ago, all recorded knowledge existed in a few libraries, curated and controlled by a tiny percentage of the world's population. Technology has opened it all up. Even more, it's helping us create new knowledge at alarming rates. Ninety percent of the world's data have been generated in the last two years, which means the rest of recorded history, from the beginning of time, represents only 10 percent of what we know today.

While open access to knowledge is a good thing, this glut of information brings new challenges that technology has yet to solve. For example, it's impossible to curate the 2.5 quintillion bytes of data created each day or evaluate its accuracy. (For some perspective, this means the world will create enough data to fill up thirty-nine million 64 GB iPhones today alone, and to fill up fourteen billion iPhones within a year.) Further, even if there were a way to curate, evaluate, and consume that information, people now realize that new knowledge doesn't equate to ability. They know that "I've watched a video on how to play the piano" is very different than "I can play Chopin's Nocturne in C-sharp Minor."

For these reasons, and more, wisdom has become such an important thing. People have either already consumed all the information they need, or they know how to get it. Yet they don't know how to make sense of it, prioritize it, or put it in action. That's why they're looking for someone to help. When you can calmly, wisely do that, your reputation will grow faster than you'll believe.

REPUTATION PRINCIPLE 8

OPERATE WITH *UNFLINCHING* INTEGRITY AND *Authenticity*

One of my good friends, Tony, is a university professor, researcher, writer, podcaster, and speaker. I've always admired him because, among other things, he "shows up" the same way in his articles, on stage, and in his daily life with friends and family. No matter the context, his principles—even his "voice," which is articulate, interesting, witty, and wise—remain the same.

This unique brand of authenticity (i.e., knowing who he is and being true to that) and integrity (i.e., acting in a way that's consistent with his own values) makes him memorable. His audiences, students, colleagues, clients, and friends always know what they're going to get and trust it.

Even though both authenticity and integrity have become buzzwords, it's important to not lose sight of their value. When you become the kind of person who always does what you say you'll do, whose principles and values are made clear, who acts in alignment with those values without deviation, and who does all that in all contexts, you'll stand out as the kind of professional others respect and admire. You'll become the kind of person people want to hire or collaborate with. Even more, you'll hold *yourself* in high regard. And learning to recognize, and be proud of, your own virtues is one of the most undervalued features of a successful career and life.

That pride doesn't come from merely "being yourself," though. Rather, it comes from "being your *best* self." Earlier in this chapter, I mentioned how, in my twenties, I was exposed to social dynamics, applied to the "pick-up community." In their literature, they often called into question this commonly offered social maxim: "Just be yourself." The argument: If "yourself" is awkward, uninteresting, and unskilled socially, if "yourself" is rude, abrasive, or condescending, if "yourself" is prejudiced, entitled, elitist, then definitely *don't* be yourself. Rather, spend time on your "inner game," building the qualities and characteristics required to become your best self.

Your best self can only emerge when you've learned to practice:

active listening,

leading with compassion and understanding,

delivering feedback with care and perspective,

over-delivering without expecting anything in return,

seeing all experiences as opportunities to grow, and

showing up with honesty, humility, and integrity.

In the end, as mentioned earlier, reputation is a human factor. Which means it's developed by getting better at being with humans. No one is born with these skills already mastered. Each of us has to believe that these skills are important to develop, trust that practicing them will be worth the effort, and then get to the practicing.

Of course, mastering all eight isn't possible overnight. It takes years of practice. However, mastery isn't necessary. The simple fact that people see you working on them will attract them to you, your products, and your services. Keep working and people will start sending friends and family too.

Q&A with JB: Reputation

To support what you're learning, I've compiled end-of-chapter Q&As that are full of real, thoughtful questions I've gotten over the years. In each one I share my unfiltered take on the challenges you'll undoubtedly face as you grow your career.

⊕ You can check out all the Change Maker Q&As at www.changemakeracademy.com/questions.

This chapter's questions include:

Q: In one of your seminars I heard you talk about your "Google the Opposite" strategy as a way to seek out feedback on certain ideas. Can you share more about it? (Answer: ~400 words)

Q: In this chapter, you talk about "being yourself." How does appearance play into that? "Myself" is wearing board shorts and T-shirts, but I don't think too many people would think that's professional. (Answer: ~400 words)

Q: What about cursing? I know a coach who drops f-bombs every other word. I can't imagine that's too smart for reputation. (Answer: ~225 words)

Q: I once had a client tell me that my website didn't look professional. How important is all that stuff to developing my reputation? (Answer: ~275 words)

Q: You mention inclusivity when it comes to different sizes, shapes, races, genders, and ability levels. How important is that? (Answer: ~500 words)

Reputation IS A HUMAN FACTOR
IT'S WHAT OTHER PEOPLE think OF you

TO BUILD A great REPUTATION:
Earn UNIMPEACHABLE CREDENTIALS
CONSISTENTLY do GREAT WORK
SHOW UP AS AN authentic HUMAN

LIKE GETTING stronger IN THE GYM,
REPUTATION SKILLS ARE strengthened THROUGH
patient PRACTICE AND a growth MINDSET

All FEEDBACK HELPS you GROW
THAT MAKES IT A precious GIFT
NO MATTER HOW it's DELIVERED

THE FASTEST LEARNERS HUNT feedback
THIS INCREASES growth OPPORTUNITIES

AS you GET BETTER AT TAKING feedback
YOU could GET WORSE AT GIVING IT
GUARD against THIS

Turn YOUR fear OF DIFFICULT CONVERSATIONS
INTO EXCITEMENT FOR GETTING practice
AND MAKING improvements

ALWAYS KEEP YOUR goal IN MIND
DON'T let DISTRACTIONS (OR EGO)
TAKE you AWAY FROM WHAT'S important

AS YOU GROW IN wisdom
you'll LIVE A BETTER LIFE
AND HELP others AROUND YOU
Do THE SAME

DON'T JUST "BE YOURSELF"
DEVELOP YOUR best SELF
AND BE THAT

CHAPTER 7

EDUC

ATION

A COMPLETE
CURRICULUM FOR
Becoming THE Ultimate
CHANGE MAKER

As a kid, I hated school.

I'm not sure if I hated it because school was mandatory, because we had to sit at desks all day, or because we had to learn the same things, at the same pace, regardless of our aptitude. But, even now, after a long and successful postsecondary run, "education" can still give me the shivers.

What about you?

Did you love your high school years? Or spitball your way to detention? Think your chemistry teacher was a wizard? Or worry about your lit teacher's relationship with Chaucer? Love solving algebraic equations? Or, like me, *hate it all* (but discover the fountain of knowledge later)?

Either way, regardless of your past experiences with academics, becoming the ultimate health and fitness change maker depends on a new relationship with learning, one where your continuing education balances excitement and inspiration (*I can't wait to learn that!*) with relevance and usefulness (*And I get to use it in my practice tomorrow!*).

Contrast this with what I see from many trainers, dietitians, health coaches, rehab specialists, and functional med docs. After they complete specialty training, their learning is disjointed. There's a seminar here, a course there. A textbook here, a journal article there. A conference here, a webinar there. Maybe there's *a little* excitement and inspiration. But mostly it's going through the motions, taking courses they think they *should*, earning CEUs to check the boxes for qualification renewal.

Yes, they're acquiring new knowledge. But that's not the point. Without a master plan that connects all their learning together, they end up wasting their time, money, and energy gathering tools that they'll never quite know how to use in the context of their actual practice.

Plus, many of the courses they take are so highly specific (three days on the neuroanatomy of the left extensor digitorum longus?), it's hard to see how they'll translate into client and patient results, business growth, or a remarkable reputation.

The good news? This chapter offers a better plan.

It outlines the essential information *you'll* need to create an inspired and reputation-building learning curriculum. One that puts you on track for a long-lasting, fulfilling, and successful career.

Don't think an ongoing continuing education curriculum is *that* important?

Consider the 40 percent annual turnover rate in the health and fitness industry. By this time next year we'll have lost four out of every ten professionals. They'll have ditched a career they were initially so passionate about. They'll have forfeited an opportunity to find meaning in their work. They'll have given up the chance to change, maybe even save, lives.

And why? Because they weren't prepared. Because no one taught them the who, what, where, when, why, and how of continuing education and lifelong learning.

That's the point of this chapter: to help *you* craft an educational plan that's intentional, practical, forward-thinking, and success-oriented so you don't become another health and fitness statistic. To help you shape your path to becoming the ultimate health and fitness change maker.

Why IS A CAREER CURRICULUM Important?

At first, clients and patients will look for "credibility indicators" and "social proof" like: which university you attended, what degree(s) and certification(s) you have, whether you've been written up in the media or appeared on the radio or on television programs, whether you can show them testimonials from satisfied and enthusiastic clients.

But, after that, they immediately start caring more about who you are (as a coach and as a person) and how you can help *them* achieve *their goals*. Why, then, does *your* continuing education matter?

Is it to get a first job? To get a better job? To earn the respect of your peers? To show off your skull-popping brains (to go along with your sleeve-stretching biceps)?

Continuing education *might* help with those things. But I consider those collateral benefits. In other words: Don't read books, attend seminars, complete certification programs, and earn degrees because you expect they'll produce some sort of external benefit and validation. Rather, engage in lifelong education because of the internal benefits.

Learning changes you. It helps you become a better student, questioner, and thinker. It helps you become more curious, interested, and aware. It helps you develop an all-important growth mindset. And it helps you become a more well-rounded, confident, and fearless change maker.

When that happens, sure, it could lead to your first job, or a better job, or more success, or any of the other external things young people expect from education. But if your motive is credential shopping or job chasing, you'll miss out on the real benefits.

I emphasize this because, all too often, cynics deride the value of degree programs, certifications, and other structured continuing-education pathways. "Clients don't care about your degree!" "Do you really think that certification is going to help you get a job?!?"

They're right, to some extent. Once they're satisfied with your credibility, clients won't care much about the details of your latest course. And that certification you worked so hard on? It might not help you get a job. But that doesn't make degrees and certifications worthless. Again, the value isn't external. It's internal.

That's why you should understand the *why* of education before the *what*. The why establishes how to think about your educational path, and it helps you create well-considered criteria for the courses you'll select. From there, instead of trying to accumulate an alphabet's worth of letters after your name to impress others, search for the task-specific knowledge, wisdom, and insight you'll need to master yourself and your profession.

Eric Cressey—a good friend, one of the world's premier strength coaches, and a highly successful entrepreneur who runs sport-training facilities in Hudson, Massachusetts, and Jupiter, Florida—shares these questions for evaluating any continuing education opportunity.

Evaluating Continuing Education

Next time you're wondering whether you should sign up for a specific course (or not), ask yourself the following:

Will it provide me with specific information I wouldn't otherwise have?

> ⊕ To do this exercise, and all upcoming ones, please download our printable + fillable worksheets at **www.changemakeracademy.com/downloadable-forms**.

Will it provide info I can immediately apply in my interaction with clients and staff?

⊕

Is it delivered by one of the best? Can they speak from an experienced, in-the-trenches perspective? Or are they academics who haven't worked with clients in years?

⊕

I'd add one additional question that I think is important:

Is it part of a comprehensive long-term personal development plan designed to help me achieve a deep mastery of my craft and lead to my ultimate career goals?

⊕

I include this last one because I think continuing education needs to fit into your own career domination plan. It has to map to *future you*, the kind of professional you'd like to one day become.

I liken this to the long-term athlete development models published by national sport governing bodies around the world. My daughter is trained in gymnastics and my wife is a figure skating coach. Having been exposed to both, I love how they *clearly* outline: a) which skills will be required, b) which lessons should be delivered, c) which training modalities to use, and d) which specific steps will transform an unskilled toddler into an Olympic champion over ten to fifteen years.

Whether the athlete knows it or not, whether the parent knows it or not, whether junior coaches know it or not, they're all executing a decade(s)-long plan well-known to lead to a particular outcome. Every lesson, every course, every practice, every skill is building toward the goal of producing a masterful athlete, one who could compete at the highest level of sport.

Why not think about your own career in the same way?

What could you accomplish with your own long-term professional development plan? How much would your probability of success increase if you didn't choose education opportunities randomly, but as part of a master curriculum?

BUILDING your
PERSONAL *CURRICULUM*

In Chapter 1 I said that the health and fitness field will eventually morph from a place of focused specialists to a place of broad generalists. Clients and patients will increasingly expect a one-stop health and fitness experience. And that's what professionals of the future will deliver.

Of course, you don't have to give up on your dream of being the world's foremost expert on asparagus smoothies. But it does mean you need to approach your education with a broader stroke. And widen your base of competency to support all aspects of health: movement, nutrition, supplementation, sleep, stress management, and more.

You certainly won't be an expert in each area, nor will you diagnose or prescribe in each area. But you will need the training to confidently deliver a basic summary of each topic. Plus, when you have questions, or if someone needs more help than you can provide, you'll have built a contact list full of professionals you can turn to or refer clients to.

Here's an example: When I used to consult with elite professional and Olympic-level sports teams, my main focus was sport science and nutrition. Fitness and food, no problem. We had that locked down. Unfortunately, some athletes still felt bad: tired, lethargic, full of aches and pains.

I realized that we couldn't get the most out of them until we looked at their lives holistically. Many of these athletes traveled so often (with so little knowledge of sleep hygiene and circadian rhythms) that it didn't matter how well their training was structured or how many grams of protein they consumed. Their recovery, body composition, and performance would never be what they wanted until we took care of their sleep needs. When I finally started sharing basic sleep and circadian management strategies, our fitness and fueling protocols had the chance to work, and they did.*

Again, I'm not suggesting you need a PhD in sleep medicine to talk about this. But helping people feel better is what you do. If sleep were a limiting factor, wouldn't it make sense to share basic sleep hygiene ideas?

One of my favorite ways to think about this approach is the T-shaped learning model:

---

* For those athletes who required more help, I referred them to a trusted sleep expert.

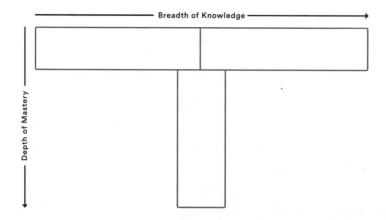

Using this model, the horizontal bar represents all the subjects you'll need to learn and understand to become a complete, well-rounded, elite professional. This could include client-specific domains like exercise, nutrition, supplementation, sleep, and stress management. It could also include professional-development domains like change psychology, coaching philosophy, marketing and sales, customer care, business systems and processes, reputation management, and more.

The vertical bar represents your specialty, where you have deep, subject-specific knowledge. This could be in any one of the client areas like movement, nutrition, rehab, medical diagnostics and treatment, etc. It could also be in a professional development area like marketing and sales.

My health and fitness career, for example, could be illustrated as follows:

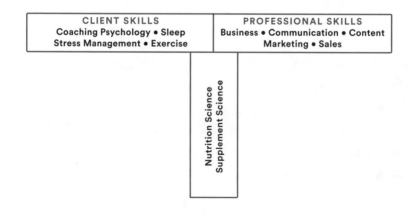

I have master's and doctoral training in nutrition and supplementation, and I've also sought out education and mentorship in all the areas along the horizontal bar to become a well-rounded and successful speaker, writer, entrepreneur, coach, and business owner.

Now it's your turn.

As you start thinking about your own T-shaped learning, keep in mind the goal. You'll want to know a little about a lot (particularly the things that contribute to career success). And a lot about a little (particularly the things you can master). You'll also want to put together a network of T-shaped allies with different specialties (who know a lot about the things you only know a little about). This way your network can cover all the bases. You can reach out, or refer out, when required.

Think about some of the most interesting people you've met. They're usually folks who can converse on a wide range of subjects—be it current events, home-gardening techniques, local breweries, superhero movies, French history, the environment, whatever the conversation circles to. But they also usually have one area where they add value, where they're a deep expert.

Often cited as an exemplar of a T-shaped individual is American novelist Ernest Hemingway. His deep mastery of writing (the vertical bar of his T) was "rounded out" by his interests in hunting, fishing, sport, languages, camping, backpacking, travel, art, music, history, wine, social dynamics, and much more (the horizontal bar of his T). According to those close to him, he had a "strange power of presence" and left folks "falling into fits of admiration."

So, not only will living a "T-shaped life" contribute to a leveling up of your career, it'll also contribute to a leveling up of your personal life. As a professional, you'll become the coach your clients need you to be. And, as a person, they might even talk about *your* "powerful presence" and fall into "fits of admiration" for *you*.

Of course, you probably already know your main area of focus—the vertical bar of your T. It could be exercise programming, nutrition coaching, diagnostics, prescription, etc. You've probably also invested a lot of time and money into deepening this area of knowledge. Yet maybe it's time to focus more on the horizontal bar of your T and filling it out with training in some different areas.

AREAS TO DEVELOP BEYOND YOUR SPECIALTY

EXERCISE AND FITNESS.
To develop a deeper understanding of how different exercise modalities can contribute to massive improvements in health, fitness, disease resistance, and performance.

NUTRITION AND SUPPLEMENTATION.
To more deeply understand how your clients' eating decisions and supplement choices influence their energy levels, physical health, quality of life, and performance.

HEALTHY MOVEMENT AND MOBILITY.
To discover how movement and mechanics play key roles in the daily health and functional capacities of office workers, to manual laborers, athletes, children, and more.

STRESS MANAGEMENT AND MENTAL HEALTH.
To learn how mental health and stress influence who we are, how we see the world, how our bodies function at rest (vs. during performance), and what we're able to do (vs. not do).

SLEEP.
To understand how sleep amount and quality are closely interconnected with exercise (ability and capacity), eating (choices and digestion/absorption), mental health, and more.

COACHING AND CHANGE PSYCHOLOGY.
To realize that knowing all about cellular function, movement, nutrition, sleep, and stress won't get you far *without* knowing how to help people change their actions and practices.

MARKETING, SALES, AND BUSINESS.
To learn how to attract people to your business, convince them you're the right fit for them, and deliver exactly what you've promised in a way that exceeds their expectations.

Curious which courses are the best in each domain? At the end of the book you'll find examples in each category. But, before rushing to that, consider filling out the following empty T with the categories you think are most essential to achieving your career goals.

Your T-Shaped Curriculum Worksheet

The T-shaped model helps you visualize your depth and breadth of knowledge as well as map out the skills you'll require to move from *today you* to *future you*. To this end, fill out the following empty T with the categories you think are most essential to achieving your career goals.

The horizontal bar should be filled with the categories you'll need to be fluent in to become *future you*—the ultimate change maker you want to become.

The vertical bar should be filled with the category you'd like to (or already do) specialize in—where you'll achieve mastery.

Either can include the categories listed above, as well as other professional skills (like having crucial conversations, giving and receiving feedback) or clinical skills (like reading and interpreting blood labs, diagnosing and treating special conditions).

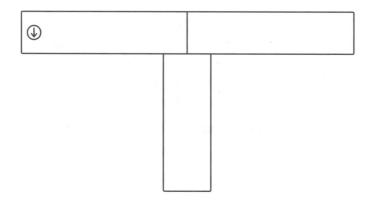

THE PROS AND CONS OF
DIFFERENT *Learning* FORMATS

Now that you know which domains you want (and need) to receive more training in—hopefully, over a long and productive career, you'll seek out training in *all* the domains above—let's talk about the different learning formats available, their pros and cons, and their value.

Before starting, however, it's important to remember that—just like everything else in life—the educational choices you make have trade-offs.

(Want to get married? If so, marriage will probably help you gain companionship. But you'll probably lose some independence. Want to stay single? If so, you get to keep your independence. But you'll be missing companionship.)

To help you understand the trade-offs for each of seven popular learning formats below, I've created a ranking system based on the following criteria:

EASE:
10 represents education that's simple to consume

AFFORDABILITY:
10 represents education that's free or very low cost

CONTEXTUALLY RELEVANT:
10 represents education that's put in its proper context

SKILL BUILDING:
10 represents education that will help you build practical skills

CREDENTIALS:
10 represents education that will give you credentials

CAREER VALUE:
10 represents education that will make a difference in your career

Learning Format #1: Articles in magazines, journals, trade publications, or online

With publications for every interest and profession, plus an explosion of online publications catering to every subniche within every niche, articles are everywhere! If you've found a trusted, honest, authoritative source, their ease of access and cost is hard to beat. In addition, articles can be published quickly in order to deliver cutting-edge, timely information. This is why so many people read articles online as part of their personal and professional education.

However, since articles are designed to be short and specific, they don't always help you orient what you're learning in its proper context, within the larger field of knowledge. Not all articles are equally authoritative and credible, of course. And articles rarely help you develop practices that reliably lead to new skills.

So choose wisely. Also remember that if you spend all your personal development time reading articles, you won't have time left over to develop the skills you'll need in your daily practice. Reading doesn't produce the same kind of learning as doing.

EASE		
AFFORDABILITY		
CONTEXTUALLY RELEVANT		
SKILL BUILDING		
CREDENTIALS		
CAREER VALUE		

Learning Format #2: Books and e-books

Once upon a time, having a published book was a marker of authority and credibility because books could only be published through a small group of information gatekeepers (i.e., publishing houses). This made publishing more difficult for individuals, but it largely helped protect readers from unqualified authors and fraudulent information.

Nowadays, the gatekeepers are gone. Traditional book publishing decisions are driven primarily by the likelihood that a book will sell and not necessarily by a book's trustworthiness or credibility. Plus, self-publishing requires no permission or review whatsoever. So buyer beware. Just because someone's written a book doesn't mean that the book is original, valuable, or useful.*

With that said, good books, written by trustworthy and believable authors, can deliver valuable information set in its proper context. As books are usually ten to twenty times the length of articles, they can allow deeper exploration of particular topics. And, while books almost never produce transformative change on their own, they often do introduce us to new ideas that, explored more deeply in other learning formats, can lead to transformation.

Because they require a sizeable time investment (days, weeks, or months depending on how much time you devote to reading) and still aren't particularly oriented to skill development, make sure you're clear on what you need most before picking up a new book: more information about a topic you know little about or more practice doing what you already "know" but haven't implemented.

EASE		
AFFORDABILITY		
CONTEXTUALLY RELEVANT		
SKILL BUILDING		
CREDENTIALS		
CAREER VALUE		

Learning Format #3: Free online videos, lectures, podcasts

I rate free online videos, lectures, and podcasts similarly to free articles as they share some of the same pros (inexpensive, easy to consume) and

---

* Except this one, of course. This one is immune from all criticism.

cons (lacking context, low on skill development unless they offer exercises for you to do at home).

Similar to articles and books, the lack of credibility gatekeepers means you have to be very diligent in finding trusted, authoritative, and honest sources who base their work on a balanced review of the research (as opposed to agenda-driven opinion pieces).

As with both articles and books, since video content is ubiquitous, cheap, and easy to consume, it's important not to mistake consumption for progress, especially if you require skill development even over information gathering.

EASE		
AFFORDABILITY		
CONTEXTUALLY RELEVANT		
SKILL BUILDING		
CREDENTIALS		
CAREER VALUE		

Learning Format #4: Live seminars (paid)

Weekend seminars in the form of summits (multiple speakers delivering thirty- to ninety-minute presentations on a variety of topics) or workshops (single speakers delivering one or two days on a specific topic) are popular in the health and fitness industry. Depending on the quality of the event and the speakers, attendees usually come home with a mix of new information, new things to try, and (sometimes) hands-on experience.

Workshops often allow us to explore a particular topic in depth, as well as interact with subject-matter experts. This means you might find that the content more closely meets your specific needs and interests than what you'd get in books, articles, and online videos.

However, the value of these events has to be weighed against the time commitment, cost (of travel plus event fees), and usefulness at the present stage of your career. For example, an advanced program-design workshop for athletes, while interesting for certain personal trainers, may not be relevant if most of their clients are recreational exercisers. Similarly, if a functional medicine doctor's main limiting factor is getting clients, another biochemistry workshop might have to come later.

Often, the real value in attending live events is getting to meet people. Attending a one-hour talk on nutrition for seniors will probably be less instructive than reading a book on the subject by the same author. However, having the chance to interact with the author, and with others interested in the same topic, could help expand your network or simply help you connect with other like-minded professionals. As most experienced conference-goers know: The best conversations happen during the coffee breaks.

Learning Format #5:
Certification programs

Certification programs in health and fitness give professionals the chance to not only learn a tremendous amount about a particular subject, but also to earn a credential in the chosen area. For example, earning a pre- and post-natal certification demonstrates that you've passed the minimum standards required to work with women before, during, and after pregnancy.

In addition, well-done certification programs do an excellent job of surveying the entire field of knowledge, reviewing all the available research, and helping to place the information in its relevant context. For example, a well-done nutrition certification program will help you figure out exactly how a low-carbohydrate diet works biochemically, who it might be appropriate for, who it might not be appropriate for, and when it might (or might not) be appropriate. Compare this to one-sided articles, books, or video lectures from individuals arguing for or against such an approach, and you'll better understand the idea of context here and why it's so important.

In my opinion, short of degree programs, if you hope to develop fluency in a particular discipline, choosing trusted, balanced, authoritative certification programs offers the best value for your investment. Although the investment of time and money is sometimes significant, if you can afford both, you'll come away with deeper knowledge, more relevant practice, and a more balanced view than if you'd simply read articles, books, or attended one-off seminars.

Two caveats.

First, there are a lot of bad certification programs out there. So you'll want to use the triangulation method described ahead (page 300) to help you separate the good from the bad.

Second, don't assume certification always means accreditation or getting hired. For example, without earning a degree in dietetics, there are some things in nutrition even a certified professional cannot do (i.e., medical nutrition therapy). Also, while many employers do accord higher value to certain certifications when hiring candidates, being certified doesn't guarantee you'll get a job or even more clients.

As discussed earlier, education is about the internal benefits, not the external ones. And it's a long-term play, not a short-term one. **Invest in developing your inner game through learning and education and, over time, you'll become more desirable to employers and clients alike.**

EASE		
AFFORDABILITY		
CONTEXTUALLY RELEVANT		
SKILL BUILDING		
CREDENTIALS		
CAREER VALUE		

Learning Format #6: Internships and field experiences

Internships and field experiences undertaken with high-profile professionals or with high-performing facilities can offer tremendous practical, hands-on, task-relevant skill development. That's because they require you to actually *do* the thing instead of just *learning* about it. (Consider the difference between *reading about* how to do a deadlift and actually *trying* your first deadlift.)

In addition, internships and field experiences can give you a one-of-a-kind opportunity to see if you actually enjoy the specific work they're providing. This was particularly huge for me because, at one point in my academic career, I considered becoming a pharmacist. Thankfully, I first took a part-time job at a pharmacy, where I learned it wasn't a good fit for me.

While internships and field experiences can offer a lot of value, they may require you to relocate (at least temporarily), which could come at a high cost, especially if they're unpaid internships. Further, not all internships are created equally. Some are simply poorly structured attempts to get young people to perform free labor for the professional or facility, while others are designed beautifully to expose you to all aspects of their practice and walk away with a tremendous amount of practical learning in a short period of time. So evaluate internship opportunities critically.

EASE		
AFFORDABILITY		
CONTEXTUALLY RELEVANT		
SKILL BUILDING		
CREDENTIALS		
CAREER VALUE		

Learning Format #7:
Academic programs

In some occupations, you need a degree to actually practice in the field. (For example, you can't practice dietetics without having earned a dietetics degree; you can't practice medicine without having earned a medical degree; you can't practice chiropractic care without having earned a chiropractic degree.) So, if you're choosing a health and fitness career that requires a college or university degree, this is a must.

In addition, academic programs with a well-built curriculum usually offer the broadest contextual look at the subject you're studying (i.e., many courses in different areas of your specialty, including hands-on practicums, taken over many years). These programs can offer a broader understanding of a range of other topics, too, including giving you more experience in learning, thinking critically, writing, evaluating ideas, and more.

As great as academic training can be, it can also be extremely time-consuming (four years to complete a standard degree program) and expensive (hundreds of thousands of dollars in direct costs plus the opportunity cost of not working for those four years). In addition, it isn't always relevant for certain career paths, nor is it likely to help you get a job in others. So do your research to figure out if what you want to do for a living is enhanced by university training (or not).

Bonus resource: Mentors

I didn't include mentors in the learning categories above because I consider mentorship something every professional should have at every stage of their career.

If you're reading this and you don't have a mentor today, I urge you to begin looking for one who can help you reach the next stage of your professional journey. Someone who's thoughtful, experienced, wise. Someone's who's just a little further along the path than you are (but not so far along the path that they can no longer relate to the challenges and opportunities before you today).

Wondering how to find one? In my life I simply keep on the lookout for amazing people I'd like to emulate, people who've accomplished some of the remarkable things I'd like to accomplish myself.* If I get the chance to connect with them, whether by email or in person, I do. And I follow the advice I shared in Chapter 6, showing up as a respectful, grateful, open, compassionate, honest, and curious human. Then I let nature take its course.

Finding Mentorship

My friend Nate Green, a master connector who's been mentored by a who's-who list of interesting and successful people, takes a much more proactive and intentional approach. Here's how he thinks about approaching possible mentors, plus some of the strategies he'd recommend for you.

SEND THE EMAIL.

Nate emailed Lou Schuler, the fitness industry's most well-known journalist, when Nate was just nineteen years old. He proceeded to tell Lou that he wanted his job, asking how he got it.

"It wasn't my best email," Nate told me. But Lou surprised him by writing back and offering career advice. "That meant a lot to me. I would have never met him (or many other people who've helped shape my career) if I didn't first reach out."

Here's an updated script he recommends if you plan to reach out to a potential mentor via email.

> *Hey NAME,*
>
> *My name is Nate, and I'm a big fan of your work.*

---

* These don't only need to be professional accomplishments, although they could be. I'm just as excited to learn from someone who has a great family life as I am from someone who's grown a billion-dollar business.

> *Specifically, your (article/book/podcast) about (A, B, C) really helped me to (X, Y, Z).*
>
> *I know you're busy, but I'm hoping you have a minute to answer a very short and specific question for me.*
>
> *INSERT VERY SHORT AND SPECIFIC QUESTION HERE*
>
> *If you don't have time, I completely understand.*
>
> *Thanks again for your work.*

APPROACH AN EQUAL AND NOT AS A "FANBOY."
Whether you start with an email, or you get the chance to meet a potential mentor in person, make roughly 5 percent of the next interaction about how much you love their work. The remaining 95 percent or so is all about talking to them like a friend would. (This works better in person, of course, but applies equally to email.)

Nate recommends never fawning over people, hanging around them for too long, or coming across as needy. "It's like dating that way," says Nate. "No one wants to hang out with someone who's constantly like, 'OH MY GOD I LOVE YOU' and clings on in a needy way."

Also, when meeting people in person, *never* ask to take photos with them. ("It's too fanboy-ish," according to Nate.) Yet feel free to bring people small gifts, such as a book you really enjoy and think they'd like too.

ASK IF YOU CAN FOLLOW UP.
If you end up meeting someone at a professional event or social function and have a good initial conversation, Nate

recommends asking if you can follow up. Here's how you can approach the subject.

> *It was really nice chatting with you, NAME.*
>
> *I know you're busy, and so I want to respect your time.*
>
> *That said, if I have a VERY specific question about (X, Y, Z), are you open to me sending you a short email?*
>
> *If you don't have time to answer, that's fine.*
>
> *But I really respect your opinion and think it could really help my career.*
>
> *You have my word that whatever you tell me to try, I'll give it a shot.*

If they say yes,

> *Thanks so much. What's the best way to get a hold of you?*

If they say no,

> *Thanks so much. Keep doing good work. You're helping a lot of people.*

IF THEY SHARE SOME ADVICE, TAKE IT.

More than gifts or financial rewards, a mentor's greatest pay-off is knowing that a mentee respects their time, takes their help seriously, and isn't afraid of hard work.

"Let's say I'm at a conference and meet someone I respect and want to learn from. Maybe we have a five-minute conversation and they give me a small piece of advice. I write that advice down (later, when I'm back in my hotel room). Then I *follow their advice*. If they tell me to read a certain book, I read it. If they tell me I should consider starting a blog, I start one."

Whatever it is, Nate does what they recommended. Later, he tells them about it. "I'll email to follow up. Then I'll ask for a next step, something else they'd recommend I put into action."

ALWAYS CONSIDER: "WHAT CAN I OFFER THEM?"

You may have no idea what that is. But it helps to think this way—to constantly be on the lookout for how you can do something, anything, to express your gratitude for their help, guidance, and support.

If you're wondering why mentors would even spend their time helping you like this, the answer is easy. The right mentors *want* mentees, badly. They want to share what they've learned. And they want to share it with young, smart, curious people who are likely to do something valuable with their advice (and honestly report back on what they did and how it worked out).

And, keep this in mind, they're not looking to be "impressed." Frankly, if you're mentoring with someone worth learning from, you *can't* impress them at your level of development. So you're not there to be the expert, or to show them how smart you are, or to impose your own limited insights. You're there to show up with a great attitude and a growth mindset. To listen carefully, ask great questions, and put what you're learning into action.

Yet, while you're there to learn, you do get points for being curious, thoughtful, and adding value to the relationship in other ways, for expressing gratitude for the advice and the opportunity. To this end, I often send my mentors handwritten notes, short reports of how I used their advice to my advantage (as Nate does), and small tokens of my gratitude. I love it when my mentees do the same.

Choosing THE RIGHT COURSES AND RESOURCES

Now that you know which areas you want (and need) to receive more training in, as well as the pros and cons of different modalities you could choose to learn from, it's time to discuss how to select the right resources, people, and companies to pursue your education with.

Whether you're looking to level up your nutrition knowledge by doing a nutrition certification, or to improve your knowledge of anatomy by taking a fascial dissection course, there are *so many* options out there. To help you choose which are right for you, I highly recommend a method I learned from Phil Caravaggio. It's called triangulation.

Using the "triangulation" method

When Phil gets into something, he *really* gets into it. Recently, he's gone deep into coffee—to the point where he decided to set up a world-class coffee bar in Precision Nutrition's Toronto headquarters. Of course, he could have done some Googling, talked to a few local experts, and consulted a few coffee equipment manufacturers to figure out how to set up the coffee bar.

But that's not how Phil does anything. When something matters to him—whether it's hiring the best coffee machine or hiring the best CEO—he uses a particular, highly effective formula.

1 Find at least three *believable** people with *demonstrated* competence** who are passionate about the subject matter.

2 Prepare thoughtful, insightful, deeply curious questions to ask them. Creating these questions might take some research and "homework" beforehand—for instance, he might review a particular person's career path, read materials they wrote, and so forth.

3 Use these questions to interview them in person (preferably) or on a video conference; listen closely and absorb everything they teach, taking extensive notes.

4 Pay particular attention to areas where the experts don't agree. (This is important.) Then follow up with each to figure out *why* they disagree.

5 Only then, taking everything into account, make your decision.

In the case of his coffee bar, Phil called three people (including a world-champion barista, a highly regarded coffee grower, and a thought leader on coffee hardware/machinery) and asked them pointed questions on everything from beans to machines to brewing process. Through the interviews, it turns out they agreed on a lot of things. However, two of them strongly disagreed on which machine (and process) Phil should use in his coffee bar. This was awesome because understanding *where and why* experts disagree can provide the best learning.

* People who have repeatedly and successfully accomplished the thing in question, who have a strong track record with at least three successes, and have great explanations of their approach when probed.
** Showing that you deserve the title of "authority" or "expert" with consistently high-level performance.

When Phil brought up this disagreement, Expert 1 mentioned that, while he respects his colleague, Expert 2 is really fixated on using robotics to achieve coffee-making consistency. As a result, his priority is making a reliable, reproducible cup of coffee every time, regardless of the variable conditions that could influence coffee making (altitude, ambient temperature, water quality, and so on). His recommendation was biased by a particular set of interests he has. When Phil spoke with Expert 2, he mentioned that, while he also respects his colleague, Expert 1 is interested in craftsmanship and the human factors involved in coffee making. He doesn't mind a little variability as long as every cup is excellent. So his recommendation was biased by his own (very different) interests.

For Phil, this was especially enlightening because it became clear that this disagreement wasn't about which approach was "right" or "wrong," "better" or "worse." Rather, it was about personal style and preference. Since each approach had merit, it was up to Phil to decide which trade-offs he was willing to accept at his coffee bar, based on his own goals.

This is what triangulation gets you: the ability to hear from world-class experts, to look for areas of agreement, and to learn from their areas of disagreement. And, as mentioned, I *highly* recommend using this process, especially as you try to evaluate which people and companies to learn from while building your educational curriculum.

Find a few believable people. Ask them the best learning opportunities in each domain. Take note when they agree. And probe deeper when they disagree.

Here's a great example that's come up in my work. People often ask me whether they should do one of two particular nutrition certifications: the Precision Nutrition (PN) Certification or the International Society of Sport Nutrition (ISSN) certification. Of course, they expect me to recommend the one I co-authored, the PN program. They're often surprised by my answer.

When asked, I tell them that *both* programs are valuable and well respected and that any health and fitness professional who's deeply interested in nutrition will eventually do both. So don't ask, "Which is better?" but, rather, "Which should I do first?"

The answer: the one that addresses your current limiting factors.

The PN certification is a nutrition *coaching* certification. While the first half of the program focuses on the science of nutrition, the second focuses on coaching and change psychology. The ISSN certification, on the other hand, focuses on the science of sports nutrition and supplementation, in theory and in practice.

So, if you need advanced sports nutrition and supplement protocols for highly disciplined, nutritionally compliant athletes *more* or *more urgently*, you might tackle the ISSN program now and the PN program later.

On the other hand, if you need to help clients *change their behaviors*, address limiting factors, build habit systems, grapple with the natural ambivalence of growth, and improve their nutritional quality within the context of their everyday lives, you might tackle the PN program first.

But don't take my word for it. In the spirit of triangulation, ask a few other believable people to help you come up with a few options. Once you've narrowed your selection, based on the experts you've spoken with, here are two additional steps to building confidence in your decision.

Crowdsourcing

Ask friends, colleagues, or social media connections for their opinions. You could even post surveys in your Facebook groups. See what others think the best option is for you, making it clear exactly what your goals are and why you're considering the programs you're considering.

(Just be sure to do this after triangulation. It's better to ask people to help you choose between two or three options instead of asking for open-ended recommendations.)

Online reviews

If you already know the programs you're trying to choose between, search Google for program reviews by typing in the name of the program and "reviews" after it, such as "Precision Nutrition Certification reviews," or "ISSN certification reviews."

Keep in mind that you don't exactly know the believability of the online reviewers or whether their goals align with yours. To this end, weight your original experts highest, using crowdsourcing and reviews to add to your decision-making process but not as your only criteria.

MAKING TIME TO Prioritize EDUCATION

After helping new health and fitness pros build out their T-shaped learning curriculum with specific educational categories, and helping them decide on which courses (or resources) they'll use in each of those categories, the inevitable question they ask me is:

"How the heck am I going to do all that?!?"

Trust me, I get it. I used to be riddled with anxiety about how little I really knew compared to how much I had yet to learn. I felt behind, impatient, and stressed out. Like I'd never get to where I wanted to be. At some points I wondered if I should leave the industry altogether.

If you're feeling that way yourself, remember: It's not a race. You're not behind. And there's nothing to "catch up" to. Education is, truly, a career-long process. If you do it right, it won't ever stop.

For example, I'm twenty-five years into my career and am exposed to more seminars and workshops now than I was early on. With four young children, less interest in being on airplanes, and a $200 million company to run, I generally choose online or prerecorded ones (rather than attending in person). Nevertheless, I end each with pages full of ideas and new things for our team to try when I get back to my office.

In addition, I pick three impressive people and/or companies to closely follow each year. And when I say closely, I mean *closely*. I visit every page of their websites, read all their communications, and buy all their products with the goal of understanding what makes them special. Of the companies I follow, one is usually bigger than ours, one is the same size, and one is smaller. If I'm following an individual, it's usually someone talented but younger. I do this because, by following them, I get to see how they use new strategies and technologies to leverage timeless and unchanging principles. As I learn how these people and companies operate, I share the best insights with our team.

Then there's my "brain-picking fee." Taught to me by my late friend Charles, whenever there's something specific I need to learn, I find one of the world's leading thinkers on that subject—whether scientist, educator, or in-the-trenches practitioner—and offer them an hourly fee to pick their brain on their subject of expertise. People like scientists and professors, especially those working for public institutions, are often eager to spend an hour or two talking with someone deeply interested in their area of expertise, especially if that person comes well-prepared* and is willing to pay for their time.**

Finally, I'm now in a unique position where I can *create new knowledge* through research trials (laboratory experiments with small groups of volunteers and clinical trials with large groups of consenting Precision Nutrition clients), business-related pilot projects (exploring new organizational structures and launching new beta products), or marketing-related projects (testing price sensitivities and exploring new launch models).

As you can see, my education continues to this day, even if it's different than my early days of academic programs, structured coursework, and guided mentorships/internships. I have a hard time imagining a time where I'll feel "done" when it comes to learning, growing, and developing.

---

* Being well prepared is critical to make sure a) I'm not wasting my own time and money and b) they don't feel like I've wasted their time. This means becoming very familiar with their work, understanding what they're excited about now, and coming up with important, insightful questions.

** I usually offer between $100 and $200 USD per hour for their time. Sometimes they ask for more. More often, though, they waive the fee altogether.

I suspect my T-shaped curriculum will continue to evolve until the day I die.

If you plan *your* career well, your T-shaped curriculum will also continue to evolve. It will always represent *future you*. It'll never be finished. Because, for ambitious people, the mountain *always* gets taller as you approach its summit. When you reach the heights you now aspire to, no matter how high you think they are, there will be *many* new things you'll want to experience, learn, and do.

That's why, for now, the only path forward is to take it one step at a time. One course at a time. When time and money are tight, maybe you only invest in one course, event, or certification per year. If you have more of either resource, consider more than one learning opportunity per year. Go at your pace, though, because that's the only pace you can go at.

So how do you choose your very next course?

Here's what I recommend:

BEGIN WHERE YOU ARE TODAY.
Be honest about where you are in your career, your baseline knowledge and experience, and what your prospects and clients need most right now. For example, signing up for a super-elite physiology course after completing your basic specialty training might not be a great move if you still know very little about client acquisition or change psychology.

CHECK YOUR GAPS.
You drew your T, right? Look at the areas you're lacking. Once you have your specialty training, build out your horizontal row before throwing the kitchen sink at your vertical row. Go broad before going deeper. Additionally, recognize and respect the power of the so-called Dunning-Kruger effect, a psychological phenomenon that means when we're less experienced, we don't realize how little

we know, or how relatively unskilled we are. So if you notice yourself thinking you already "know it all" or "have everything mastered," be on your guard and make sure to calibrate your own skills and performance against that of world-class experts.*

DO A LIMITING FACTOR ANALYSIS.

Now that you know what you're missing, ask yourself the most important question in the process: Which weak point is holding you back the most? In other words, which factor is most limiting for your personal and professional growth? This is called a **limiting factor analysis**. It forces you to be critical about your information and skill gaps and to prioritize learning in the areas that'll make the biggest difference to your career immediately.

For example, if you're like most health and fitness professionals (who have to get their own clients), marketing and sales may be your limiting factors. Without the ability to attract, register, and retain clients, you won't be able to stay in the field very long. Or maybe you know a lot about how the body works but don't have strategies for working with living, breathing humans in the context of their actual lives. Your limiting factor might be change psychology. Or, maybe you're a fitness model with an extensive exercise and nutrition background, plus one hundred thousand followers, but you're not sure how to turn that into a business. Your limiting factors might be business systems and strategy.

---

* But don't fall prey to the opposite problem: "I'll never be at the level of so-and-so! There's no point trying! It's too much!" Calm down, figure out a plan, and fill those gaps one by one, slowly and steadily.

RUN A TOURNAMENT.

Once you've identified your limiting factor(s), it's time to prioritize learning in those areas. However, as we saw earlier in the book, prioritization is difficult. Even after following the steps above, you'll still likely end up with a not-so-short list of courses that feel important to your career development. As mentioned, it'll be a list that takes years to check off. Instead of being stressed out by this, or paralyzed into inaction, make your list items compete, like in a bracketed sports tournament, as mentioned in Chapter 5.

Here's an example of what that could look like:

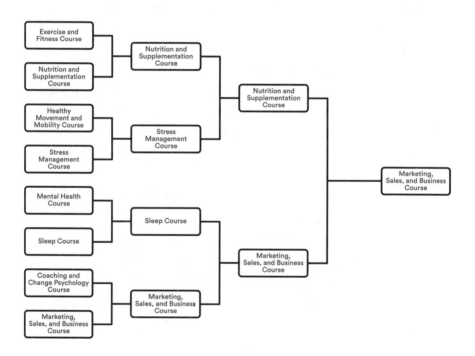

Of course, *your* tournament may look very different from this one. But the process is the same.

Your Educational Tournament

Fill out a blank tournament bracket to decide on your next course or learning opportunity. Pair up items from your list, make them compete for the next precious spot in your learning calendar, and see what wins. (Then, of course, take action and do the learning.)

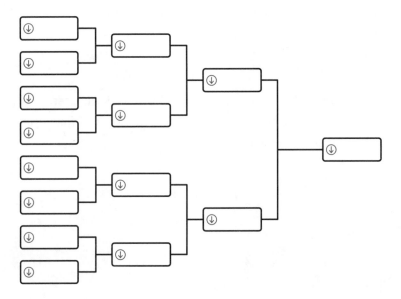

Important: Once you complete your latest learning adventure, be sure to rerun the tournament. You'll want to be sure your original list, your brackets, and your winners are as up-to-date as possible and are based on what you've learned since your last time running it.

Sometimes even making time for one new course a year can feel daunting within the context of your own life, especially if you're trying to juggle work, a social life, family, or other commitments and responsibilities. This is where the same prioritization skills (as discussed in Chapter 5) are so important. When overwhelmed with options and opportunity, errands and busy work, the only reliable way to make time for the most important thing is to reevaluate how you're spending your time and prioritize the tasks that have the potential to make the biggest difference.

Prioritizing the Big Rocks

One helpful method of identifying and following your priorities is to think of your time as a jar, which you can fill with a finite number of rocks, pebbles, and sand. To the right is an example.

Everyone's rocks, pebbles, and sand will look different. But, regardless, if you fill your jar with too much sand first, the rocks and pebbles won't fit.

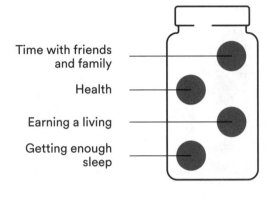

Time with friends and family
Health
Earning a living
Getting enough sleep

Your Big Rocks represent the stuff that's most necessary to feel fulfilled in life. They often relate to family, health, and livelihood.

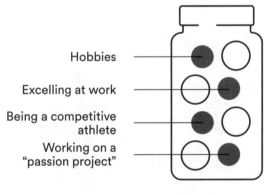

Hobbies
Excelling at work
Being a competitive athlete
Working on a "passion project"

Your Pebbles add extra fun and satisfaction to life, but aren't totally necessary.

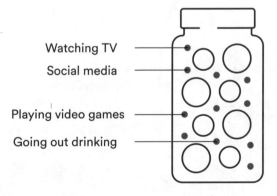

Watching TV
Social media
Playing video games
Going out drinking

Your Sand is purely "bonus" activity. It can be enjoyable, but it's not crucial to your survival or fulfillment.

Spend some time thinking about your "big rocks," "pebbles," and "sand" and fill out the following:

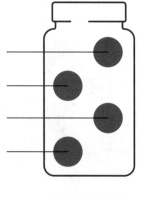

Your Big Rocks represent the stuff that's most necessary to feel fulfilled in life. They often relate to family, health, and livelihood.

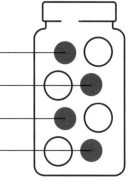

Your Pebbles add extra fun and satisfaction to life, but aren't totally necessary.

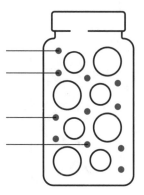

Your Sand is purely "bonus" activity. It can be enjoyable, but it's not crucial to your survival or fulfillment.

Another great way to make time for the most important things is to keep a time diary, also mentioned in Chapter 5. Your schedule reflects how you're prioritizing the activities in your life. So, when you track your time for a few weeks, you'll find out if it's consistent with your goals and values.

To do so, begin by tracking your day in fifteen-minute increments. For example:

> **7:00–7:15 Woke up, brushed teeth, washed face**
> **7:15–7:30 Checked Instagram**
> **7:30–7:45 Still on Instagram**
> **7:45–8:00 Made coffee and breakfast**

Then, analyze it.

ACTUAL

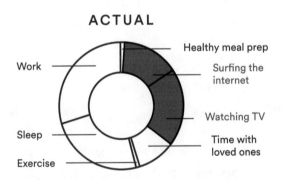

DESIRED

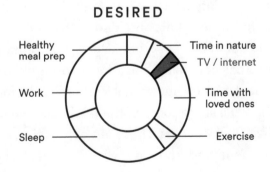

Without judgment, ask yourself if your schedule reflects your true priorities and what you know will help you reach your personal and professional goals. If not, make some adjustments to clear time for your most important personal and career tasks (including continuing education).

MY FAVORITE EDUCATIONAL RESOURCES IN EACH CATEGORY

A few years back I sought out a supplement partner for Precision Nutrition. I didn't actually want to sell supplements. Rather, I wanted a *trusted, reliable partner to refer clients to* when they asked about safe, effective products.

I did a lot of diligence. I visited a host of companies' headquarters, packaging facilities, and materials suppliers. After an extensive search, I found one I was proud to recommend. They had a long track record, great sales, and were doing things right. Sadly, three years later, they were acquired and stopped making the products our clients needed at the quality I demanded.

It's for that reason—even the best of companies come and go—I decided not to include a comprehensive list of books, seminars, courses, and certifications in this section. Sure, I would love to help you design your curriculum with some trusted recommendations. However, Precision Nutrition has been around for fifteen years and, during that time, I've seen companies go out of business, books go out of print, and once-relevant resources get staler than a four-month-old bagel.

With that said, in the Educational Resources section at the end of this book I'll share some of the resources I've found to be most beneficial in *my* career. These are companies, people, and programs I've benefited from, as have our students. (That's why they skew toward nutrition and fitness.)

By the time you read this book, they could be long gone. (I hope not.) If they are, that's okay. Because you now know how to evaluate learning modalities, triangulate among believable experts, and use crowdsourcing and online reviews to choose and prioritize the right courses for you.

THE **VALUE** OF *education*
IS **INTERNAL** NOT **EXTERNAL**

EDUCATION *changes* YOU
IT LEVELS UP **YOUR THINKING,**
learning, **AND** QUESTIONING

Your EDUCATIONAL **CURRICULUM**
SHOULD **MAP** TO **FUTURE** *you*
AND *who* **YOU'D** LIKE **TO BECOME**

LOOK FOR THE **TASK-SPECIFIC**
KNOWLEDGE, *wisdom,* **INSIGHT** TO
MASTER *yourself* **AND** YOUR *profession*

BECOME **A T-SHAPED PROFESSIONAL**
Learn **A LITTLE** ABOUT **A LOT**
AND *a lot* ABOUT **A LITTLE**

PLUS, PARTNER WITH PEOPLE who
know A LOT ABOUT WHAT
YOU know A LITTLE ABOUT

YOU DON'T finish YOUR EDUCATION
AND MOVE ON TO doing YOUR job
Doing AND LEARNING GO HAND IN HAND

WHEN making IMPORTANT DECISIONS, triangulate
Listen TO THREE WORLD-CLASS EXPERTS
BE ESPECIALLY curious WHERE THEY DISAGREE

PRIORITIZATION IS DIFFICULT
but IT'S THE ONLY WAY TO MAKE TIME
FOR THE MOST important THINGS

THERE'S NO HURRY
IT'S NOT a race
YOU'RE NOT BEHIND

CONCLUSION

A Person in Such a Hurry Seldom Gets Good Results

There was once a young man named Matajuro. Like his father, he wanted to be a great swordsman. So he packed his things and went to Mount Futara to find the famous swordsman Banzo.

"You wish to learn swordsmanship under my guidance?" asked Banzo.

"Yes," said Matajuro. "If I work very hard, how long will it take to become a master?" he asked.

"Oh, I see you cannot fulfill the requirements," said Banzo, and he rejected Matajuro's request.

"But . . ." he pleaded, "I'm willing to pass through any hardship if you'll teach me! If I become your devoted servant, how long will it be?"

"Oh, maybe *ten years*," Banzo relented.

"But my father is getting old and soon I must take care of him," said Matajuro. "If I work more intensively, how long would it take me?"

"In this case, maybe *thirty years*," said Banzo.

"What?!? First you say *ten* years and now *thirty* years. I will undergo any hardship to master this art in the shortest time!" exclaimed Matajuro impatiently.

"Well," said Banzo. "In that case you'll need to remain with me for *seventy years*. A person in such a hurry seldom gets good results."

As we come to the end of this book, I share this story—one of the world's most famous Zen koans—as a gentle reminder that as passionate as you might be for all things health and fitness, and as excited as you might be to take on this life-changing work, your path to mastery will also require strategy, clear-thinking, and *lots* of patient practice.*

---

* Probably a lot more than you're thinking right now.

If that sounds like challenging work, it is. Although, as I teach my students, we all—like Matajuro—tend to *overestimate* how difficult things will be and *underestimate* how long they'll take.

Hopefully the curriculum laid out in this book will help you calibrate both.

Even more, I hope it helps you minimize time-wasting, dream-squashing detours on your road to success by constantly drawing you back to what's most important. To the few things, carefully chosen, that can make all the difference for you and the people you hope to serve.

Becoming the ultimate change maker will require you to think differently about who you are, why you're here, how you can make a great living, and how you can make a real difference. This begins with asking new questions like:

What's my purpose, unique ability set, and value system?

What do the people I hope to serve really want?

How can I serve those needs while also respecting mine?

Which skills must I build to turn my passion into something sustainable?

And don't forget these most crucial ones:

When I die or retire, will I have worked toward something valuable, meaningful, satisfying?

Will all my efforts have made any difference at all?

How will I know?

I grew up in an immigrant family. My parents came to North America from a tiny farming village in central Italy, one in which most of the homes, including theirs, had no electricity or running water. As a child I watched them work tremendously, sometimes backbreakingly, hard while expecting, and receiving, very little in return. It was the same with most of the other families I knew.

This is one of the reasons I continue to be astonished by the rich rewards *I've* received by following the lessons in this book.

This isn't me trying to seem humble. I am *legitimately* in awe of the kind of alchemy that can transform a little boy, with a funny accent, growing up in a tiny apartment over a run-down garage into . . . me.

My daily commute is ten steps to my home office. I have a healthy family that I can spend as much time with as I choose to, and I choose to spend a lot. I have interesting friends and deep friendships. I'm paid handsomely to consult with the largest companies in the world. I started, and stay involved with, one of the most respected health and fitness organizations. I'm passionate about what I do. And I believe my work has made, and will continue to make, a difference.

While the work ethic I learned from my family certainly has something to do with this magical life I'm living, I'm also certain that success is about a whole lot more than "embracing the grind." Because every immigrant I grew up around worked ten times harder than you can possibly imagine. Every morning, noon, and night. Weekends too. And most barely earned a living wage.*

Observing this mismatch between "work ethic" and "success" made me realize that if I wanted to do better, I couldn't just try *harder*. I'd have to try *different*. In the beginning I had no idea what this "different" might look like. Now, nearly three decades later, I'm starting to get it. In fact, I've come to believe that, if there were a "formula" for personal and professional success, it might look like this:

---

* Although this was enough reward for many of them. Because, depending on where they came from, their goals were to escape unemployment, abject poverty, persecution, and/or death.

STRONG PERSONAL **MISSION** and
deeply **HELD** MOTIVATION
(UNIQUE abilities **AND** VALUES)

+

A HIGH level OF **COMPETENCY**
AND **SKILL** (countless **HOURS**
of PATIENT **PRACTICE)**

+

SYSTEM for **EXECUTING**
every **DAY** (A STRATEGIC,
CLEAR-THINKING plan
to **APPLY** YOUR **CRAFT)**

=

PERSONAL AND
CAREER Success

Over the course of this last year, in the writing of this book, I've tried to outline, with as much clarity as I can muster, the rationale for each element in that formula. Some days the writing came easy. Other days it was challenging. I continued on because I believe these lessons have the power to not only change your life but reshape an entire industry.

Yet learning isn't the same as doing. Not for your clients. Not for you.

That's why I'll once again encourage you to visit, if you haven't already, www.changemakeracademy.com/downloadable-forms and download the free exercises, activities, questions, and worksheets I've provided. They're there to transform your knowledge into career-changing action. To show *today you* the path to *future you*. To bring forth the ultimate change maker you've set out to be.

As you work through them, always remember this: It's not a race. You're not behind. And there's nothing to "catch up" to. As Banzo wisely knew, patience, mastery, and success walk hand in hand.

QUICK REFERENCE GUIDE TO WORKSHEETS, THOUGHT EXERCISES, AND RESOURCES

Once I completed the first draft of this book, I gathered fifteen friends and colleagues—people at different points in their health and fitness careers, even people working in different careers—to do sort of a peer review of the material. Using the thinking-aloud process outlined in the Q&As from Chapter 3, they spent countless hours reading, considering, and commenting. The result? Close to a thousand ideas and comments to review and decide whether (or not) to incorporate in the book.*

The number-one request? Worksheets and summary pages. They wanted a way to quickly find the exercises most relevant to them. Plus the ability to share the ones that could most benefit friends and colleagues. So that's what this quick-reference guide is all about. I've included a list of templates, scripts, and worksheets for the most important exercises, and instructions for the most important processes.

To download free printable and fillable PDF versions of these, please visit: www.changemakeracademy.com/downloadable-forms.

Here's a complete list of these resources:

---

* Yes, it was painstaking and time consuming. It was also 100 percent worth it. This book is far better for the effort. I'm eternally grateful for each of them and their care.

CHAPTER 1: OPPORTUNITY

CHAPTER 2: CAREER

CHAPTER 3: CLIENTS

CHAPTER 4: COACHING

CHAPTER 5: BUSINESS

CHAPTER 6: REPUTATION

CHAPTER 7: EDUCATION

Again, you can download printable and fillable PDF versions of each worksheet and summary at: www.changemakeracademy.com/down loadable-forms.

QUICK REFERENCE GUIDE TO Q&As

To support what you're learning throughout this book, I've compiled end-of-chapter Q&As that are full of real, thoughtful questions I've gotten over the years. In each one I share my unfiltered take on the challenges you'll undoubtedly face as you grow your career. To save space, we've hosted these online and you can download them (for free) at www. changemakeracademy.com/questions.

The questions include:

Chapter 2: Career

Q: I'm excited about getting into the health and fitness industry. I feel like my purpose is here and my unique abilities will allow me to make a difference. But it does feel really crowded, like a lot of people want to be involved. Should I be worried about competition? (Answer: ~375 words)

Q: Earlier, you talked about using your purpose, unique abilities, and values to help determine what to say yes to and what to say no to. Is that true for every stage of your career? (Answer: ~700 words)

Q: I understand the value in turning down certain opportunities at certain stages in my career. But how can I turn them down without seeming ungrateful, disappointing the people who might be counting on me to say yes, or ruining future opportunities? (Answer: ~650 words)

Q: It sounds a lot like you're saying that passion should drive one's career. I've heard that's not a good idea and you need to be more practical. What do you say to that? (Answer: ~150 words)

Chapter 3: Clients

Q: The ideas in this chapter are mostly qualitative and I'm more of a quantitative person. Don't you collect measurable data when planning your marketing, advertising, and products? (Answer: ~275 words)

Q: You mentioned a technique called "thinking aloud." What's that, and how does it work? (Answer: ~425 words)

Q: My business is relatively new, I don't have many clients yet, and I only offer one service. I'd love to get deeper insights but don't really feel like I have the time, am not sure I can afford to pay people for interviews, and wonder if what I learn will be useful. What should I do? (Answer: ~350 words)

Chapter 4: Coaching

Q: You outlined seven coaching principles, and they all sound important. I'm feeling a little overwhelmed with what to do next. What do you recommend? (Answer: ~200 words)

Q: I find accountability to be a big part of why people hire coaches, but I think they also get frustrated when things don't go their way. How do I balance holding clients accountable without sounding like I'm nagging or bothering them? (Answer: ~200 words)

Q: Clients are always giving me this vague goal of wanting to lose weight, which is great. But now that I know I'm supposed to ask more questions, where do I go from here? (Answer: ~300 words)

Q: What do you do when clients resist nearly everything you suggest? (Answer: ~200 words)

Q: Okay, let's talk results. How do you track them? (Answer: ~225 words)

Q: Got any tips for clients who seem impatient or frustrated by plateaus? (Answer: ~175 words)

Q: I have a handful of clients who are just plain lazy. They simply don't want to put in the work no matter what I try and how easy I make it for them. Now what? (Answer: ~575 words)

Q: Sometimes my clients have elaborate, and incorrect, theories on what works for them and what they should do next. How do I deal with that? (Answer: ~450 words)

Q: So you took a shot at the cheerleader types of coaches. I pride myself on being motivating and positive, and people tell me they like it. So you're saying I shouldn't be like that? (Answer: ~200 words)

Q: You want me to be silent sometimes? I'm supposed to have answers. (Answer: ~425 words)

Q: I'm very frustrated by people coming in and saying they want to try something they've seen on TV. Any advice? (Answer: ~200 words)

Q: My clients swear they're "doing everything right" but I have my doubts. What can I do to challenge them without seeming adversarial? (Answer: ~125 words)

Chapter 5: Business

Q: I love the whole tournament idea to help with prioritization and I'm going to start doing it. I'm just not always sure which to-do should win out over another. Can you help? (Answer: ~300 words)

Q: What if I'm still having trouble? (Answer: ~300 words)

Q: In health and fitness, I see a lot of people with side gigs. Either their coaching is the side gig for another job or they have other side gigs to supplement coaching. Is this a good idea? (Answer: ~175 words)

Q: There seem to be a lot of people making careers out of being internet or social-media famous. Is that a reasonable business model? (Answer: ~425 words)

Q: Are there any other business lessons you've learned over the years? (Answer: ~625 words)

Chapter 6: Reputation

Q: In one of your seminars I heard you talk about your "Google the Opposite" strategy as a way to seek out feedback on certain ideas. Can you share more about it? (Answer: ~400 words)

Q: In this chapter, you talk about "being yourself." How does appearance play into that? "Myself" is wearing board shorts and T-shirts, but I don't think too many people would think that's professional. (Answer: ~400 words)

Q: What about cursing? I know a coach who drops f-bombs every other word. I can't imagine that's too smart for reputation. (Answer: ~225 words)

Q: I once had a client tell me that my website didn't look professional. How important is all that stuff to developing my reputation? (Answer: ~275 words)

Q: You mention inclusivity when it comes to different sizes, shapes, races, genders, and ability levels. How important is that? (Answer: ~500 words)

Again, you can download all the questions, and my answers, for free at www.changemakeracademy.com/questions.

EDUCATIONAL RESOURCES

Precision Nutrition has been around for fifteen years and, during that time, I've seen companies go out of business, books go out of print, and once-relevant resources get staler than a four-month-old bagel. For that reason I decided not to include a comprehensive list of books, seminars, courses, and certifications in this book

With that said, I did want to share some of the resources I've found to be most beneficial in *my* career. These are companies, people, and programs I've benefited from, as have our students. (That's why they skew toward nutrition and fitness.)

By the time you read this book, they could be long gone. (I hope not.) If they are, that's okay. Because you now know how to evaluate learning modalities, triangulate among believable experts, and use crowdsourcing and online reviews to choose and prioritize the right courses for you.

EXERCISE AND FITNESS:

ACSM Certified Personal Trainer (certification)

ISSA Certified Personal Trainer (certification)

NASM Certified Personal Trainer (certification)

NSCA Certified Strength and Conditioning Specialist (certification)

Personal Trainer Development Center (website)

NUTRITION AND SUPPLEMENTS:

Examine.com (website)

The Examine Research Digest (subscription)

International Society of Sport Nutrition CISSN program (certification)

PrecisionNutrition.com (website)

Precision Nutrition Level 1 Certification program (certification)

MOVEMENT EDUCATION

Functional Movement Systems certification program (certification)

ISSA Corrective Exercise Specialist (certification)

MobilityWOD.com (website, seminars, and courses)

Postural Restoration Institute (website, seminars, and courses)

Z-Health Performance Solutions certification program (certification)

COACHING, COMMUNICATION, CHANGE PSYCHOLOGY

Crucial Conversations: Tools for Talking When Stakes Are High (book)

Girls Gone Strong (website)

Girls Gone Strong Level 1 certification program (certification)

PrecisionNutrition.com (website)

Precision Nutrition Level 2 Certification program (certification)

Switch: How to Change Things When Change Is Hard (book)

Thanks for the Feedback (book)

SLEEP, STRESS, MENTAL HEALTH

CAMH course in Mental Health

CAMH course in Motivational Interviewing

CAMH course in Cognitive Behavioral Therapy

Motivational Interviewing: Helping People Change (book)

Motivational Interviewing Network of Trainers (seminars)

The Sleep Revolution (book)

SleepEducation.org (website)

Why Zebras Don't Get Ulcers (book)

BUSINESS, SALES, MARKETING

Business for Unicorns (articles, business courses, coaching programs)

OnlineTrainer.com (website)

Online Trainer Academy (online training certification)

Net Profit Explosion (articles, courses, coaching programs for fitness)

Results Fitness University (live fitness business mentorships)

Strategic Coach (entrepreneurship coaching and mentorship)

HIGH INTENSITY/GROUP TRAINING

Training for Warriors (various levels of certification)

CrossFit (various levels of certification)

TRX (various levels of certification)

SPECIAL POPULATIONS

CrossFit Kids (certification)

Girls Gone Strong Pre- and Post-Natal certification program (certification)

ISSA Senior Fitness Specialist (certification)

INTERNSHIP OPPORTUNITIES

Altis (elite sport coaching courses and internships)

EXOS (human performance courses and internships)

Cressey Sports Performance (elite strength and conditioning internships)

ACKNOWLEDGMENTS

The idea that the person whose name rests on the front cover of a book is the one responsible for "creating" said book is misleading, if not comical. Phil Caravaggio, my longtime friend and business partner, calls it "the myth of authorship." And this project certainly destroyed whatever remaining ideas I had about being "the author" of "my own" book.

Don't get me wrong; I spent more than a year struggling over the manuscript. Almost daily. For most of my working hours. Yet a huge list of people were responsible for me getting to the point where I could struggle in the first place. Without them, I'd have never learned the lessons within, started writing, or completed the work. I owe them all a big debt of gratitude, including:

Phil Caravaggio, my friend and partner of twenty years. Without him, this book would never exist. Not in this universe or any other. Because, without him, I'm not the kind of person who could write it.

The leadership team at Precision Nutrition, including Timothy Jones, Erin Weiss-Trainor, Luke Galea, Tracy Simpson, Robert Lombardi, Lorinda Nepaul, Belinda Hudmon, and Adam Campbell. Their work, and their character, have influenced me in powerful ways too numerous to count. I'll forever be grateful.

The Precision Nutrition team members I've worked closely with, including Aaron Hughes, Alex Cimino, Alex Picot-Annand, Jason Crowe, Jason Grenci, Jennifer Nickle, Kate Kline, Lance Jones, Lee Walker Helland, Morgan Kennedy, Nate Green, Angela Self, Holly Monster, Jen Schwartzenhauer, Janet Filipenko, Krista Schaus, Sarah Masi, Ailbhe Keys, Eva Tang, Nadia Fisher, Ruby Bennett, Alaina Hardie, Cheryl Stinson, Doug Estey, Graham Anthony, James Herdman, Jason Dreher, Jenny Brook, Justin Giancola, Kelly Shea, Kyra Aylsworth, Mattia Gheda, Adam Feit, Brian St. Pierre, Craig Weller, Denise Allen, Dominic Matteo, Gillian Hagg, Jason Bonn, Jen Cooper, Jessica Christensen, Jonathan Pope, Kate Solovieva, Krista Scott-Dixon, Lisanne Thomas, Pam Ruhland, Ryan Andrews, Sarah Maughan, Scott

Quick, Toni Bauer, Tracy Reck, and Zach Moore. Each of these people believe in the Precision Nutrition mission and execute it enthusiastically every day. In doing so, they've taught me many important lessons about work and life. And changed me in the process.

Scott Hoffman and Steve Troha, my agents extraordinaire. Both have trusted my ideas, represented me unfailingly, and guided this newbie through the publishing process with experience, grace, and wisdom. I can't tell you what it means to have "representation" that gets you, and your ideas, from the start.

Ted Spiker, my writing partner. When it comes to understanding the writing and publishing process, Ted's wisdom has to be measured in dog years. Without his talent, experience, and regular prompting, this book may never have been completed. And, if it had, it certainly wouldn't have been as compelling.

My peer review team, including Adam Campbell, Bryan Krahn, Camille DePutter, Carter Schoffer, Casey Sasek, Craig Weller, Geoff Girvitz, Geralyn Coopersmith, Krista Scott-Dixon, Nate Green, Stuart McMillan, and UJ Ramdas. Each turned their talented and critical eyes on the first draft of this manuscript. And each shared "thinking aloud" feedback that led to important changes to the book's structure and delivery. When I asked each to help in this way, they responded enthusiastically and affirmatively within a day with no expectation of anything in return. I'm an extremely lucky guy.

The BenBella production and publishing team, including Glenn Yeffeth, Claire Schulz, Sarah Avinger, Monica Lowry, and Lindsay Marshall. They've been true partners in every sense. Over dozens of meetings, and even more interactions, not one of my ideas was met with resistance. Every step of the way I could feel their desire to work together to make the best book possible.

Rodrigo Corral and Anna Kassoway, my talented design team, and one of the best in the world. Not only are they design geniuses, they're also authentic, reliable, and accommodating collaborators, a rare combination. Together we created something beautiful that I'm extremely proud of. The icing on the cake? We had a lot of fun creating it.

Andrea Hayes who acted, in equal parts, as assistant, project manager, and partner while we worked on the completion and marketing of this book as well as launching the Change Maker Academy brand. Her enthusiasm for ideas, and commitment to seeing them through, was refreshing every step of the way.

Last, but not least, Amanda, Amalynn, Raelon, Graydon, and Ambria, my family, to whom I've dedicated this book. Through the hours spent cloistered in my office, and the cranky moments when I finally came out, they supported me unwaveringly as I did my best to shape this work and get it out into the world. Simply watching them move through life inspires me and has provided me with some of my best learning and teaching moments, as well as some of the best stories in this book.

INDEX

ABOUT THE AUTHOR

John Berardi is a Canadian-American entrepreneur best known as the co-founder of Precision Nutrition, the world's largest nutrition coaching, education, and software company.

He's also the founder of Change Maker Academy, devoted to helping would-be change makers turn their passion for health and fitness into a powerful purpose and a wildly successful career.

Berardi has advised organizations like Apple, Equinox, Nike, and Titleist, teams and athletes like the San Antonio Spurs, the Carolina Panthers, US Open champ Sloane Stephens, and two-division UFC champ Georges St-Pierre, and was named one of the twenty smartest coaches in the world and one hundred most influential people in health and fitness.

Berardi lives in Ontario, Canada, with his wife and four children.